Bridal BARGAINS

Secrets to throwing a fantastic wedding on a realistic budget.

DENISE AND ALAN FIELDS

WINDSOR PEAK PRESS

All rights reserved. **Copyright © 1994, 1995 by Denise and Alan Fields.** This book may not be reproduced in whole or in part by any means without the express written permission of the authors. Published by Windsor Peak Press, 1223 Peakview Circle, Suite 7000, Boulder, CO 80302.

Distribution to the book trade by Publisher's Group West, 1-800-788-3123.
Amazingly accurate marketing advice by Mark Ouimet & Diane Levinson.
Lead guitar and keyboard programming by Alan Fields.
Lead vocals, bass guitar and funk by Denise Fields.
Intense chain sales and hand claps by Anne Brooks and Lori Garrabrant.
Harmony vocals and Ingram interface by Stacey Hoover.
Hair by Charlie Winton.

To order this book, call (800) 888-0385 or write to
Windsor Peak Press
1223 Peakview Circle, Suite 7000
Boulder, CO 80302
Quantity discounts are available.

If you have a question or comment,
feel free to contact the authors at (303) 442-8792.
Or write to them at the above address.

Library of Congress Cataloging-in-Publication Data

Fields, Denise, 1964-
Fields, Alan, 1965-
  Bridal Bargains: Secrets to Throwing a Fantastic Wedding on a Realistic Budget/Denise and Alan Fields.

  Includes index.
  1. Wedding—United States—Planning. 2. Consumer education—United States. 3. Shopping—United States.
                                        93-093752 LIC
ISBN 0-9626556-1-9

Cover, illustrations, and interior designed by Archetype, Inc.

A Record of the Wedding

BRIDE

_____

GROOM

_____

WEDDING DATE

_____

HOW WE FIRST MET

_____

OUR FIRST ARGUMENT WAS OVER

_____

_____

PARENTS' REACTION TO ENGAGEMENT ANNOUNCEMENT

_____

_____

PARENTS' FIRST DISPARAGING REMARK MADE ABOUT FIANCE/FIANCEE

_____

_____

FIRST ARGUMENT OVER WEDDING

_____

_____

MOST STUPID REMARK MADE BY A WEDDING ATTENDANT

_____

DATE AT WHICH YOU KNEW THINGS HAD GOTTEN OUT-OF-HAND

_____

DATE AT WHICH EITHER OF YOU UTTERED:

*"But I thought planning a wedding was
supposed to be a happy experience!"*

_____

Special thanks to our
editors panel of wedding professionals
who provided invaluable advice!

Extra special thanks to all the
brides and grooms who have provided
their personal insights on how to throw
a fantastic wedding on a realistic budget.
Without you, there would be no
Bridal Bargains.

Thanks!

Overview

Your Wedding teaches you how to find the best deals on bridal apparel for the bride and the wedding party. Then, you learn how to shop for your ceremony site, wedding flowers, and invitations. Each chapter gives you indepth money-saving tips and shopping strategies.

Your Reception shows you how to save money on everything from catering to entertainment. Our chapter on wedding photography gives you six creative ways to save money plus 10 important questions to ask any photographer. You'll also learn how to find the best deals on wedding cakes and wedding videos.

Weddings Across America is a fascinating look at how couples are tying the knot in over 20 U.S. cites. You'll learn how bridal traditions and customs vary from region to region in the United States. We'll show you what's hot and what's not for nuptials in towns from coast to coast.

Table of Contents

Part II: Your Reception

Part III: Weddings Across America

Icons

What the Icons Mean

 What Are You Buying

 Sources

 Top Money-saving Secrets

 Getting Started: How Far in Advance

 Biggest Myths

 Step-by-step Shopping Strategies

 Questions to Ask

 Pitfalls to Avoid

Chapter 1

STOP! READ THIS FIRST!

AAAAAIGH!!! So, you're engaged? Well, fasten your seatbelts! Soon you will travel through a bizarre and crazy world, where the boundaries of good taste and sane thought are only fuzzy lines. Yes, you've done it now.

You've entered the WEDDING ZONE.

See, that's why we are here. We're sort of your tour guide through this wondrous journey of things bridal and ideas nuptial. Of course, right off the bat, you probably will notice a basic difference between this and all those other wedding books—this book contains actual COMMON SENSE.

Sure, we know we're going out on a limb here but what the heck? Why not write a book you can actually use to plan your wedding? Hey, it's the least we can do. At this point you may have a question: so, who are you guys? Let's put that into bold.

So Who Are You Guys?

When we got engaged, the first thing we did was trot down to our local bookstore. There has got to be a book that will help us survive this process, we thought. What we wanted was a consumer guide that would show us how to plan a wonderful wedding without spending an amount equivalent to the Federal Deficit. From recently-married friends, we heard all the horror stories—that wasn't going to happen to us. We would find out how to shop, what questions to ask and how to avoid scams and frauds. A small request, we thought.

Ha! All we found were etiquette books last revised when Eisenhower was president. Plenty of books wanted to tell us what was "proper," what was "socially acceptable" and what was "never to be done except under threat of death." Gee, that's nice, we said, but what we need is help, not useless etiquette.

So we left the bookstore with our heads down. Now what? Then the idea hit us: hey, why can't we write this book? There must be a few other engaged couples going through this experience needing practical advice too.

To make a long story somewhat shorter, we were right. In the past four years, we have "mystery shopped" more than 1000 wedding businesses, from bridal shops to caterers, and photographers to bakeries. From these anonymous visits, we learned a lot about planning a wedding. We now know how to spot a truly talented wedding photographer and which bakery will produce the best wedding cakes. At the same time, we learned how to identify dishonest merchants who will try to rip off brides with inferior products or dubious service.

Basically, we took those experiences and wrote six books that have become best-selling wedding books in the Southwest. But we didn't stop there. For this book, we spent three years interviewing bridal professionals and wedding "experts" across the country. We then spoke to hundreds of engaged couples, carefully documenting problems and challenges they had planning their weddings. When you read this book, you get not only our opinions but also the wise advice of many recently married couples who have gone before you.

If you find this book helpful, please recommend it to your friends. If they can't find it at a local bookstore or library, call us toll-free at (800) 888-0385. Also feel free to write to us at 1223 Peakview Circle, Suite 7000, Boulder, CO 80302. We value your opinions, comments and experiences—we plan to revise this book for future editions, so please feel free to contact us.

The Four Truths About Weddings You Won't Read in Etiquette Books

1 SO YOU THINK YOUR WEDDING IS FOR YOU AND YOUR FUTURE SPOUSE? Ha! Forget it. Unfortunately, weddings often become less a celebration of marriage and more like a huge social event for the participants. Parents, and even some brides and grooms, are frequently guilty of turning weddings into spectacles to impress their friends or business associates. Money can become the sticking point since whoever pays for the wedding may feel a divine right to influence the proceedings with their own tastes.

Sometimes parents and relatives try to make your wedding into the wedding they never had (and always dreamed of). Your friends may be guilty of pressuring you to make your wedding fit some predetermined mold. Put another way, while you may be the stars of the show, you and your fiance may not be the wedding's directors, producers, or choreographers.

Recognize this fact early and learn to negotiate without giving ultimatums. Yes, it is YOUR day, but remembering that others (parents, friends, relatives) are on the stage with you may prevent excessive bloodshed.

2 WEDDINGS ALWAYS END UP TWICE AS LARGE AS ORIGINALLY PLANNED. If only we had a dime for every couple we met who said "all we wanted was a small, intimate wedding and what we got was a huge affair for 500 guests." A wedding often takes on a life of its own, expanding into a hideous creature several times larger than you ever imagined. Other weddings start as informal gatherings and turn into formal spectacles that rival Princess Diana's shindig.

This process usually begins with what we call Guest List Inflation. Here the guest list grows because each family simply must invite personal friends, close business associates ,and people whom they haven't seen for 15 years. The main problem: Adding to the guest list has a direct, negative impact on your budget.

Several weddings have nearly unraveled when families have insisted on inflating the guest list without offering to help pay for the additional cost. We suggest you and your families be allowed to invite a certain number of guests each. Any invites beyond those targets must be financed by the offending party. Careful negotiations are often necessary to avoid open warfare on this point. Good luck.

3 PERFECT WEDDINGS DON'T EXIST IN THE FREE WORLD. No matter what anyone tells you, understand that the "perfect wedding" is an impossibility on planet Earth. That's because weddings always involve human beings who, on the whole, tend to be less than perfect creatures.

We know everyone tells you that you must have the perfect gown, perfect flowers, and perfect cake unless you want to catch the Bridal Plague and die an agonizingly painful death. Don't listen to these demons. Instead, we suggest you aim for a "fantastic" or "wonderful" wedding. Or even just a fun wedding!

Since it's impossible to perfectly script something as complex as a wedding, we say why try? Attendants will miss cues, things will go wrong—if you need any proof of this just watch "America's Funniest Home Videos." Ever wonder why so many of those clips are of weddings? Hmmmmm.

Aiming for a wonderful wedding will also give you another benefit—you probably will be able to maintain your sanity.

4 THE "WEDDING INDUSTRY" ISN'T AS INNOCENT AS IT LOOKS. You might think the wedding industry is a col-

lection of sweet old ladies whose only desire is to see young couples in love, but the reality is quite the opposite. Instead, think the bridal business as a group of cut-throat small-business persons who, in some cases, will do anything for a sale.

Columnist Dave Barry once wrote that the motto of the wedding industry is, "Money can't buy you happiness, so you might as well as give your money to us." Quite true. Weddings are big bucks. According to *Modern Bride* magazine, more than $30 billion will be spent this year by couples tying the knot. That's *billion,* with a "b." Making matters worse is the fact that many wedding businesses own a mini-monopoly in their city over gowns, cakes, photography, etc. These firms viciously block any new competition. Why should that matter to you? Because by blocking the competition, businesses can effectively stop discounters and keep the prices high.

Now, we aren't against people in the wedding business making money. The problem we have is that too many wedding businesses have the morals of a slug. Many simply don't realize that federal laws prevent price fixing. Others are surprised to learn that consumer protection laws outlaw deceptive marketing and advertising practices such as "bait and switch." "No kidding," they say, "it's illegal to rip people off?"

So, we say, be careful out there. We hope this book will teach you how to spot the scams and rip-off artists.

The Goal of This Book:
To help you save money and still have a fantastic wedding!

Consumer justice doesn't have to be a somber topic. Getting a great bargain should be fun. Outfoxing dishonest merchants should be a joyful experience. That's why we try to keep our perspective about this wedding stuff, and we urge you to do the same. Not maintaining your sense of humor during wedding planning may be hazardous to your health. That's why we've liberally sprinkled what could be loosely described as humor throughout this book.

In each chapter we give you pitfalls to avoid. As you learn about these bridal scams and wedding frauds, realize that just because you are a bride does not mean you have to be a victim. By using our consumer tips, you can protect yourself from losing hundreds, if not thousands, of dollars and have a good time doing it!

This book is for brides and grooms who want to hire

professionals for their wedding. This book doesn't teach you how to sew a bridal gown or give you a recipe for a wedding cake. Instead, we'll show you how to get a nationally advertised designer gown at a 20% to 40% discount. We'll also show you the secrets to finding an affordable baker who will bake you the best wedding cake you've ever tasted.

There's No Advertising in This Book?

There are no paid advertisements in this book. Furthermore, no company paid any consideration or was charged any fee to be mentioned in it. The publisher, Windsor Peak Press, derives its sole income from the sale of this book and other consumer guides. As consumer advocates, the authors believe this policy ensures objectivity. The opinions expressed in this book are those of the authors.

So, How Much Does a Wedding Cost Anyway?

Unless you are a certified public account, you may not be inclined to use the words "fun" and "exhilarating" to describe setting the budget for your wedding. As you might expect us to say, however, this is a critical (albeit painful) part of the planning process.

Whether you're spending $100 or $100,000 on your wedding, every bride and groom have a limited amount of money to spend. This means you'll have to make tough choices regarding how you want to allocate your limited resources. In the appendix, we provide an in-depth look at setting a budget. Hopefully, this will help make this process easier.

So how much does a wedding cost? Here are the average costs for a formal wedding for 200 guests:

THE AVERAGE COST OF A U.S. WEDDING
(Based on industry estimates for 200 guests)

APPAREL	$ 1,175
FLOWERS	750
CAKE	400
RECEPTION/CATERING	8,000
PHOTOGRAPHY	1,500
VIDEOGRAPHY	850
INVITATIONS	350
MUSIC	1,000
MISCELLANEOUS	1,000
TOTAL	**$15,025**

When you add in the engagement and wedding rings, the total bill could top **$18,000!** Wow!

Now, if you are a bride-to-be in New York City or Los Angeles, you may be looking at the above numbers and laughing (or crying). That's because everything there costs at least two to three times the average. Keep this in mind throughout the book when we quote "average prices."

As a side note, we have seen dramatic inflation in the costs of some wedding services. For example, the cost of a professional wedding video has gone up dramatically—in the mid 1980s, the average cost was about $400. Now, it's more than double that. Likewise, many photographers have been jacking up their prices at an alarming rate of 20% or more per year.

On the upside, we've noticed deflation in the costs of some bridal apparel. Intensive competition and the recession of the early '90s prompted the introduction of several lower-cost lines of bridal apparel. Price hikes for other goods (such as invitations and flowers) have been held to a minimum, too.

Now, if you're going to spend the kind of money mentioned above, perhaps you'd like to know who it's all going to. Our recommendation: Get yourself organized.

This doesn't mean you have to buy the $50 "bridal organizers" that the wedding industry hawks. We've received great suggestions about how to get organized from some of our past readers. For example, one bride suggested going down to a local office supply store and buying a plain accordion file for all the contracts, proposals, and receipts every bride collects. The unglamorous brown file was a mere $5—significantly less than the $35 price for a "bride's" accordion file with taffeta-fabric and a satin bow, advertised in a bridal magazine.

Another bride organized her wedding using a three-ring binder. She hole-punched all the contracts and bought pocket inserts for her receipts, photos, and fabric swatches. Total cost: $4 to $5. If you bought a similar product specially designed for brides, with lacy inserts and full-color photos, you'd spend as much as $35.

Regardless of the method you use to organize your wedding, keeping all your receipts and contracts in one place is vitally important. Also, make copies of any written correspondence you have with the businesses you hire. Even keep a telephone log of your phone conversations.

Although chances are your wedding planning will be a smooth process, if any problems do crop up, you'll be glad you spent the time and money to be so well organized.

The Bridal Clock

"I'm late! I'm late for a very important date!" said the rabbit in Alice in Wonderland. At times, as you plan your wedding, you might feel a bit harried your self. (Admittedly, that was a very bad pun).

Of course, the first real crisis of any engagement is the realization that you must accomplish 1.6 million things in about 13 seconds in order to get to the church on time. The second crisis is wondering which of those 1.6 million things you should do first.

To solve this problem, we have invented our BRIDAL CLOCK, which is displayed below. Think of the numbers of the clock as months in the wedding planning process. At high noon is your wedding.

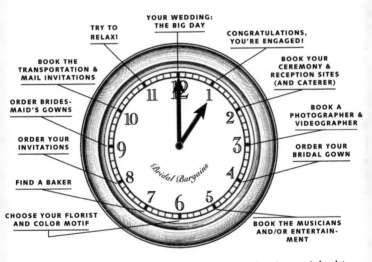

Start with reserving your ceremony site (one o'clock). Next, find and book a reception site and a caterer. From there, shop for your wedding gown...and so on.

In each chapter in this book, you'll find specific advice on how much time you need to order everything from invitations to a wedding cake. Of course, the BRIDAL CLOCK gives you a general sense of how far you've gone—and how much further you need to go until the bewitching hour!

PART I

Your
Wedding

Chapter 2

Apparel for the Bride

Wonder how you can save 20% to 70% off those fancy designer bridal gowns? In this chapter we'll show you how, plus teach you 16 steps to buying the right bridal gown. Then you'll learn 12 valuable money-saving tips. Finally, we'll expose how dishonest bridal shops rip-off brides, and we teach you how to outfox them. Last but not least, we'll take a candid look at the country's biggest bridal designers, rating them on prices and quality.

The Bridal Gown. Nothing symbolizes a wedding more than the bridal gown. Prospective brides are taught from birth to fantasize about this ultimate dress, sparkling with beads, sequins, and pearls delicately sewn into French lace. Of course, the designers who make those gowns are well aware of this—their ads are laced with references to "fairy-tale" weddings and "storybook" brides.

Okay, I admit to falling into this fantasy stuff head first when I was a bride. But, hey, how often do you get to wear a piece of clothing that costs $1000? Finding the right bridal gown (at a price that doesn't resemble the federal deficit) is often the overriding priority for brides. And why not? Bridal gown shopping is the ultimate battle between women and the evil apparel industry. This is the Olympics of shopping.

And, gee, wouldn't you have figured? Shopping for a bridal gown is perhaps the most perilous and tricky task in this journey we call wedding planning. You didn't expect this to be easy, did you?

The reasons for this degree of difficulty are complex. In this chapter we explore the reasons that buying a bridal gown generates the biggest number of complaints from engaged couples. We'll teach you how to find the gown that's just right for you and how not to get ripped off doing it.

Where do brides buy bridal gowns? According to a magazine survey, 70% of all brides purchase a gown at a bridal shop, a specialty store that focuses on bridal and formal apparel. Another 12% purchase a dress from a department store, while 10% have a gown sewn by a professional or friend. The remainder wear a gown that was a family heir-loom (2%), borrow or rent a dress (2%), or buy through a discount service or mail order (3%).

In this section, we will focus on buying a bridal gown from a traditional bridal shop. Of course, there are several little-known but quite fascinating alternatives to this route. We'll discuss them later in the chapter.

What Are You Buying?

 At the simplest level, you are buying a dress. But not any dress. This is a darn expensive dress. The average bridal gown costs $800 in most stores, no matter where you live. Many of the premium designer gowns sell for much more, topping $1000 and even $2000.

So what do you think you would get for $800? Well, before you answer this question, we ask you to shift your mind into BRIDAL MODE. That's because if you think in the REAL WORLD MODE you're going to be in for a shock. For example, if we gave you $800 and told you to buy a nice party or cocktail dress you'd expect a few things for that amount of money. Fine fabrics like silk? Sure. Quality construction with a lining and finished seams? Why not. How about sewn sequins and detailing? Hey, you'd expect that for $800! Right?

Well, BRIDAL MODE life isn't like that. To put it mildly, $800 buys you garbage. For that amount of money, all you get is synthetic fabric, shoddy construction with unfinished seams and no lining. Want sequins, pearls and beads? Expect them to be just glued on, not sewn—especially for gowns that are under $600.

Frankly, we can't figure out why this is. Perhaps the entire bridal apparel industry (from the powerful designers to the lowly local bridal shop) think that when women get engaged they collectively lose all sense of reality. Like zombies, brides are supposed to walk into bridal shops and plunk down a cool $1000 for a gown they wouldn't even consider buying for $300 if they saw the same design at a department store.

As a side note, don't forget that the bridal gown is just the beginning. You'll also need undergarments, a petticoat, shoes and the ubiquitous headpiece and veil. If you think bridal gowns are overpriced, wait until you see the prices for accessories. The "average" headpiece and veil runs $150, while you can add another $150 for accessories. Hence, the total ensemble may cost you $1100.

We should also note that most shops require a 50% deposit on all special orders. (We'll explain later why most gowns are special-ordered instead of bought off-the-rack.) That can be a sizeable financial hit several months before the wedding. The balance is due when the dress comes in.

Sources to Find a Bridal Shop

 Finding a bridal shop is easy. Finding a good bridal shop is somewhat more challenging. Beyond the basic sources, there are three important ways to locate local shops:

❧ *Bridal Magazines* The major bridal magazines are literally plastered with ads from apparel manufacturers. On the page next to the dress, you can often find a list of shops that carry the designer. Just look for your city, and bingo! There will be at least one candidate for your search. Before you put much stock in magazines, however, read our section on them later in the chapter.

❧ *Friends* Ask everyone you know whether they know someone who was recently married. Call several recent brides and drill them on their experiences. Any shops they recommend? Any shops they recommend you should avoid like the plague? Listen carefully to their advice—we know one couple who were repeatedly warned by friends not to buy at a particular shop. They bought anyway, and, wouldn't you know, they fell victim to a scam and lost $500.

❧ *The Better Business Bureau* Check to see whether any shops you have heard about have a record of complaints. Any complaint (even if the company resolved it) is a big red flag.

Games Bridal Shops Play

(Not all bridal shops are guilty of the following dishonest practices. However, after visiting more than 200 bridal shops, we have encountered several disturbing practices you should be aware of.)

Once you decide which shop carries the type of gowns you want, the fun begins! It's time to shop! Before you go, realize that once you step inside some bridal shops, you are entering the DARK AGES OF CONSUMERISM. For some reason, bridal shops exist in a time and space where their owners think they're exempt from such silly concepts as honesty and ethics. Buying a bridal gown is a "one-shot" deal—you won't be back next week to buy another. Let's take a look at the appalling tactics that some shops use to confuse you, the consumer.

1 MYSTERY GOWNS. Many bridal shops rip the tags out of their sample dresses to keep you from knowing who designed and manufactured the gown. In other cases, shop owners simply refuse to tell brides who made the dresses, even when the brides ask point blank. Why would they do this? We've interviewed many shop owners who basically

admit they do it to prevent price competition. Hey, they argue, if we tell you the designer, then you'll go down the street to our competitor and get the dress at a discount.

We say this is a bunch of bull. What the shops are trying to do is keep you ignorant. All designers are not equal; some offer better quality work than others. Keeping the designer from you is a sneaky way for them to pass off an inferior gown as "comparable" to a premium design.

What is most perplexing about this deceptive practice is the fact that most brides find out about the shop from a designer's ad in a bridal magazine. Designers spend millions trying to get brides to recognize their brand name, and for what? To have their retailers tear out the tags is stupid, especially under the guise of stopping price competition.

Not only is it stupid, but it's also illegal. A federal law called the Textile Fiber Products Identification Act of 1960 requires all apparel (yes, even bridal) to be properly labeled. This must include the name of the manufacturer (or their "registered number," assigned by the Federal Trade Commission) as well as the fiber content and country of origin. Sadly, many bridal shops flagrantly violate this long-standing consumer law, thanks to lax enforcement by the FTC.

You'd be offended if you walked into a grocery store only to find all the labels torn off the food. We say you should be just as offended if a bridal shop does this. If a shop doesn't clearly label their gowns (or refuses to identify the designer of the gown when asked), we suggest you go elsewhere.

SOLUTION: Find a few dresses you like in a bridal magazine. Then walk into the shops listed in the ads and ask to see those specific dresses. If the salespeople say they don't know who makes which gowns, don't believe them. Before you walk out, you may mention to the salesperson that she just lost a big sale.

2 SECRET CODES. We've visited many shops that secretly encode the tags on their dresses to hide the manufacturer and style number from you. The reason is the same as the above deceptive practice. Many shops don't want you to know what you're spending those big bucks for.

3 THE BIG FUSS. No matter what gowns you try on, the salesperson who helps you will invariably gush and say something like, *"You're sooooo beautiful!"* Sometimes I wonder if I tried on a gown made out of potato sacks whether the salesperson wouldn't say something like, *"Wow! That natural look! It's so you!"*

As you might have guessed, most salespeople at bridal shops work on commission. Hence, it's to their advantage to get you to buy any gown, preferably an expensive one. Some salespeople go overboard, taking advantage of brides-to-be by playing on their emotions. For example, at one store we visited, the salespeople couldn't stop saying how wonderful one particularly expensive designer gown looked on me. One salesperson came up to me and asked if she could take my picture for "an album of all their brides." After the picture, the salespeople put the camera down and helped me back in the dressing room. That's when my fiance looked at the camera and noticed that it didn't have any film! Later we visited the same store again and saw no picture album. The whole shtick was a clever ploy to convince me to buy that dress. A word to the wise: Don't get caught up in all the false flattery that will be heaped on you by the bridal shop.

SOLUTION: On your shopping trips, bring a trusted friend or relative (just one!) with you whose opinion you value—this ensures a more objective critique.

4 KILLER MARKUPS. The profit for bridal shops doesn't stop at the 100% markup they charge on gowns. Alterations are also a big profit center, averaging $100 to $200 per gown. Euphemistically called "custom fitting," alterations to make the gown fit perfectly are very expensive. One industry newsletter we saw recommended bridal shop owners triple the cost of the seamstress and pass that along to the brides. Hence, if the shop pays a seamstress $7 per hour to alter gowns, the charge to you, the consumer, is $21 per hour—a bit greedy in our opinion.

Accessories are another major profit area. Shops sell everything from bras, shoes, and slips to ring pillows, garter belts, and champagne glasses at steep markups. Veils and headpieces are extraordinarily expensive.

5 FALSE DISCOUNTS. In what is a patently illegal practice, many shops mark their gowns higher than suggested retail and then offer you a "discount." Gee, thanks! For example, we visited one shop that was offering a 10% discount off all special-order gowns. One gown we saw had a price tag of $1100—we later learned the suggested retail for the gown was just $1000. Their big 10% discount knocked $110 off the gown, bringing the price down to $990. The real discount was just $10 off the real retail price—a puny 1%.

6 ELUSIVE EXCLUSIVES. Some bridal designers occasionally give one shop in a city an exclusive on certain dresses. These dresses are termed "confined," and you can't find them anywhere else in town. Or can you? Many bridal shops skirt these exclusive rules by a process called trans-shipping.

You may run into "trans-shipping" on your visits to bridal shops. We visited several shops that told us they could order any gown, even if they didn't carry it in their store. How do they do this? Let's assume Bridal Shop 1 carries Dresses A, B, and C brands. But you want a Dress D brand. So Shop 1 calls Shop 2 (usually in a nearby city) which just happens to carry Dress D. So, Shop 2 places the order and then ships the dress to Shop 1.

Trans-shipping, which is not illegal per se but is in a gray area of interstate commerce law, occurs because most bridal shops can only carry and stock 10 to 12 lines of bridal apparel. But there are more than 200 apparel designers out there, and odds are a customer may want a dress the shop doesn't carry. Instead of losing the order, the shop places the order through back-door channels. By the way, shops often add a small markup for the trouble of ordering a dress from another shop.

The use of exclusives in the bridal industry is quite controversial. Store owners love them since they limit competition and help stop discounting. The apparel designers, on the other hand, are divided. Some believe exclusives are the only way to control who resells their gowns. Others claim they can't make a profit by granting exclusives. Giving certain designs to just one shop in a city doesn't generate enough orders to make financial sense.

In fact, that's why we've noticed many designers talk with two tongues. While they flail against the evils of trans-shipping and discounting (keeping their retailers happy), the apparel designers then quietly sell to discounters. Others turn a blind eye to trans-shipping since, of course, they end up selling more dresses and making more profit.

The propaganda war has reached new heights lately, with traditional bridal shops displaying "authenticity" certificates that certify they are "authorized outlets." Bridal manufacturers are advertising in bridal magazines that only legitimate dealers will have these certificates. One flyer from a bridal shop we received said that if you don't buy from an authorized outlet, you will get inferior quality or a counterfeit gown.

Is this true? Of course not. In fact, the same shop that distributed the flyer also said they could get gowns that they do not regularly stock "from another source." Obviously, they are trans-shipping these gowns. Frankly, the duplicity of some of these bridal shops is disgusting.

What does this mean for you? Be careful of bridal shops that promise they can get in "any dress you want." Check with past client references and the Better Business Bureau to make sure the shop has fulfilled its previous promises.

Getting Started: How Far in Advance?

 Most brides are surprised when they learn how far in advance they must place an order for their gown. At the bare minimum you need at least three months. Ideally, you should order your gown any-where from five to nine months before your wedding. That's right, nine months! The "average" time that brides order their dress is eight months in advance of the wedding.

Why do you need so much time? Well, the big factor is the kind of gown you want. Some gowns take as little as six weeks to order, while others can take up to six months. Later, we'll explain why it takes bridal apparel manufactur-ers so darn long to fill an order. But first, let's take a look at the five stages of buying a bridal gown:

1 SHOPPING. Hey, don't forget that you need time to look for that gown which is just right for you. Sure, you can do this in as little as one day, but most brides we have interviewed said they took two to three weeks. That's because it takes time to visit a handful of the area's best shops and more time to make a final decision.

2 ORDERING. Once you place your order, the shop sends it to the manufacturer. Some designers have six-week turnaround times. However, several "upper-end" designers can take as long as six months. A few manufacturers have quick delivery that can get you a gown in a couple of weeks, not months. That's why it's important you know the designer of the gown in order to make sure the gown will arrive in time for your wedding—see the reviews of designers at the end of this chapter for the scoop. Some manufacturers offer "rush ser-vice," but the extra fee for this may bust your budget.

3 ALTERATIONS. After the gown comes in, you must leave another month for alterations. Some shops may be able to do "rush" jobs but the quality may be rushed too. You may have several time-consuming "fittings," appoint-ments with the seamstress where you inch closer and closer to getting the gown to fit just right.

4 PORTRAIT. In some areas, brides have a formal portrait taken before the wedding which is displayed at the reception. In order to leave enough time to view the proofs and get the final print framed, most photographers suggest doing the portrait four to six weeks before the wedding. That means the dress has to be altered and ready to go four to six weeks before your wedding.

5 SAFETY ZONE FOR MISTAKES. Yes, mistakes can happen, especially here. Apparel is most prone to problems since there are more people involved in this process than any other. Orders can be botched at several points between the store and the manufacturer. Leaving time (perhaps two weeks) in your schedule to correct problems is prudent.

Whoa! That's a lot of time! The time guideline we recommend is six months. If you want an elaborate designer gown, allow for even more time. However, don't panic if your wedding is around the corner. Look for our TOP MONEY SAVING TIPS later in this chapter—-many of these strategies can quickly unite you with a gown.

Step-by-step Shopping Strategies

 ❧ Step 1: After you've set the date, sit down with your fiance to talk about your wedding. The key decision is how formal you want the event. Now, the bridal magazines have all kinds of crazy rules to tell you what to wear for each formality degree but just remember this: your gown should reflect your ceremony and reception. The gown that is perfect for an intimate garden ceremony held in the afternoon probably won't work at a evening ceremony for 200 close friends at a big church with a sit-down dinner reception following.

❧ Step 2: Now that you have an idea of how formal your wedding is, look through those ads for bridal designers. Which gowns intrigue you? Which ones make you sick? Key on the elements of the dresses—the silhouettes, the necklines, waistlines, train length, amount of lace, etc.

❧ Step 3: Before you head out to local bridal shops, ask your ceremony site coordinator if there are any restrictions on the amount of skin you can show in the sanctuary. Some churches frown on low-cut, off-the-shoulder or even strapless gowns. Determining what's appropriate before you fall in love with the "wrong" gown is prudent.

❧ Step 4: Listen to the advice of recently-married friends and acquaintances about local bridal shops. Their insights on selection, service and prices may be valuable. Using our other SOURCES listed above, draw up a list of three to five stores that offer the gowns you want. Don't forget that a store's service (how you're treated when you come through the door) is almost as important as the selection of dresses.

❧ Step 5: Try to visit the stores on your list on any day other than a Saturday. Weekends at bridal shops are crazy—everyone tries to shop on Saturday. If you can go during the week (some stores are open in the evening), you'll find better service, less-crowded dressing rooms, etc. Call ahead—some shops require an appointment. Go with just one other person (your mom, a friend, even your fiance) whose opinion you value. Having more than one other person will give you too many opinions.

❧ *Step 6:* When you visit the shop, be prepared to answer a few questions. The first is probably the most critical: how much do you want to spend? We recommend lying here. Most salespeople will try to "up-sell" you slightly, so we recommend you under-estimate your price range by 10%. If you really have budgeted about $1000 for a gown (not including alterations, headpiece/veil and any accessories), tell them you want to spend $800 to $900. Undoubtedly, they'll show you a few dresses closer to $1000.

❧ *Step 7:* Next you'll be asked about your wedding date and how formal your wedding will be. We recommend fudging about your wedding date—push it forward about three to four weeks. For example, if you're real wedding date is June 18, tell the shop the "big day" is May 21. This insures that your gown will arrive (and any potential problems will be fixed) in time. The wedding date will also help determine whether you'll want long or short sleeves, for example. Also, they'll ask you what "style" of gown you prefer: Sheath or mermaid-style? Traditional floor-length skirt or tea length? High or low neckline? Long train or no train? Obviously, you won't know all the answers but try to give the salesperson an idea of your preferences.

❧ *Step 8:* Keep an open mind. Many dresses pictured in bridal magazines on those anorexic models look different in real life on real women. Try a few different styles, with a friend (your mom, a bridesmaid, etc.) taking notes on which gowns you like the best. Be careful of "gown overload:" trying on too many gowns in one day can confuse you, blending into a blur of lace and sequins. Our advice: don't try on more than five gowns at each shop. Besides you'll become exhausted.

❧ *Step 9:* Narrow down your choices to two or three gowns. Make an appointment with the same salesperson you talked with on your first visit. Now, it's decision time! Don't be rushed by anyone but also remember that time is of the essence—you need time for alterations, etc.

❧ *Step 10:* Congratulations! You've selected your bridal gown! Now, before you put down that hefty 50% deposit, ask the bridal shop the questions we list later in this chapter. Get measured (bust, waist, hips and from the base of your throat to the hemline) with a vinyl tape measure and ask to see the manufacturer's sizing chart. Given your measurements (and remember your bust measurement is not your bra size), select the gown size that corresponds to the largest of your measurements. Remember you can make a gown smaller but you can't expand it. It's important that you make the decision of what size to order—don't let the bridal shop make it for you. We'll explain why later in our PITFALLS section.

❦ *Step 11:* If you're unsure whether the shop is an authorized dealer for the gown you want, call the manufacturer (several designers' phone numbers are printed later in this chapter). Most manufacturers will tell you if the shop is a legitimate re-seller for their gowns. If the shop won't tell you the manufacturer of the gown, we suggest you go elsewhere. If the manufacturer tells you the shop is not an authorized dealer, the shop may be sewing counterfeit gowns or trans-shipping the gowns from another source. Ask the owner about this and if you don't get a straight answer, go elsewhere. Don't worry: you may be able to get the dress from another more honest shop even if the first shop claims they have an "exclusive."

An exception to this rule: many discount mail order and ware-house companies are not "official" authorized outlets, according to public statements by bridal manufactures. While the discounters often purchase gowns through legitimate channels, the designers don't want to admit that they're selling to them.

❦ *Step 12:* When you place an order, get a receipt with the price, color, size, manufacturer, style number, and most importantly, the promised delivery date. Also, listed on the ticket should be any extra special-order requests (some dresses can be ordered on a rush basis, with extra beading or length, different fabric and detailing, etc.). All these requests cost extra. If the store recommends a size for you, write on the ticket "Store recommends size." Then, if the gown comes in needing extensive (and expensive) alterations, you're in a better negotiating position. When you place your order, also get a written estimate on alterations. Be sure you ask about the store's refund policy, as well as any extra charges for pressing and so on.

❦ *Step 13:* One to two weeks after you place the order, call the bridal shop for a "confirmed shipping date." The shop receives this date from the manufacturer after it places the order.

❦ *Step 14:* Starting two weeks before your dress is due in, call the bridal shop to confirm the date your dress will actually arrive. Delays at the factory (imported lace arriving late, a larger number of back-orders) can delay the delivery of your gown, as well as the bridesmaids'. Bridal shops are usually aware of such delays. Calling ahead will help avoid surprises.

❦ *Step 15:* Hooray! The dress has arrived! Now, inspect the dress carefully. Gowns have been known to come in with flaws, stains, tears—you name it. Don't rely on the bridal shop to inspect the dress for you (many let problems slip through the cracks). Also, confirm the size of the dress by actually measuring it. Incorrect sizing is a major problem with some manufacturers.

❦ *Step 16:* Finally, it's time for alterations. Whether you have the shop or an outside seamstress alter the gown, give the alterations person a firm deadline. Be sure to confirm the experience level of the seamstress—how familiar are they with bridal fabric? How long have they been altering gowns? See the PITFALLS for more advice on alterations.

Questions to Ask a Bridal Shop

1 WHO IS THE MANUFACTURER OF THIS DRESS? As we previously mentioned, some shops try to hide this from you. Even though they have torn out the tags from the dress (in an illegal effort to keep you from comparison shopping), you can still ask them who makes the dress. This is important for several reasons. First, you can determine whether the store is an authorized dealer for the gown by calling the manufacturer. Second, you know what you are buying—some designers offer better quality than others. If the shop refuses to tell you, or if the salesperson says she just "doesn't know," go elsewhere.

2 HOW LONG WILL IT TAKE TO GET THE DRESS IN? This is a critical question since the delivery times for different manufacturers vary greatly. If you choose to fudge your wedding date (moving it forward a few weeks from the actual date), be careful here. If you move the date up too early, the shop may not be able to order the dress in time for the early date. In general, bridal gowns take anywhere from six weeks to six months to special order. Bridesmaids' gowns take about two to four months.

3 WHAT ARE YOUR PAYMENT POLICIES? Can you put the deposit on a credit card? This is a very important point, as you'll learn in our next section. Also, confirm the store's refund policy. Nearly all bridal shops have a no-refunds policy on special-order dresses—even if the wedding is called off or there is a death in the family. Read the receipt (or contract) carefully before you sign.

4 CAN I HAVE A WRITTEN ESTIMATE FOR ALTERATIONS? Before you order, get this in writing. Remember that you do not have to use the store's in-house alterations department (even though they will strongly encourage you to). Quality

alterations are extremely important—we've seen too many unskilled seamstresses (many at bridal shops) botch alterations. Whomever you decide to hire, try to meet the seamstress who will alter your gown. Ask them about their experience with bridal gowns. How long have they been doing this work? Have they ever worked with the fabric and lace on your dress before? If you detect any problems here or can't get a written estimate, consider hiring another seamstress.

5 WHAT FREE SERVICES ARE AVAILABLE? Some stores throw in a free "steaming" with all bridal gown orders. Other freebies might include free delivery and even ceremony coordination (especially when you place a large order with the shop). Some of these services might be offered quietly. Ask and ye shall receive.

Here's a little consumer tip that can protect you from getting ripped off by unscrupulous bridal shops: use your credit card (instead of cash or a check) to pay for your bridal gown. Most brides and grooms do not realize that a special federal consumer protection law protects all deposits and payments made with credit cards. The law, called Federal Regulation C, entitles consumers to receive refunds if the merchandise delivered doesn't live up to what's promised.

Specifically, the law says that if you have a problem with the quality of goods or services that you purchased with a credit card and you have tried in good faith to correct the problem with the merchant, you may not have to pay the bill. (As a side note, this only applies to purchases over $50 and if the purchase was made in your home state or within 100 miles of your mailing address).

So what does that mean for you? Well, let's suppose two brides put $500 deposits on the exact same dress at BRIDAL SHOP XYZ in their town. One bride puts the deposit on her MasterCard (or any credit card) and the other writes a check. Delivery will take four months (which is not an unusual amount of time).

Let us tell you that four months may not seem like a long time to you but it's an ETERNITY to retailers. Much can happen in four months. In fact, BRIDAL SHOP XYZ has now gone out of business. The owner of the shop has left town without a trace. So what's happened to our two brides? Well, the bride who put the deposit on her credit card will contact the bank that issued her card and, most likely, she will receive a refund.

And what happens to the other bride who paid with a check (or cash)? Her $500 is probably lost forever. Sure, she can sue the owner in small claims court—if she can find the owner. She can also report the incident (which is technically theft) to the local authorities. But, if the shop owner has left town, the bride may never see her money again.

Does this sound far-fetched? Well, it happens more often than you think. In one city we researched, for example, no less than ten bridal shops have gone out of business in the past three years! While four closed "responsibly" (they stopped taking deposits and turned their special orders over to other shops in town), the other six bridal shops did not. Their owners took deposits until the day they closed and then quickly left town. We know dozens of brides who lost hundreds of dollars in deposits because they paid cash (or by check) instead of with a credit card.

In 1992, a couple who owned a chain of Detroit area bridal shops was indicated on 60 counts of fraud in a "bridal scam." Over 5000 brides were bilked out of $1 million in deposits when the shops failed to deliver dresses. And this isn't an isolated case: sources in the bridal industry tell us not a week goes by when there isn't a shop somewhere in the country that closes and takes brides' deposits.

According to several credit card-issuing banks we've talked to, deposits paid with credit cards for bridal apparel (or any wedding-related purchase) are protected by Federal Regulation C. Be aware that the rules apparently vary slightly with each issuing bank. One bank we talked to had a requirement that complaints have to be filed within 60 days of the purchase. The fact that a deposit isn't really a "purchase" clouds the issue somewhat. Another bank told us they would refund money (credit the account) to a bride under a scenario like the one above even if more than 60 days had elapsed from the date the deposit was processed.

What if you've already paid the bill? You still may be able to get a refund—contact your card-issuer for more info. What if the shop only takes cash or checks? Here's a sneaky solution: many credit cards also give you checks (which work like cash withdrawals) for purchases. Purchases with these credit card "checks" may be covered under the same law.

Now we are not telling you this to scare you. The odds of you getting ripped off by a dishonest bridal shop are not great, but...BE CAREFUL! This advice applies to other deposits too, not only for bridal apparel. If you can, don't pay for any other "wedding" deposits (the cake, flowers, photographer, etc.) with cash or a check. A WORD TO THE WISE: USE YOUR CREDIT CARD.

Top Money-saving Secrets

 Many of our top money-saving tips for bridal apparel involve alternatives to traditional bridal shops. The savings we calculate are based on a gown that retails for $1000.

1 RENT A GOWN. Since the mid 1980s, bridal apparel rental stores have opened in most major cities (look in the phone book under "Bridal Shops"). Rental prices for bridal gowns range from $75 for simple dresses to $600 for expensive designer gowns. That's right, you typically can rent one of those exquisite designer gowns dripping with pearls and lace that would retail for $1000 or $2000 for less than $600. Most rental shops require a $100 to $200 deposit. The dresses, which are professionally cleaned after each rental, can be altered to fit. The only drawback to renting may be the search required to find a good rental shop—there are typically only one or two in each city. For example, while you'd expect to find a rental shop like Just Once in New York City (292 5th Ave., 212-465-0960), what about a smaller town like Litchfield, IL (pop. 7500)? Even here we found a rental shop, Formals Etc., (217) 324-4513. The message: check your local Yellow Pages or call the rental companies listed in the next chapter for local dealer information. Total savings = $400 or more.

2 PURCHASE A GOWN FROM A "BRIDAL BROKER." Most brides don't realize they can order nationally advertised gowns from bridal brokers at a substantial discount from retail. These brand-new gowns, discounted 20% to 25% off retail, are shipped directly to you, cutting out the middlemen. For more information on one of the most popular discounters, see "Discount Bridal Service" later in this chapter. Total savings = $200 to $400.

3 CHECK THE CLASSIFIEDS. We've found some incredible bargains listed right in the Sunday classifieds. Sometimes weddings are cancelled or postponed. In other cases, recent brides who need extra cash are willing to part with their gowns. Most of these gowns are in excellent shape; some have never been worn before! Best of all, the prices we've noticed are often 50% or more off retail. Of course, you'll need to carefully inspect the gown before buying. Total possible savings = $500 or more.

4 CONSIDER "CUSTOM-DESIGNING." If you want a gown that costs over $1000, consider having a local seamstress create a copy of the original. We've seen several beautiful gowns that were custom-designed by talented seamstresses. Why is this a money-saving tip? Well, first a seamstress can often buy the fabric at wholesale (or at a discount from retail). Second, there are no costly alterations—your gown is made to fit. Certainly the labor costs for an expert seamstress can be substantial, but the results can be striking. Total savings here will vary but we priced one exquisite silk Jim Hjelm gown at $2700 retail which cost only $1400 to reproduce with a local seamstress.

5 SEW IT YOURSELF. If you have a flair for sewing (or know a good friend who does), consider making your gown yourself. Patterns for bridal gowns are readily available at local fabric shops. One fabric shop pointed out to us that the exact materials (fabric, lace, pattern) to make a popular designer dress would cost $225. The retail of this dress was $995—not counting an extra $100 for alterations. One note of caution: sewing with bridal fabric is challenging so be careful if you go this route. Total savings = $775, less your time and labor to sew the gown.

6 BUY A "SAMPLE" GOWN. Bridal shops often sell their "samples" throughout the year at substantial discounts from retail. Most gowns are marked down at least 50%, some even more. Since many shops sell most of their gowns by "special order," they need these "demonstrator" samples to entice orders. What happens when a gown is discontinued or they need more room for new styles? It's sale time! Check your local paper since some shops have big sample sales throughout the year. However, most shops have a rack of discounted "sample" gowns year-round. Before you use this tip, read our PITFALLS section for special tips on buying a sample gown. Total savings = $500 or more.

7 WEAR YOUR MOM'S DRESS OR BORROW A FRIEND'S GOWN. You'd be surprised how a seamstress can inexpensively restore a vintage gown. Even if you spend $100 to $200 to have the gown altered or jazzed up, this will be much less than buying a gown at retail. Borrowing a gown from a friend is another great money-saving option. Total savings = $800 or even more!

8 ASK FOR THE "BIG 8" DISCOUNT! If you order from a traditional bridal shop, here's a little-known discount you can ask for: some designers (including Alfred Angelo) give retailers an 8% discount if they pay their bills on time. While some designers don't offer the discount or have lowered the percentage recently, this is still a break the store owners get on some gowns. So we suggest they pass it on to you! For example, a $1000 gown really costs the store $500. If the shop gets the "Big 8," the real cost of the gown is $460. Using the standard mark-up in the industry, a fair price for the gown is now $920—a savings of $80 off the original retail. We should add a caveat to this tip: some of our readers have told us that the Big 8 Discount is sometimes difficult to negotiate—a few stores deny it exists and refuse to pass it along.

9 ORDER A BRIDESMAID'S OR LESS FORMAL GOWN. Most brides don't realize that many bridesmaids' gowns can be ordered in white. For a less formal wedding, you can get a plain bridesmaid's gown for just $75 to $150. Beautiful, less-formal gowns (without trains, sequins, pearls, etc.) are available from ready-to-wear clothing designers like Jessica McClintock. Her stunning line of bridal dresses start at just $200 (ranging upward to $600).

10 SHOP AT BRIDAL OUTLET STORES. Scattered across the country are outlet stores for bridal designers and retailers that offer substantial savings. See the Best Buy section later in this chapter for more information.

11 BUY A CONSIGNMENT GOWN. These pre-owned gowns are often fantastic bargains. Many apparel consignment shops have popped up in major cities across the nation. In San Antonio, Texas, for example, we found not only one, but four consignment shops that carried bridal. in Boston Best of all, these shops often carry a wide assortment of quality gowns by the top designers. One shop we visited had over 50 gowns, including one beautiful Priscilla of Boston gown with exquisitely beaded Venice Lace. The gown, which originally retailed for $2000, was only $400! Or you could rent it for just $200! Now, that's a bargain.

If you want to sell your gown after your wedding, many shops accept consignments from across the country. Zazu (800) 872-0346 in Boston is a pioneer in the industry. If you're looking for a local consignment store, you can write the Bridal Special Interest Group of the National Association of Resale Stores at PO Box 144, Brookline, MA 02146.

Biggest Myths about Bridal Gowns

 Myth #1 "*Considering how expensive those designer bridal gowns are, I assume they are being hand-crafted by skilled seamstresses.*"

Wrong. We spoke to a bridal apparel industry veteran who painted a very unflattering picture of how most bridal gowns are manufactured. First, the bridal manufacturer waits until they receive a certain number of orders for each size (that's why it takes so long to get a gown). Let's say they wait for 10 orders of size 8 gowns in a particular style. When the orders come in, they stack on a conveyer belt 10 layers of fabric, which are then cut by a laser. Later, machines sew the seams together. Even the lace added to the dress may have been machine-beaded at another location. Basically, that's why so many gowns look like disasters, with unfinished seams, no lining and shoddy construction. The assembly process has more to do with factory assembly lines than human beings lovingly hand-sewing the gowns. As a result, gowns are not custom-made to your measurements but rather are rough approximations which often require additional alterations (read: money).

Myth #2 *"I'm a rather contemporary person but when I visited a bridal shop, all I saw were boring, traditional gowns. Do I have to choose a gown that says "Hi! I'm young, and innocent?"*

Getting married does not require you to lose all your fashion sense. Too often, the bridal apparel industry stereotypes all brides to fit certain molds. You must look like Cinderella or, if you're daring, perhaps Snow White. Well, we say, no Virginia, you don't have to look like TRADITIONAL BRIDE on your wedding day if that's not your style. Consider some snazzy alternatives. Watters and Watters has several tailored suits and "informal" gowns that are striking sheaths with delicate portrait collars. In taffeta, satin and silk shantung, the gowns retail for $300 to $600. Another of our favorites is Jessica McClintock, whose cotton and linen suits are wonderfully sophisticated. Several other "ready-to-wear" women's apparel designers have entered the bridal market with splashy and contemporary gowns. Among the best are Scaasi and Carolina Herrera.

Myth #3 *"I know brides must always wear white but I've tried on several white gowns and they make me look like death warmed over. My mom says I have no other choice—it's white or nothing."*

Tell your mom you do have a choice. Almost all gowns also come in ivory (also called candlelight and, believe it or not, egg shell). But that's not all the color possibilities. Several gowns now are available in subtle blush colors like peach and pink. These creamy hues are simply breath-taking.

Helpful Hints

1 SHOPPING FOR A GOWN IS AN EXHAUSTING PROCESS. Take frequent breaks and don't try to squeeze too many shop visits into one day. Limit yourself to two to three shops, leaving time to think about which gown you like most.

2 SOMETIMES THE FIRST DRESS YOU TRY ON IS THE ONE YOU PICK. We're always surprised by the number of brides we've met who buy the first gown they tried on. Perhaps the first impression you get from that first gown is the one that most sticks in your mind.

Pitfalls to Avoid

Pitfall #1
BAIT AND SWITCH WITH ADVERTISED GOWNS.
   "I fell in love with this dress in a bridal magazine. I called the local shop listed in the ad—they told me they didn't have that design, but had others 'just like it.' I was so furious…is this a scam or what?"

Well, it certainly isn't ethical. Believe or not, the designers do not always require their dealers to carry the advertised gown— even if the store is listed in the ad! While the shop may have other gowns by the same designer, the dress you fell in love with is sometimes nowhere to be found. Usually the shop comes up with some excuse (our favorite is "the designer decided not to cut that sample yet") and then subtly tries to "switch" you to a "similar design we have in stock." We urge the industry to stop this practice. Don't patronize shops who pull the "bait and switch" scam. And shame on the bridal magazines for allowing this charade to happen in the first place.

Pitfall #2
OVER-SIZING TO MAKE EXTRA MONEY ON ALTERATIONS.
   "I wear a size 6 in street clothes and I was rather surprised when the saleswoman at the bridal shop told me I needed to order a size 10. In fact, the sample gown was a 10 and it really didn't fit. What should I do about the size I order?"

First, understand that bridal sizes do not correspond to real-world sizes. However, a favorite ploy of dishonest bridal shops is to order a dress way too large for the bride. Then, when it comes in, guess what? It needs expensive alterations! Here are our tips on this very common deceptive practice:

❦ Don't pay attention to the sample gown. Most sample gowns are tried on so many times that they stretch—what once was a 10 may now be a 12 or even a 14!

❦ Instead, get measured with a vinyl tape measure. Needed measurements include bust, waist, hips, and from the base of the throat to the hemline. Don't let the bridal shop use a cloth measuring tape, since these can stretch over time and give inaccurate measurements.

❦ Ask to personally see the manufacturer's sizing chart. Each manufacturer has their own sizing chart that is sent to each bridal shop that carries their gowns. As you will see, just because you wear a size 8 in "street clothes" does not mean you will wear a size 8 in bridal gowns. Complicating this process is the fact there is no standard for bridal sizing—all manufacturers do their own sizing.

For example, a bride with the measurements of 36, 26,38 (bust, waist, hips) would be a size 10 in a Bianchi, size 12 in an Ilissa, and a size 14 in a Mori Lee. According to a survey of 35 top manufacturers, this same bride would need to order a size 8 in 3% of the designers, a size 10 in 34% of the designers, a size 12 in 45% of the designers, or even a size 14 in 18% of the designers! Isn't this crazy?

❦ Given your measurements, pick a size that closely matches your largest measurement. Remember that gowns can only be altered in, not out. Make sure the size you pick is clearly marked on the sales receipt.

Brides encounter problems in this area when they let the shop pick the size for them. Instead of measuring you, they'll just guess what your size is (usually over-guessing). Other cases we've seen involve intentional fraud—the shop knowingly orders a size too large in order to make extra money on alterations. Be careful. If you accept the shop's "advice," write on the receipt that "Shop Recommends Size." If the dress comes in way too big or too small, you have more leverage in negotiating a solution.

Pitfall #3
MANUFACTURER GOOFS ON SIZING.

"I ordered four bridesmaids dresses from a local bridal shop. When they came in, they were all the wrong sizes— three were way too small and the other was floor length instead of tea length. The shop owner just shrugged her shoulders and told us their seamstress could fix the problem ...for a hefty charge. What should I do?"

First of all, the manufacturer is fully responsible for shipping the correct sizes. If the order is incorrect, the manufacturer should fix it free of charge. If there is not enough time before the wedding to send the dresses back, we believe the manufacturer should pay the bridal shop to alter the gowns to the correct size. The bride is definitely not at fault and should never be charged. In order to protect yourself from this pitfall, make sure all ordered bridal merchandise is inspected and measured when it comes in. Actually take a tape measure and make sure the gowns are the sizes that correspond to the sizing chart. We recommend this since many incorrectly-sized gowns are marked with tags that indicate the correct size. Sizing goofs are a common problem; we've seen numerous cases of gowns that came in too big or too small.

Compounding this rip-off are some shops that refuse to fix defective merchandise. Whether it's the wrong size or botched lace detailing, we've encountered some merchants who refuse to make good. Some claim "there's not enough time before the wedding to send the dress back." This points up the need to order a dress early.

How many dresses come in flawed? One major retailer who sells 10,000 bridal gowns a year told us that, shockingly, two out of every three dresses comes in with a flaw. In about half of those cases, the problem is minor and can be easily fixed. However, the other half include such serious problems as the wrong size or poor workmanship. These must be sent back to the manufacturer to correct.

Pitfall #4
THE BIG SWITCHEROO.

"My bridal gown came in yesterday and boy was I surprised! The lace and fabric looked nothing like the sample gown I tried on or even the magazine picture. What recourse do I have?"

"After four months of waiting, my special-order gown finally arrived. However, it looked suspiciously like the used sample I tried on four months ago. Have I been taken to the cleaners?"

This scam often appears in two flavors: the lace/fabric switcheroo and the "sample gown shell game." First, you must realize that many manufacturers reserve the right to change the lace, fabric and trim on any bridal gown. We've seen several cases where a manufacturer substituted a cheaper lace when they ran out of the more expensive lace. If you're unhappy with the substitutions, ask the bridal shop to go to bat for you. Reputable bridal shops may be able to negotiate a solution (free alterations, a partial refund, etc.) with the manufacturer. If time permits, the gown may be sent back to the manufacturer to make it correct. (Note: many manufactures can ship overnight a correct dress—don't let the shop bully you into thinking you need more time).

We urge all bridal manufacturers to deliver what they promise. If they can't, the bride should be notified and given the opportunity to cancel the order. Substituting lace, fabric or detailing is a deceptive practice and should be stopped.

What about the "sample gown shell game"? This is when a store promises to order a brand new gown, but instead tries to pawn off the used sample dress you originally tried on. The bottom line: you are duped into paying full price for a used gown—clearly an unlawful deceptive trade practice. We've heard reports that this insidious scam is rampart at some shops in Chicago and Detroit, though it can happen anywhere.

Here are some rather ingenious ways to spot this rip-off, as submitted by our readers. First, take a needle and red thread with you to the bridal shop. While you're in the dressing room, sew this thread inside the sample dress in an inconspicuous location. If the shop tries the scam, you can spot the used "sample" by the thread.

Another protection is to take a picture of the gown. But most shops don't allow pictures, you say? Sneak a small camera in your purse and snap a few pictures in the dressing room, after the salesperson leaves. The pictures will help you remember all the details and styling of the sample dress—just in case the shop tries to substitute that used sample or a different gown altogether. One bridal shop employee tipped us off to this scam, saying they often substituted cheaper dresses on brides since they could never remember what they ordered several months ago!

Pitfall #5
WHOOPS! WE FORGOT TO PLACE THE ORDER!

"I ordered a gown from a bridal shop four months ago and was notified yesterday that the shop forgot to place my order! I couldn't believe it! And now they won't give me a refund, instead suggesting I buy a gown out of their stock. What should I do?"

Contact your attorney. When a shop fails to place an order, they are breaking a valid contract and should give you a refund. A pitch to buy a sample gown is terrible. Unfortunately, we have heard of several cases in which bridal shops just simply forgot to place the order. They simply shrug their shoulders and say "we're sorry!"

Protect yourself by dealing with a reputable shop (find one using the sources we list earlier in this chapter). When you place an order, get a promised delivery date. A few weeks before the anticipated delivery date, call the bridal shop to confirm the shipping date (they receive this from the manufacturer). The more communication you have with your shop the more likely you will get your gown.

Pitfall #6
BOTCHED ALTERATIONS.

"My bridesmaids gowns came in three weeks ago and they were beautiful! However, when we picked them up after alterations, we couldn't believe our eyes! Those same

gowns were a disaster, poorly altered and sewn! How could we have prevented this?"

Bridal shops love to pitch their "expert alterations" service to brides as the only alterative for their gowns. In reality, their "expert seamstress" is sometimes a person they hired last week for $5 per hour who has only altered her daughter's prom gown. No wonder this is one of the biggest problem areas consumers have with bridal shops.

The main problem is the skill level needed to alter bridal gowns. The fabric is slippery and intricately-beaded gowns can make even the most simple jobs challenging. Some bridal shops ask for these problems by hiring inexperienced seamstresses who then botch the alterations.

You can prevent this problem by asking to meet the seamstress before you do the alterations. Ask them about their experience with bridal gowns. Ask to see their work area. If it looks like a sweatshop or if you sense the seamstress is unqualified, get the gown altered somewhere else. Many communities have "free-lance" seamstresses who do excellent work at much more affordable rates. One note of caution: don't skimp here. You want the best alterations money can buy.

Pitfall #7
SAMPLE GOWNS MAY NOT BE BARGAINS.

"I don't have enough time to order a gown before my wedding. I was thinking of buying a sample gown. Are there any things I should watch out for?"

Sample gowns may be a terrific buy or a terrible nightmare. As we explained earlier in this chapter, sample gowns (just like demonstrator models) are cleared out periodically to make room for new styles. Many are marked 50% (or more) off the retail price. The big pitfall here: most sample gowns are in less than great shape. That's because most have been tried on dozens (if not hundreds) of times by different shoppers. Sample gowns may be dirty, stained (especially from makeup) and beaten up. We've seen several that have beads missing and lace that is falling off. Furthermore, the gowns are stretched out and often in no way resemble their original size.

Of course, the condition of sample gowns varies greatly from store to store—some simply take better care of their merchandise. If you go this route, go over the dress with a fine tooth comb. If the shop agrees to clean the gown, get a written guarantee that the purchase is contingent on your approval of the gown after the cleaning. Cleaning a bridal gown is tricky since some dry-cleaning chemicals can discolor the glue used to affix beads/detailing. An inexperienced cleaner can destroy a bridal gown.

Pitfall #8
SALON-STYLE SHOPS.

"I went to a bridal salon where they kept all the gowns in the back. They told me they'd bring out the gowns they thought I would like. Is this kosher?"

We're not big fans of bridal shops that operate "salon-style." In most cases, these shops keep all their gowns out of sight and then ask you for your likes, dislikes, and price ranges. Unless you know exactly what you want, salons can be trying. First of all, the salesperson brings out what she thinks you want to see. We've been to several of these salons and they've yet to figure out what I want. Instead, they tend to bring out what they want to sell (i.e., an expensive gown). We suggest you shop at stores that allow you to see the merchandise. While you can't get a whole picture of what a gown looks like when it's on a hanger, you can tell which detailing (necklines, bodices, beading) you like, and you can get a better feel for prices.

Pitfall #9
HOTEL SALES, FLY-BY-NIGHT COUNTERFEITERS,
AND "UNAUTHORIZED RETAILERS."

"I saw an ad in our paper for a big sale of bridal gowns at a local hotel. They offered large discounts and unbelievable prices. Are these people for real?"

Well, yes and no. Most bridal gown sales at hotels are sponsored by liquidators who are looking to dump merchandise from bankrupt bridal stores. Some of these people are less than reputable, promising all kinds of service only to leave town quickly after they collect their money. The merchandise for sale is mostly sample gowns. Particularly a problem on the East and West coasts, hotel bridal gown sales are often too good to be true.

Another problem is counterfeit gowns. We have seen reports that several disreputable bridal shops sold brides gowns that were cheap knock-offs of designer gowns. The brides thought they were getting designer originals. You can prevent this problem by calling the manufacturer of the gown to confirm the shop is a legitimate dealer.

A different twist on this scam is shops selling gowns bought on the "gray market." In the past few years, "buying offices" have sprung up to supply gowns to bridal shops that want to skirt the industry's "minimum purchase" requirements. In a couple of cases, we've seen brides stung by these shops, when the gowns they ordered never arrived. Such bridal shops will tell you it takes an incredibly long time (say, 6 months) to order in a gown that typically takes only 12 weeks. While there are exceptions to this rule (Discount Bridal Service is a reputable discounter that we review later in this chapter), many of these "unauthorized" shops are nothing but trouble.

Pitfall #10
RIP-OFF CHARGES FOR LARGE SIZES, PETITES AND RUSH ORDERS.

"Okay, I'm not one of those anorexic models you see in the magazines. However, when I visited a bridal shop, all they had were size 10 dresses to try on! Then, they told me they charge extra for 'large sizes!' Is this salt in the wound or what?"

Yes, the bridal industry slaps brides who need a large size with a "penalty fee" that can be as much as $50 to $200 or more. But don't feel too singled out, there are also extra charges for petites. The industry claims the extra costs come from "special cuttings" and "increased fabric costs," but we haven't bought that line. Another rip-off: rush charges. Even if your wedding is still three months away, some designers still insist on "rush fees" to get you the dress on time. However, just because the manufacturers can't figure out how to sew a gown in less than three months, doesn't mean you should pay a premium. One solution: if you're a petite, order a regular size dress and have it altered. Our sources say it just isn't worth it to shell out the extra charges to get a petite.

Pitfall #11
DECEPTIVE DISCONTINUATIONS.

"I saw a great gown in a bridal shop last week. Yesterday, they called me to tell me my dress has been discontinued, BUT if I placed my order by Friday, they could still get my gown. Is this legitimate?"

Probably not. This is a common tactic by some dishonest bridal shops that try to pressure brides into quick decisions. Now while it is true that some gowns are discontinued every season, shops can't order a gown after they've been notified of its discontinued status. Hence, they're pulling your leg, trying to get a sale. If you doubt a shop's veracity, call another shop that also carries that same manufacturer. Or call your local Discount Bridal Service Representative.

Pitfall #12
SHOPS THAT HOLD BACK ORDERS.

"I ordered a bridal gown that the shop said would take three months to get in. Four months later, I have no gown and just excuses from the shop. When I asked for a confirmation that they placed the order, I get stonewalled. While my wedding is still two months away, I'm worried."

And you should be! This is another common scam perpetrated by some shops. Instead of immediately placing the order with the manufacturer, they hold on to it. Why? Well, financially strapped stores may be tempted to use your money to pay other bills—ordering the gown immediately means having to pay the invoice that much faster. How common is this problem? Even Vincent Piccione, president of Alfred Angelo, recently acknowledged how widespread the tactic is. "A major problem that concerns us is retailers who hold on to orders. This is one practice that should be eliminated, thereby putting an end to the root cause of so many horror stories that plague the industry," Piccione said in an industry trade journal.

A parallel scam is the "involuntary lay-away" rip-off. In this case, the bridal shop claims it will take much longer than it really will to get in a special-order dress. Most designers fill orders within three or four months, with six being the maximum. Yet, some of our readers report shops that claim it will take *eight or ten months* to get in their dress. What's happening? Perhaps the shop is using your money to pay their electric bill or other expenses—and plans to order your dress a few months later. In a sense, this is like an involuntary lay-away plan, where the shop holds your money for several months longer than necessary.

How can you avoid this problem? First, put the deposit on a credit card. Ask the bridal shop for a confirmation that the order is placed—most manufacturers provide this paperwork. On the order ticket, write "the shop promises to provide an order confirmation or a confirmed shipping date (from the manufacturer) within two weeks." If the shop fails to do so, cancel the order and go elsewhere. Be suspicious of retailers who claim they need more than six months to deliver a bridal gown.

Pitfall #13
IT AIN'T OVER IF IT'S OVER.

"My fiance and I fell on hard financial times and had to postpone our wedding. The problem is I had already ordered a gown. When I contacted the shop, they told me I couldn't cancel the order. Help!"

Most (if not all) bridal shops have "no refund, no-cancellation" policies on special-order bridal gowns. Wedding called off? Death in the family? It doesn't matter—you're still on the hook to buy the dress. That means the shop can also take you to court to force you to pay the balance due on the dress.

If you're merely postponing your wedding, ask the shop if you can get store credit. At least you might be able to use this in the future, or sell the credit to a friend.

Reviews of Selected Bridal Manufacturers

Here is a look at some of the best manufacturers of bridal gowns. Since there are more than 200 manufacturers of bridal apparel, we don't have the space to review everyone. Instead, we decided to concentrate on those that are the best and most visible. Our rating system (the key is given below) is based on our extensive research into bridal apparel. In the past five years, we have visited more than 200 bridal shops and tried on hundreds of gowns from dozens of manufacturers. The ratings reflect our opinion of the manufacturer's offerings, creativity, prices and quality at the time of this writing. Remember that styles and prices are constantly changing.

The past few years were a period most bridal designers want to forget. Despite public pronouncements that the wedding industry is "recession-proof," many designers were reeling from sales declines. As a result, most played it safe with new collections—few introduced new designs. On the upside, many designers didn't raise prices this season—some even rolled prices back. Here's a wrap-up of what we think are the best of the best.

The Ratings

★★★★ EXCELLENT — *our top pick!*
★★★ GOOD — *above-average quality, prices and creativity*
★★ FAIR — *could stand some improvement*
★ POOR — *yuck! Could stand major improvement*

Alfred Angelo ★★ One of the country's largest bridal designers, Angelo offers just about something for everyone. Most gowns are in the $300 to $700 range, but a few "couture" gowns run up to $1300. One typical gown we saw was a satin design with an off-the shoulder neckline and cap sleeves. Lace appliques adorned the beaded bodice and train edge. Price: $799. While some of Angelo's upper-end gowns have been favorably compared to Bianchi's elegance, others are less impressive—you get what you pay for with Angelo. The designer is still stuck in the "teal taffeta" dark ages for bridesmaids—many designs ($100 to $240) are sorely in need of updating. Large sizes are available (18-20 are $20 extra and 38 to 44 are 10% more). Only selected styles are available in petites. One negative that tempers our recommendation of Alfred Angelo: we find some of the company's marketing practices (such as requiring dealers to sign agreements not to rent their dresses) to be distasteful. See the box on page 68 of the next chapter for more on this story. (800) 528-3589 or (215) 659-8700.

Ange D' Amour ★★ This small designer is described by insiders as a "sleeper line with very good value." Most run $600 to $1100 and have moderate amounts of beading and lace. One interesting design that caught our eye was a "Venice lace mini-dress with detachable train" for $750. Only sizes 4 to 20 are available. Ange D' Amour is widely available. (800) 288-3888.

Bianchi ★★½   Bianchi, the Boston juggernaut that sells 50,000 bridal gowns a year, is one of the industry's preeminent powers. Bianchi is one of those designers that does something for everyone. From plain to ornate, Bianchi's beautiful, hand-sewn gowns have prices that range from $940 to $3100. Many brides we met said they chose a Bianchi because that's what their mothers wore at their weddings. One interesting design had "satin petals" edging the short, lace sleeves, Guipere lace and beads, a bustle of roses and tulle skirt. Price: $1080. Sizes go up to 20, with some petites available. While the bridal gowns are nice, most of the bridesmaids' styles are boring and over-priced ($144 to $250). (800) 669-2346.

Bonny ★★★   A small, import line with little exposure, but we've been impressed with their quality. For example, the beads and sequins are sewn on—for gowns that retail for $480 to $730, that's unusual. Bonny has one of the best ivory fabrics in the business and features gowns that are ornate but not overdone. Bonny's sister line is Sabrina, a lower-priced collection that comes in only four sizes. Sabrina gowns retail for about $400, with quick delivery available. New this year is an off-shoot line called "Essence by Esther" with prices from $780 to $990. A nice touch for Bonny: this line is one of the few that has sizes up to 44 (for $30 to $60 extra). (714) 961-8884.

Bridal Originals ★★   A good "middle of the road" designer, Bridal Originals offers a wide selection of gowns without ignoring the informal and second-time bride. The majority of the line is moderately styled (some call it plain vanilla). The original owners of Bridal Originals have recently bought back the company and revamped the dress offerings. Retailing for $500 to $740, most Bridal Original gowns average $600 and are widely available. One interesting design was a heavily beaded and sequined, mermaid-style gown. This lavish dress had floral appliques as well. Sizes up to 30 are available— Bridal Originals is one of the few designers that encourages stores to carry large-size samples. Bridesmaids ($100 to $200) are very traditional and basic. One plus: Bridal Originals has an extensive mother-of-the-bride and flower girl collections. (800) 876-GOWN, (312) 467-6140.

Carmi Couture ★★★½   "Have it your way" must be the theme at Carmi Couture Collection, an up and coming designer. Many dress designs are available in different fabric choices, beaded or unbeaded, with train or without, hem lace or no lace. This flexibility was most impressive. For example, we liked one design with a beaded bodice, portrait collar, deep-V back and a butterfly bow bustle. In silk shantung, this gown was $1600. Can't afford that? How about the same dress in polyester for $1200. All in all, prices ranged from $630 to $1630. A small drawback: only sizes 4 to 20 are available (with an extra $100 charge for sizes 18 and 20). We were most impressed with Carmi's lush fabrics and creative laces. Availability is still somewhat limited, but the designer has recently expanded the number of stores carrying its gowns. (212) 921-7658.

Carolina Herrera ★★★   The Porsche of bridal designers, Herrera first came to prominence with a recent Kennedy family wedding. "Understated elegance" is how we would describe these pricey designs, which almost have a contemporary European feel. Herrera may be the most creative of bridal designers currently on the market. Availability of these gowns is somewhat limited to tony salons and shops. One design we liked was a summery, white organza dress with daisies on the bodice and sleeves, jewel neckline and drop waist. Price: $2400, quite pricey considering the short, chapel-length train. (212) 575-0557.

Christos ★★★   *"Amazing"* is the word we'd use to describe Christos' gowns. Also amazing is the popularity of these pricey creations—in Houston, Texas, for example, brides have gone wild over Christos. This designer is mainly available at tony department stores and salons. Prices start at $300 (that's just for the headpieces!) The gowns go for $1100 to $3000! One typical design: a silk-dupioni gown with Venice lace appliques, sabrina neckline, details of lace and cut-work, and full skirt. Price: $1925. (212) 921-0025.

Country Elegance by Susan Lane ★★★½   For second-time brides or theme weddings, our pick would be a dress by Country Elegance. Designer Susan Lane has crafted a fascinating line of period-inspired dresses. Designs include Victorian-inspired motifs with high-neck lines and overlay collars in Alencon lace. Other dresses echo the 20's, 30's and 50's fashions. For example, the satin "Veronique" features a portrait color and high-low hemline for $400. All the gowns feature delicate laces and tiny flower appliques that are quite impressive. Prices range from $330 to $660, with most designs about $450. Gorgeous colors are available, including antique ivories, rose beiges, and pale blushes. With little or no trains, these mainly informal gowns are a hit with second-time brides. Another plus: Country Elegance's beautiful flower girl dresses are winners, if not somewhat pricey at about $150. If we had to criticize anything about Country Elegance, it would have to be their limited size options. Bridal gown sizes only go up to 16 and tend to run small. New this year are some styles that are available in the 18 to 24 size range (for a whopping $100 to $140 extra). Another important note: one reader called us to say that the fabric on her "rose beige" dress changed color slightly when pressed. (212) 302-5906, (818) 765-1551.

Diamond Collection ★★★ With its trend-setting designs, Diamond Collection's highly-stylized and distinctive gowns are a favorite with the haute couture set. Clearly one of the most innovative designers in the market, Diamond is designed by Robert Legere. One collection this year sports a decidedly "country and western" theme, with grooms in chaps and brides in pick-up trucks. One spectacular design that caught our eye features a tulle skirt and off-the-shoulder, scalloped-neck bodice with three-quarter length sleeves. Detailing included bands of multi-colored embroidery and beading. Price: $3350 for the multi-colored beading or a mere $2350 in white. A matching headpiece will run you $350 (white) or $500 (color). As you can tell, Diamond's dress prices aren't for the faint of heart, ranging from $1140 to $3400. Considering how expensive these gowns are, it's rather comical that the designer's ads show dresses thrown in bales of hay and immersed in water. Only sizes 4 to 20 can be ordered, with sizes 18 and 20 running an extra $100. Limited availability—most in tony bridal shops. (212) 302-0210.

Eden ★★★★ What a wonderful line! Eden has one of the largest selection of gowns in the $400 to $500 range. If you like Jim Hjelm dresses but can't afford Jim Hjelm prices, Eden has knocked off some of his designs for $790 to $1590. One stand-out gown that caught our eye was a blush-color, backless dress with a big bow at the bustle. The rosette detailing and tulle skirt completed the look. Petites are available (for an additional $30), as are large sizes (20 to 32) for $30 to $200 extra. Eden also offers a big selection of informals as well. "They ship fast and ship right," says one of our sources. "Eden is headed for glory!" And we agree. (818) 441-8715.

Eva Haynal Forsyth ★★★ This tony designer is mainly available at department store bridal salons. Several of their latest designs feature exquisite gold embroidery and detailing. Scaasi, the famous ready-to-wear designer, also designs for Eva. For example, one Eva dress was a silver brocade gown with a white mink, portrait collar and silver rhinestone buttons. Price: $3000. (212) 302-7710 or (804) 971-3853.

Eve of Milady ★★½ Extremely ornate and traditional, Eve must be doing something right: her designs are often copied by the smaller designers. Mainly available at upscale bridal shops, Eve's line doesn't change much from year to year, but it's still a crowd pleaser. Prices start at $700 (for the less-expensive

Boutique line) and range up to $3450 for Couture gowns. Bridesmaids' are no bargain either, running $170 to $280. With this season's crop, Eve is still going for a lot of drama, with heavy embroidery and beading even on bridesmaids' dresses. One bummer: Eve dropped her line of petites recently; now just sizes 4 to 20 are available, with an extra $100 charge for sizes 18 and 20. (212) 302-0050.

Fink ★★½ Fink is a small line that doesn't advertise much in the bridal magazines. Nonetheless, the designs may be worth the effort to search out. Styling is above average, yet still fairly traditional. One of our favorite designs from Fink is an Italian satin sheath with removeable, wrap-around train, bodice and hemline with Alencon lace and off-the-shoulder net sleeves. Price: $1000. Shipping is slow but worth the wait, our sources say. Prices run $500 to $1300. Add another 10% for sizes 18 and 20. Only sizes 6 to 20 are available. (212) 921-5683.

Galina ★★★½ One of our picks for best bridal designer, Galina pioneered the portrait neckline with a pleated collar. Fine fabrics are the trademark of Galina, whose dresses tend to be elegantly detailed with simple trains and plain hemlines. Most surprising is Galina's little-known budget-priced line, called Galina Bouquet. These gowns range from $700 to $1000, while the regular Galina gowns retail for $1150 to $3300. Bridesmaids' gowns are equally pricey at $140 to $240. Another plus: Galina doesn't shy away from color, making some of the most beautiful pale pink and pale peach gowns available on the market. For example, one design features a white tulle skirt over a peach lining, a collage-embroidered bodice, and scoop neckline. Price: $2000. Sizes go up to 20, with an extra $100 to $150 charge for sizes 18 and 20. (212) 564-1020.

Ginza Collection/Private Label by G ★★★ Ginza offers gowns in the very affordable under $500 range. Even more remarkable is the quality—every gown is hand-beaded! No glue! While Ginza gowns range from $420 to $490, Private Label by G is slightly more expensive, running from $530 to $1000. Most of the gowns are copies of more expensive designers like Eve of Milady and feature lace cut-outs on the trains. For example, one satin mermaid-style gown featured a sweetheart neckline, short puff sleeves, and a tulle skirt and train. The price is $650. Both Ginza and Private Label have sizes up to 42 but no petites. Large sizes (38, 40, 42) are an extra $100. New this year at Ginza is the Unique Collection of informal dresses and gowns without trains, running $290 to $370. (800) 654-7375.

Ilissa (Demetrios) ★★★ If there were a Top 40 chart for bridal gown designers, Ilissa/Demetrios would be in the Top 5 with a bullet. These guys are hot! One recent bridal magazine issue featured no less than 40 pages of ads for this prolific designer. With fairly ornate designs, Ilissa goes under a plethora of names from the budget-priced "Sposabella" and its twin sister "Sposaeuropa" (with gowns under $800) to the "Demetrios Platinum Collection" (with prices up to $2200). Our favorite line is "Princess Collection" a somewhat less-ornate collection that retails for less than $600. Considering the quality, these gowns are a best buy. We priced one gown from the Sposaeuropa Collection at $795 that was a two-piece ensemble with a short, lace sheath and satin overcoat. The only drawback with Ilissa: sizes only go from 4 to 20 (sizes 18 to 20 are $60 extra). Also, a bridal shop owner we spoke to complained that Ilissa's deliveries are erratic—some dresses arrive in a couple of weeks, while others take six months. The quality and workmanship can also be variable as well. As a result, we've lowered Ilissa's rating slightly from last year. Available mainly at mid- to upper-scale shops. (212) 967-5222.

Impression ★★½ Don't judge this designer by their lackluster ads. What the ads don't show is the opulent lace and wonderful fabrics. The designs are very traditional, with classic lines and detailing. The lower-priced "Crystal" gowns are an affordable $395 to $455, while the rest of Impression's dresses range from $450 to $1350. Petites are available, as are sizes 16-20 (for an additional $30) and 22-30 (for another $70). (800) BRIDAL-1.

Jasmine ★★★★ Here's a hot line that's a very good value. Jasmine's innovative detailing and well-priced gowns are winning many fans. The Haute Couture line is quite stylish—nice use of lace and beading, without being too gaudy. The Jasmine Collection's dresses are more simple with traditional necklines and silhouettes. One stand-out we liked was a "Haute Couture" design that had an off-the-shoulder sweetheart neckline, floral appliques on the bodice with sequins, short-puff sleeves and taffeta full skirt with Alencon hem lace. Price: $1190. Overall, Jasmine gowns range from $570 to $1250. Large sizes up to 44 are available for an additional $60 to $100. (708) 519-7778.

Jessica McClintock ★★★★ This ready-to-wear designer has won a lot of fans with her well-designed and priced bridal apparel. Based in San Francisco, McClintock's designs are fresh and innovative, described as "very feminine." Several sheath and strapless looks are stand-outs, as were four all-linen creations we viewed. The informals are fantastic, offering the most choices in this category next to Susan Lane. Few can beat McClintock's prices considering the quality: most dresses cost $216 to $680. Bridesmaids' gowns (some of which are 100% cotton, ranging from $132 to $240) are also impressive with a few styles on par with our favorite designer, Watters and Watters. The designer also has 11 affordable flower girl dresses for $56 to $92. For the prices and quality, McClintock is a definite best buy. Most dresses are available in sizes 4 to 16, although a few are available up to 24. McClintock has 14 stores in eight states, plus a large number of dealers. For even more savings, check out their bridal outlet stores—more information on that later. Delivery usually takes less than a month, much faster than other bridal designers. We should note that McClintock has cut back advertising lately—hence you may want to send for her bridal catalog by mailing a check for $6 to P.O. Box 44393, San Francisco, CA, 94144. (800) 333-5301. (415) 495-3030.

Jim Hjelm ★★★★ Perhaps the industry's quickest rising star, Hjelm has a resume that would make any designer green with envy: six years at Galina, nineteen years at Priscilla, and two years at Bianchi. Hjelm started his own company in 1987. Jim Hjelm Designs produces classic silhouettes with exquisite beading and lace detailing. Quality is impeccable; prices range from $900 to $3600. New at Hjelm this year is a lower-priced line called "JH by Jim Hjelm," with gowns from $730 to $1000. Many of these dresses are a best buy. For example, one JH gown had a sweetheart neckline, Alencon lace, basque bodice, full skirt and double-puff short sleeves. Price: $730. Sizes 4 to 20 are available, with sizes 18 to 20 running $150 extra. While Jim Hjelm's "Private Collection" (read: expensive) gowns are more fashion-forward in styling, the designer plays it safe with the JH gowns. On the down side, some of Hjelm's lower-priced gowns have glued-on beading; one bride called us to complain that her dress discolored after cleaning, ruining any heirloom possibilities. Also, Hjelm's bridesmaids designs are dull and expensive, running from $170 to $190. Despite these negatives, we still consider Hjelm one of the industry's rising stars. (212) 764-6960.

Joelle ★★½ We raised Joelle's rating this year, reflecting a similar rise in the line's styling and creativity. Joelle's designer, Zurc, has spiced up the collection this season, with some outstanding dresses. From sheaths with cap sleeves and wrap-around trains, to tulle-skirted designs with lace cut-out sleeves and delicate detailing, Joelle seems to be on a roll. The bridesmaids are also quite stylish this year, with two-piece suits and wrap-around tulip skirts. Bridal gown prices are moderate, ranging from $530 to $800. (212) 736-8811.

Laura Ashley ★★½ In a previous edition of this book, we listed Ashley's bridal gowns as a "best buy." However, recent price increases have made this very limited line less affordable. The five bridal gowns styles now retail for $475 to $950, almost double the previous prices. Still, the designs are impressive. One stunning silk dress with embroidery is $950. In the past, these designs were more on the "informal" side with no trains. Now, two of the designs feature short trains—an ivory brocade dress even has a long train. Most of the dresses are quite plain, with no beading and just a smattering of lace. Instead of polyester, fabrics are cotton "sateens and brocades." Bridesmaids (in stripes, florals and solids) are an expensive $185 to $235. New this year are "sailor boy suits" for ring bearers, at $98 to $120. An embroidered veil is available for $110. One advantage to Ashley: you deal directly with one of her own stores in 39 states (no messy bridal shops). You may want to call a local store for a bridal catalog to see the styles before you make the trip. (800) 223-6917.

Lili ★★½ This California-based importer can be summed up in one word: hot! The company claims to be the fastest growing bridal designer in the U.S. And with these prices, it's hard not to see why: nearly all of these ornate, hand-beaded gowns retail for $600 to $650. Lili also brags about quick delivery (as little as one week in some cases), since it stocks many styles in their warehouse. Our only complaint: Lili's magazine ads do not show off their dresses well. On the upside, all of their gowns are hand-beaded—an unusual sight in this price range. Sizes from 4 to 26 are available, with an additional $70 charge for sizes 22-26. (800) 258-7944. (818) 282-4326.

Marisa ★★★★ Especially popular among southern brides, Marisa is a small line of some very unusual dresses. Nothing is "run of the mill" here. Marisa's young designer does original designs, not copies. The unique lace treatments and plain skirts give these dresses a different look—you'll either love it or hate it. One design we liked had a sweetheart neckline, a silk shantung skirt and a bodice and waist are covered in a Guipure lace. Price: $1050. Overall, Marisa's gowns are expensive, with most designs running $890 to $2290. Sizes 18 and 20 are $160 additional (regular sizes four through 16 are available). (212) 944-0022.

Mary's ★★ Mary's by P.C. Mary's Inc. is a Texas-based importer that offers basic styles that are middle-of-the-road in quality. Recently, the designer seems to be concentrating on satin gowns with lace cut-outs. Styling is traditional with moderate amounts of detailing and decoration. Two of their more interesting new designs are short dresses with either a long jacket or wrap-around train. Prices range from $400 to $1478 with sizes from 4 to 30. (713) 933-9678.

Mon Cherie ★★★½ Don't look for this import designer's ads in the bridal magazines—Mon Cherie rarely advertises. Instead, the designer concentrates on lower prices for brides. Mon Cherie's strategy is to knock off the best dress designs from other manufacturers. Prices range from $400 to $1120, but most are in the $600 to $700 range. Large sizes (18-20 and 38-44) are only a $20 to $40 up-charge—very reasonable. "These dresses look better in person than in their ads," one source told us. Overall, quality is good for an import line. (609) 530-1900.

Moonlight ★★ This Chicago-based importer has a strong following in the nation's heartland. Designs are a mix of sheaths and mermaids, as well as drop-waisted and traditional full-skirted looks. Many are knock-offs of Eve of Milady gowns. One stand-out we saw featured poof sleeves with rosette bows and pearl drops, as well as a pearl choker above an open neckline. A satin skirt and cathedral train completed the look for $1500. Overall, Moonlight's prices range from $600 to $1800, slightly more expensive than in years past. The lack of design creativity, combined with the high prices, tempers our recommendation of Moonlight. On the upside, the designer's sizes go up to 44 (sizes 38-44 are $80 to $120 extra). (708) 884-7199.

Mori Lee ★★★ Here's a hot import designer that wowed insiders with their affordable gowns at the last bridal market. Designer Madeline Gardner has created some unique styles, with quality and handiwork that rival domestic designers. Mori Lee offers three collections, starting with the Boutique line that's in the affordable "under $500" range. Their regular Mori Lee line is $400 to $700, while the Regency by Madeline Gardner collection is $800 to $1000. A few designs are available in large sizes (up to 42) for $80 extra. While Mori Lee is a "best buy" for value, their deliveries are another story. Insiders call them "horrendous." "If you want a bridesmaid's dress, you better have six months and an iron stomach," says one source. As a result, we can't give Mori Lee our top rating. (212) 947-3490.

Paula Varsalona ★★ This Kansas City-based designer is famous for doing unique and original designs. One dress design we liked was a white-on-white swirl pattern with giant, leg-o-mutton sleeves and strategically scattered seed pearls. Occasionally, all that creativity misses the mark—Varsalona wins our award for the most ridiculous bridal design this year. Her sequined jump-suit with detachable tulle overskirt is a flop, in our opinion. For all those brides who want to wear a pant suit to their wedding, this design can be had for a mere $1995. (212) 221-5600.

Priscilla of Boston ★★★½ This quintessential bridal designer from Boston has captured the hearts and minds of brides for the past 45 years. Luxurious fabrics and traditional detailing are the hallmark of Priscilla, whose prices match the quality. Gowns start at $1280 and often go beyond the $2000 mark. We even saw one gown that sold for an incredible $8400. While many of the gowns have exquisite beading and lace, Priscilla thankfully avoids the "over-encrusted" look. Petite sizes are available. The designer rarely advertises anymore; the one new style this season is an informal, Irish linen dress with scattered Venice lace flowers for a pricey $990. One interesting new development with Priscilla: the designer has opened her own boutiques in several cities, including Denver. If we have one complaint about Priscilla, it would be the lack of new designs. The line, while beautiful and traditional, looks much the same from year to year. (617) 242-2677.

San Martin ★½ Ruffles! Ruffles! Ruffles! Described alternatively as the "cute fluffy look" and "the ruffle explosion," San Martin gowns are definitely, well, unique. Popular on the West Coast, San Martin's gowns range from $370 to $1500. The line is split into several collections—the newest and most affordable is the "Lorrie Kabala Signature Classics," which run about $500. Sizes run from 2 to 44. Sizes 18 and 20 are $10 extra, while sizes 38 and 44 are available "in limited styles." The designer is a heavy advertiser in "Bridal Guide" magazine (you won't see them much elsewhere.) (213) 257-5333.

St. Pucchi ★★½ Wow is about all we can say about this Texas-based designer. 100% pure silk, these top-of-the-line gowns are individually hand-cut and hand-embroidered—the detailing is just incredible! Completely lined (with sewn in bra cups and petticoats), St. Pucchi's has several collections with prices that are not for the faint of wallet—the gowns start at $1090. One gown we saw had lace cut-work on the sleeves, bodice and train. If you're looking for a gown that's heavily beaded, nobody beats St. Pucchi for their flash and panache. On the down side, delivery is slow, taking three to five months. Sizes go up to 20 (with a 20% up-charge for sizes 18 and 20). One positive development: St. Pucchi has just released a line of lower-priced gowns called "St. Pucchi Classique." These retail for $800 to $1400. (214) 631-4039.

Sweetheart ★★ Here's a very traditional designer that has an occasional flash of style. Most gowns are between $500 and $1000. For example, one gown we saw featured a heavily beaded and sequined bodice with beaded appliques cascading from a basque waistline for $650. One plus: Sweetheart has a large selection of informals. Another advantage is their delivery time—since the designer keeps all sizes (4-44) in stock, delivery is relatively quick. (212) 868-7536.

Venus ★★ A wide assortment of styles and price ranges describes this designer. Starting at $350, Venus even has a few pricey creations that go up to $1500. We liked the styles, which mainly seem like knock-offs of Demetrios/Ilissa. Two collections are available, Venus and the less-ornate (and less expensive) Pallas Athena. Informals are available for as little as $160. Widely available, Venus also has petites available (for $40 extra). 1-800-OH-VENUS. (818) 285-6528.

Spotlight: Best Buy #1

Discount Bridal Service
(Over 300 representatives nationwide)
(800) 874-8794

Discount Bridal Service (DBS) is a mail-order company that offers 20% to 30% discounts on almost all nationally-advertised bridal apparel. Hold it! How can that be, you ask?

Well, DBS has found an interesting way to get you those same fancy designer gowns without the fancy designer price tag. Here's how they do it: DBS has a central headquarters in Baltimore, Maryland and a network of over 300 representatives in major cities. The reps don't have typical bridal shops with all the high overhead and bloated inventory expenses. By cutting out expensive overhead, DBS passes the savings along to brides in the form of sizeable discounts.

For example, we priced one fancy designer gown dripping with lace and pearls at a retail of $2390. Then we called the local DBS rep in our city and found that she could order the very same dress for just $1700! Wow! That's a savings of $690 or nearly 30%! Other bridal gowns we priced were available at 20% to 25% discounts, with great deals on bridesmaids, head-pieces/veils, flower girl and mother of the bride dresses as well!

So what's the catch, you say? Well, you do have to pay

for shipping, freight, and insurance on all orders... but that came to just $30 extra on the gown we priced. Another slight disadvantage: DBS requires all orders to be paid in advance. Also, some dresses take more time than normal to order—up to six months in some cases.

When you order a gown from DBS, the merchandise is directly shipped to your home address after being inspected at their headquarters. If the gown needs alterations, DBS reps can refer you to one of several local seamstresses. Another big plus for DBS: while most bridal shops carry just 10 to 12 bridal apparel lines, DBS can order from more than 100 different manufacturers.

So what do regular bridal shops think of DBS? Well, most of their comments are unprintable here. Basically, many bridal shops are mad as all heck that brides can get gowns at such big discounts. Bridal shops are also angry that consumers come into their shop to try on the gowns and then go to DBS to buy. Of course, all this is just sour grapes—if shops provided good service and lower prices, there would be no reason to order from DBS.

Other bridal shops question the authenticity of the company, wondering how they can order those same designer-quality gowns. Surprisingly, this is a good example of the behind-the-scenes struggle between retailers and manufacturers over discounting. While everyone (except the brides) complains about discounting, many of the manufacturers are quietly selling to discounters such DBS.

Anyway, we like DBS and recommend the company highly. Perhaps the biggest challenge to ordering a gown from the company is identifying the exact dress. With many shops coding and concealing the identity of gowns, the best solution may be to find a picture of the same gown in a bridal magazine. Since many gowns are advertised at one point in their life, DBS can nail down the exact manufacturer and style by just knowing the magazine issue and page number.

Of course, Discount Bridal Service isn't perfect. Our readers complain that the company does *not* accept credit cards—as you know, an important consumer protection in our opinion. Also, when you call their 800-number to find a local dealer, you will more than likely get a voice mail message instead of a real person. After a day (some brides say it's more like three days), you finally get a call back. For a company that advertises itself as a "personal buying service for brides," that's hardly personal service. Despite these problems, we still like the company and find them to be very reputable.

As a side note, DBS representatives often offer discounts on wedding invitations and other accessories. Even if you decide not to order a gown from DBS, they may be able to save you money on another aspect of your wedding. For the DBS representative in your town, call toll-free (800) 874-8794 or (800) 441-0102. If you want a designer bridal gown but don't have a designer bank account, Discount Bridal Service may be the answer.

Spotlight: Best Buy #2

Kleinfelds

Kleinfelds, 8202 5th Ave., Brooklyn, New York (718) 833-1100, claims to be the largest bridal retailer in the country, if not the world. And all that buying power translates into lower prices on their giant selection of bridal apparel. While the store claims it isn't a "discount" store, their prices are often 10% to 25% below retail.

What if you don't live in or near Brooklyn? Well, you can order gowns by phone. Just fax them a magazine picture of the gown, along with your measurements. Kleinfelds will then special-order the gown and have it shipped to your home address. The company even takes credit cards, a big plus in our opinion. Delivery takes about three to six months.

In business since 1942, Kleinfelds even has an entire building dedicated to bridesmaids' and "special occasion" dresses. The "bridal attendants" store is two blocks from their main location, at 8209 3rd Ave. (718-238-1500).

So what do our readers think of Kleinfelds? The reviews are decidedly mixed. While the mail-order service gets good marks, an actual visit to Kleinfelds may be one more to endure than enjoy. One bride panned the store's selection of sample dresses which were in "terrible condition," she said. On a busy weekend the place can resemble a zoo, with service that ranges from "pushy" to "extremely disappointing."

Spotlight: Best Buy #3

Bridal Outlets & Discount Warehouses

If the '60s were the "we" decade and '70s were the "me" decade, then the '90s will probably be known as the "never buy retail" decade. Popping up all across the country are outlet malls where you can get designer goods at non-designer prices. Can't find what you're looking for there? Well, visit any of the warehouse clubs and buy something in bulk for a steal.

But can you get such a deal on a bridal dress? The answer is yes, if you're lucky enough to live in a city with a bridal outlet store or warehouse. Here's the scoop.

Bridal Warehouses. Frankly, most bridal designers would rather die than be caught "discounting" their past-seasons' gowns to brides. Instead of selling these goods to brides directly, they'd rather dump them to a "liquidator" who would quietly dispose of them without much fuss.

In the past, these liquidators would roam the country, setting up "special sales" in hotel ballrooms. "ONE DAY ONLY" their ads would scream, attracting flocks of brides who would peruse the used samples at the local Holiday Inn.

When the recession of the early '90s hit, the liquidators had a flash of inspiration—why not set up a "warehouse" where brides could buy these gowns? If it works for office supplies and electronics, why not bridal?

Suddenly, they began popping up like weeds. **David's Bridal Warehouse** was probably the first. David's has stores in Florida (Orlando, West Palm Beach, Tampa, and Hollandale) as well as, Baltimore, Philadelphia, and Springfield, Virginia. The average warehouse stocks 1300 bridal gowns, in sizes 2 to 24. Most gowns are sold off-the-rack.

Even regular bridal retailers have gotten into the act, figuring if you can't beat 'em, join 'em. Hence the Bride 'N' Formal chain in Texas (the largest in the state) has set up several Bridal Warehouses in Houston.

What are all these warehouses selling? Many stock hundreds of "past season" (read: old) bridal gowns. Our readers report the condition of the dresses varies between "excellent" and "trashed." While some dresses are last season's closeouts, others are used samples bought from bankrupt bridal stores.

Of course, the advantage is you can get a gown quickly. Many warehouses stock a wide variety of sizes—if you find what you're looking for, you can walk out that same day with a dress. No waiting months for a "special order" to arrive.

Critics point out that the deals aren't as good as they seem. At one bridal warehouse, we heard reports that the company was selling private-label bridal gowns with inflated suggested-retail prices. For example, the warehouse was claiming that a $300 gown had a suggested retail price of $900. Sewn in Taiwan, this gown probably would have retailed for no more than $400 or $500. Hence, the deals aren't as sweet as they may seem. Furthermore, the quality of these clone, knock-off gowns is certainly not the same as designer originals. Service is another area of conern. A reader from Atlanta wrote to say the David's in Georgia had service that was at best lackluster.

So should you visit the neighborhood bridal warehouse? Sure, why not? Just do some shopping in advance at other bridal shops so you are more aware of quality and price. Don't think you're getting a big bargain just because the store has the word *warehouse* in its name.

Bridal Outlets. While most famous bridal designers do not have outlets, there are a few exceptions.

Jessica McClintock, for example, has not one but FIVE outlets for her popular line of bridal apparel. The flagship outlet store is the Gunne Sax outlet in San Francisco (415-495-3326), which not only has 20,000 dresses discounted 20% to 70%, but includes a fabric outlet too. Also in California, the "La Petite Factory" (909) 982-1866 in Mont Clair and "Sutter Place" in Huntington Beach (714) 841-7124 are Jessica McClintock outlets under assumed names. If you live in the East, check out the Jessica McClintock outlets in Reading, PA (215) 478-0810 or Central Valley, NY in Woodbury Commons (914) 928-7474. All outlet stores carry past-season styles at a 20% to 70% savings.

Laura Ashley fans will probably be thrilled to hear that the designer has five outlets, in Secaucus, New Jersey (201) 863-3066, Woodbridge, Virginia (703) 494-3124, Myrtle Beach, South Carolina (803) 236-4244, Freeport, Maine (207) 865-3300 and Orlando, Florida (407) 351-2785. We strongly urge you to call before you make the trip—not all of the outlets have bridal and the selection changes frequently. When bridal is available, the savings can be as much as 60% off retail.

JCPenny (214) 431-0226 has several bridal outlets in a few states. Our readers have praised the selection and prices for both bridal gowns and bridesmaids dresses. Call your local JCPenny store for outlet locations near you.

Arizona brides can find deals on bridal gowns at **Affordable Dreams** in Phoenix (602) 279-4933. This shop sells first-quality over-runs from several famous designers from 50% to 70% off.

Dallas-based **St. Pucchi** is one of the few "couture" designers with an outlet. Pucchi's "wholesale warehouse" (214) 631-4039, located in a commercial district near downtown, fails the "truth in advertising" test. While it is a warehouse, everything is not priced at wholesale.

True, there is a back room with 100+ samples which range in condition from "brand new" to "torn to shreds." Mostly sizes 10's, the dresses from Pucchi's lower-priced Classique line ran $50 to $1500, about 45% to 75% off retail. A slim selection of mangled headpieces and single bridesmaids' dresses were shoved in one corner.

The biggest disappointment was the fact that a whole room of "special order" (read: new) dresses were not discounted. These dresses ranged from $950 to $4700 and delivery takes three months.

It really torques us to walk into a "wholesale warehouse" only to find the nicest merchandise is priced at regular retail—a lesson for outlet shoppers everywhere. Add on top of this the warehouse's non-existent service and you're suppose to pay full price for this? Pucchi's "outlet" is for hard-core fans only—if you can find a sample that's not too trashed, it may be a good deal. But if you're not a size 10 and don't have time to make repeat visits, you may want to skip this one. One interesting note: it appears that the gowns we saw had tags indicating the true style number—a boon for discount mail-order shoppers.

The tony **Neiman-Marcus** department store chain has two outlet stores called Neiman-Marcus' Last Call in Austin, TX (512) 447-0701, and Franklin Mills Mall in Philadelphia, PA, (215) 637-5900. The Texas outlet occasionally gets in size 10 sample gowns from N-M's bridal salons at incredible savings. For example, we saw one Jim Hjelm gown that retails for $3595 marked down to $650! Wow! An 80% savings! While the Phildelphia outlet rarely gets in bridal, it may be a good place to check for formals for mothers. Be aware that selection may vary widely from time to time. Call before you make any major trip.

Mention the address **"1385 Broadway"** to any New York City bride and you're likely to get a smile. That address is home to the "Bridal Building," a collection of showrooms and sales offices of the country's best known bridal designers. Here's the reason brides are flocking to that address: Many of these showrooms are open to the public on Saturdays and pass along big discounts to brides. That's right—the same designers who rail against discounting are themselves quietly discounting at 1385 Broadway.

We visited the nondescript office building last year and were impressed by the deals. When you enter the building, you're handed a list of which floors are open that Saturday. (This apparently changes from week to week.) After a crowded elevator ride (hey, this is New York), we arrived at the first open floor. We visited several showrooms and came away with the following impressions: designers not only are selling used samples but also are taking special orders for new gowns. Discounts for samples were up to 50%, while special orders were an amazing 20% to 25% off.

Why do the designers do this? One insider told us it's the only way the designers can keep their best salespeople happy— the commissions from "Saturday sales" are a big salary boost.

Service varied widely from showroom to showroom—in some cases staffers were relatively friendly (for New York). Other showrooms had little or no service and the attitudes of some salespeople needed adjusting.

Alterations is another issue—some showrooms include alterations in the price, while others charge exorbitant fees. One designer was charging a flat $200 fee for alterations, no matter what needed to be done.

So is it a good deal? Yes, with some cautions. Don't forget to factor in the price of parking and tolls ($15 a trip) for not only the initial visit but also any follow-up alteration fittings. Selection and which showrooms are open will vary from week to week—it's really a gamble to find the right dress. Our sources say the best pickings are after the twice yearly bridal markets in April and September. Lots of samples are available at these times, but special orders are taken all year round. So, if you live near New York, you may want to venture into the jungle and check out the bridal building.

Bridal Magazines: Friend or Foe?

One of the first things you probably did after you got engaged was trot down to your local newsstand and pick up a copy of a bridal magazine. Hoping to find answers to wedding questions, you thumb through all the glossy advertisements.

But what kind of advice are these magazines giving consumers? And who's side are they on anyway? The short answer is: not yours. And the advice is silly at best. For example, in a special section titled "A Lavish Wedding For Less," Bride's magazine reveals that "the fewer prints you choose for your photo album, the less you'll pay." No kidding.

Of course, Modern Bride Magazine is just as absurd. In an article titled, "50 ways to Stretch Your Wedding Dollars," the rocket scientists at Modern Bride suggest "hiring a professional wedding planner." Later, they advise "stick to your budget. If you want a more expensive dress, cut back in another area." You've got to be kidding!

Of course, suspiciously missing in all these articles are any real tips on saving money on such items as the bridal gown. In fact, a recent spat between the two largest magazines, Bride's and Modern Bride Magazine, produced some startling revelations about the magazines and their true aims. Among other confessions, one admitted to blocking ads by bridal discounters and gown renters, while another flaunted its anti-consumer bias.

The feud began in April 1991 when the Director of Advertising at Modern Bride, Jim Duhe, wrote a letter to all bridal retailers. We obtained a copy of this letter.

What was the subject of Duhe's wrath? Attached to his letter was an article in Glamour Magazine (April 1991) titled "Truth in Fashion: The high cost of getting married."

The article correctly points out the poor quality and inflated prices of bridal gowns. "Many dresses that cost under $2000 are made of synthetic fabric and mass-produced," the story said. Furthermore, the article points out that "many bridesmaids dresses are synthetic-fiber horrors lacking in sophistication" and that "manufacturers claim the lack of style results from having to make dresses that can be worn by

Headpieces and Veils

If you think bridal gowns are overpriced, you haven't seen anything yet! Wait until you see the price tags on headpieces and veils! You may have to be revived with smelling salts. That's because hefty markups on these items regularly push the prices of headpieces/veils over $150 and even $300.

Now, let's look at what you are actually buying here. Let's see, we have a headpiece frame, which costs about $5 in fabric stores. Then you add some lace, pearls, and beads. Top it off with veiling, which costs $2 to $5 per yard at most fabric stores. Sure, the labor involved to assemble these things isn't cheap, but we still don't comprehend how this all adds up to $200.

Our best advice on headpieces and veils is to consider going "custom" here. If you have a relative who can sew, here is where he or she can help you. Another option is resale/consignment shops that sell headpieces and veils for about $100 or less. Don't forget that you can rent a headpiece and veil at rental shops for a fraction of retail prices. One rental shop we visited had more than 20 styles that rented for $25 to $30 each. Wow!

By the way, on your visit to most bridal shops, you're going to be strongly encouraged to purchase a wide range of accessories, from lingerie to shoes. See the following page for more details.

any body type." The story concludes that the "biggest rip-off" at bridal shops are accessories such as lingerie, jewelry, and shoes that are sold at outrageously inflated prices.

Obviously, this is all true. Yet Modern Bride's Duhe claimed the "article includes several alarming statements—some are merely inaccurate; others are extremely damaging to anyone who depends upon bridal retail sales for his/her livelihood."

Duhe then notes that Glamour is owned by Conde Nast, the same company that owns Bride's magazine. He implies that Bride's was behind the article! He says, "it is incredulous to accept that Bride's magazine can do absolutely nothing to project the bridal industry in a more positive light to its sister publications."

On May 1, 1991, the publisher of Bride's at that time, Elliot Marion, shot back. "We intend to hold you responsible for your knowingly false lies," he says in a letter to Jim Duhe, a copy of which we also have obtained.

Marion called Duhe's letter "a shocking commentary on you and your view of the journalist profession. What infuriates us is

Accessories & Other Outrageously Priced Extras

If you thought the bridal gown was expensive by itself, wait till you see the prices on "bridal accessories:" head-pieces/veils, petticoats, lingerie, shoes, garters, gloves, stockings, jewelry are all available from your local friendly bridal shop at mark-ups that are quite obscene.

And, amazingly, the bridal industry makes no bones about the fat profits it fleeces from brides and grooms on these items. According to *Vows: The Bridal & Wedding Business Journal*, "Accessories are an important, lucrative part of the bridal business." One executive of a hosiery company advises shops to "go ahead and get the garters, the gloves and stockings for the entire bridal party—they're easy add-on sales. The mark-up on them is usually 100 percent and that's quite easy to achieve."

And some shops don't stop at 100%. *Glamour Magazine* interviewed one furious bride who was suckered into buying a $28 bra at a bridal shop. The boutique owner told her she *must* wear that bra. When she got home, she discovered that the manufacturer's price tag said $22. Hence the bridal shop had taken an $11 bra (at wholesale) and marked it up to $28—a tidy 155% mark-up. What a racket!

Of course, the accessories don't stop at the bride. Ring pillows, cake tops, guest books and attendants gifts are items you *must have,* says the bridal shop. Just listen to what wedding guru Beverly Clark (who, by the way, has her own collection of bridal accessories that she hawks) advises to bridal retailers in *Vows*: "Each time the wedding entourage enters your store, you have an opportunity to increase your overall dollar volume, in excess of $300 per party." And here's the kicker: "In this economy," Clark said, "you [the bridal retailer] have to get every dollar out of the bride." Isn't that nice? And people wonder why the bridal industry gets such a bad rap?

your assertions of Bride's involvement in this article are false and, because you yourself used to work at Bride's Magazine, know how things are done here, you must have known it was false."

The letter concludes "we suggest that next time you have your lawyers review your letters."

Whoa! Now things are getting interesting! But, wait sports fans, the best is yet to come!

That's because Modern Bride wasn't done yet—in another letter on May 16, 1991, the same Mr. Duhe renews his attack on Bride's. This time the target of his rantings is page 358 of the June/July 1991 issue of Bride's. The article on that page is "Shopping Secrets," which includes several widely-known money saving tips.

For example, Bride's suggests brides "negotiate price if

Avoiding the big rip-offs in this category is tricky. Nearly a third of all brides fall victim to sales hype and buy accessories at bridal shops. While brides try on gowns, owners of bridal shops often sneak out those bras, jewelry, hosiery and other do-dads. There may be subtle and not-so-subtle pressure to buy the "whole outfit." We say resist the pressure and shop around. For example, those $50 shoes at bridal shops (which *Glamour Magazine* says are "usually made of poor-quality, dyed-to-match satin") may be much cheaper at chain shoe stores. Those stores also offer a wider selection, too. Catalogs are another affordable option.

Forget the jewelry at bridal shops. Much of it is fake and grossly over-priced—sometimes two to three times the retail prices of other stores. Other, non-bridal stores are likely to have better prices. The same goes for gloves, lingerie, guest books and more. The best shops will rent slips and petticoats for a fraction of retail prices.

And don't think the bridal industry has forgotten about the groom either. One of the biggest profit areas in formal-wear rental has nothing to do with the tuxedo—it's the shoes that are the money-makers. Yes, we're talking about those cheesy, plastic black shoes that bridal shops and tux places buy for $14 each. The shops turn around and rent them for $10 a pop—since the shoes can be rented out 20 times or more, each pair can reap revenues of $200!

According to *Vows*, the magazine conservatively estimated the profit from shoe rental at a fat 55%. "That is over three times the profit that most operators enjoy on a tuxedo rental." And the key word in that sentence is *enjoy*. Our advice: skip the shoes and buy a nice pair of black shoes. Since you'll wear them again and again, in the long run, you'll probably come out ahead.

you've found the same dress for less at another shop." Now, it doesn't take a brain surgeon to recognize this is a way to save money. The article also suggests "borrow a slip," "compare catalog shoe prices," and "the groom's tuxedo may be free with a rental of usher's tuxedos."

All of the above are very common tips. But, of course, that doesn't thrill Mr. Duhe of Modern Bride who has seems to have appointed himself as the Keeper of Correct Political Thought in the bridal industry.

He says, and we're not making this up, that "the majority of information included in this section is either blatantly inaccurate or in direct conflict with standard bridal retailing practices."

The kicker comes in the next paragraph when Duhe of Modern Bride *says* "Bride's could and should have been

Alterations

One of the best euphemisms in the bridal business is what the shops refer to as "custom-fitting." Whether called by this name or another more common moniker (alterations), there's no denying that this is a high-expense area.

After shelling out $500 to $1000 (or more) for a gown, many brides are surprised to learn that their gown requires "custom-fitting" (read: more money). That's because few gowns are made to your measurements—most are made on assembly lines to correspond to a standard size. This may be close to your measurements—close, but not close enough.

Remember the survey we quoted earlier in the chapter, when we revealed the same bride would be a different size in different designers' gowns? Well, the other news from that survey is that 60% of the time, the bride will need additional alterations—er, "custom-fitting."

So, what's a fair price for a little tuck here and there? For that answer, we looked at another survey, this one by *Bridal Information Resource*, an industry newsletter. In 1991, the publisher surveyed 130 bridal shops to determine "average" cost for such common alterations as a bridal gown hem and bridesmaids dress alterations.

For example, the survey revealed that an average bridal gown requires $62 in alterations—some shops charge as little as $30 and others more than $125. A hem for the gown averaged $28, with prices from $20 to more than $100.

Bridesmaids' dresses didn't escape the needle, either. The bridesmaid is socked with an additional $17 in alterations, with some shops charging a whopping $50 or more. A simple hem for a bridesmaids' dress can run $10 to $30.

Here's the biggest rip-off: shops that raise the price of alterations for more expensive gowns for no reason at all. According to an article in *Vows: The Bridal Business Journal*, "shops that have a higher price point, charge more for alterations. These more expensive dresses are not more difficult to alter, nor do they fit badly. It's a matter of what the market will bear."

Wow! Can you believe this? Just consider it a little gift from the bridal industry—for those of you who purchase expensive (i.e., anything over $500) dresses, you get the privilege of being overcharged for alterations.

So, how can you avoid these problems? First, realize that some shops offer alterations for free. Of course, you can also take your gown to an independent seamstress (local fabric stores often have recommendations). This avoids the bridal shop altogether and, in some cases, may be the best route.

more sensitive to the needs of the retailers it purports to serve. All of us in the bridal business must concentrate on minimizing confusion in the marketplace and projecting full-service bridal retailing in a positive light."

Now, that last statement is quite revealing. Given the argument Duhe lays out, one is left to assume that "projecting the bridal industry in a positive light" means covering up problems in the bridal industry. Of course, one could also "minimize confusion in the marketplace" by censoring consumer-oriented tips that save brides and grooms money. If you as a consumer are armed with smart shopping tips, the only "confusion" will be in the retailer's mind—wondering why they aren't able to rip-off brides with inflated prices and dubious practices.

Which brings us to the bottom line of Modern Bride's thinking here—money saving tips and true consumer information are, in Mr. Duhe's words, "an affront to every full-service bridal retailer and may have an extremely negative impact on your (the retailer's) business." Well, at least we know where their true loyalties are.

Meanwhile, Bride's was next to put their foot in their mouth. In a truly shocking letter to bridal retailers on May 6, 1991, Bride's drops a bombshell. In trying to prove how much they support the wedding industry, the publisher Elliot Marion states an official policy that is still in effect as of this writing: "While other bridal publications carry discount bridal retailer ads, as well as bridesmaids rental ads, Bride's has NEVER accepted these ads, [we] believe that these can only hurt your business."

Wow! There it is folks, in black and white from the guy at the top—Bride's doesn't want you the consumer to save money from bridal discounters. If someone wants to offer you a discount on wedding gowns or any other merchandise, that's not the kind of merchant Bride's wants you to find. Hmmmm.

Perhaps even more amazing is the fact that Bride's blocks ads by bridesmaids rental firms. Well, take a look at any recent issue of this magazine. Notice anything funny? Surprise! We see many ads by companies that rent formal-wear for MEN! But what if a company wants to rent formal-wear for women, sparing them from shelling out big bucks for taffeta bridesmaid nightmares? Nope, you won't see that in Bride's Magazine.

What an amazingly sexist policy from a magazine whose readers are 98% women! Why would they do that to you? That's because the magazines know where their bread is buttered—these letters show without a shadow of a doubt that their #1 concern is not you, the bride. Nope, the most important interest in their eyes are dollars signs—the big money bags of the wedding industry. Forget about journalistic integrity. If you're a $10 billion industry, maybe you can buy off a few magazines too.

Clone Gowns: Is Your Gown a Knock-off?

Here's an ominous new trend in bridal fashion: clone gowns. Yes, it's happened with computers and now it's coming to a bridal shop near you!

So, what is a "clone" gown? As you might expect from the name, these gowns are knock-offs of designers originals. Most are made in Taiwan and then are imported into the U.S. We've noticed a flood of these gowns in the past year or so—one import company has even opened up a retail shop in Houston, Texas that sells nothing but clone gowns.

Many "traditional" bridal shops have also jumped on the clone gown bandwagon. Why? Clone gowns are cheaper for the store to buy. Does that mean they are passing along the savings to consumers? Don't bet on it—our sources indicate stores are taking larger mark-ups on clone gowns. This helps boost profit margins that have been sagging due to competition from discounters.

For example, we found one clone gown in a bridal shop for $900. We were shocked to find the gown's true cost was just $275.

What is the down-side with clone gowns? Fixing problems with special orders is one challenge. Since the gowns are imported, it may take longer to fix snafus. Also, most clone gowns are marketed by import companies with only skeletal U.S. operations. Legitimate designers (even those that manufacture in the Orient) have U.S. sales offices and warehouses. If a problem develops, they can get a replacement gown much quicker.

Of course, buying a clone gown off-the-rack will avoid such problems. But, how can you spot a "clone gown'"? Typically, they have obscure names and are never advertised in bridal magazines If you must special-order, ask the store for information on the manufacturer—where are they located? Can you call them to confirm their customer service commitment? The store should readily give you information on a designer/manufacturer—it's your guarantee that the store is on the up and up. If they balk, then walk.

Call for updates! By calling our special hotline, you'll hear the latest bridal bargains, trends and news! (See inside back cover for price information.)
(900) 988-7295

Chapter 3

Apparel for the Wedding Party

Y es, there are bridesmaids' gowns out there that don't look hideous! We'll tell you in this chapter who are the best bridesmaid gown designers and give you several surprisingly affordable alternatives. We'll also give you valuable tips on tuxedos for the guys.

Bridesmaids' Gowns

What Are You Buying?

 Perhaps nothing symbolizes what's wrong with the wedding industry more than the bridesmaid's gown. Have you seen any of these abominations to fashion? Cheap polyester fabric, ugly colors, absurd detailing like gargantuan puff sleeves—it seems like a bridesmaid's gown can transform any woman into a taffeta nightmare. What's most appalling about bridesmaids' gowns is that they are actually designed that way! No kidding!

We're not sure why bridesmaids' gowns are designed as "throw-away" gowns and disposable dresses, meant to be worn for only one day. One thing we are sure of is their high prices; even the low-end gowns sell for $100 to $150. That's too much money to "throw away," in our opinion. To get a gown of any quality that would actually look half decent, bridesmaids might have to shell out nearly $200—and that doesn't even include expensive alterations.

The most hilarious part of this travesty is the suggestion by bridal shops that (are you ready for this?) most of their bridesmaids' gowns can be worn again as formals! Yeah, right. How many New Year's Eve parties have you been to where women wore bridesmaids' gowns? Please, we wish these bridal shop owners would stop saying such drivel. Ninety-nine percent of all bridesmaids' gowns are banished to the back of the closet within hours of the wedding.

Anyway, your bridesmaids have to wear something to your wedding. So here are our suggestions.

Our Recommendations for Bridesmaids' Gowns

❦ Buy the cheapest bridesmaids' gowns you can stomach. Some of the basic styles sell for about $90. The nicest thing you can do for your bridesmaids who are on a tight budget is not burden them with paying for a $180 gown that they can only wear once.

❦ Consider an alternative to typical bridesmaids' gowns. Yes, there are several beautiful gowns your bridesmaids could actually wear again. As you might expect, these gowns are designed not by bridal designers, but by "ready-to-wear" manufacturers. One good example is Lanz, whose attractive floral dresses are profiled later in this chapter.

Money-saving Secrets

1 PACKAGE DISCOUNTS. If you order your gown from a bridal shop, they may offer a discount if you also order all the bridesmaids' dresses from that store. This discount can range from 10% to 20%. Sometimes this is negotiable, so ask.

2 CONSIDER ALTERNATIVE SOURCES. Resale/consignment shops often carry matching bridesmaids' gowns at attractive prices in a range of sizes. Rental stores rent bridesmaids' gowns at a fraction of retail prices. At the end of this section, we will review two national companies that offer bridesmaids dresses for rent!

3 CALL DISCOUNT BRIDAL SERVICE. With savings of up to 40% and dresses that are shipped directly to each bridesmaids, you can't go wrong. For more details, see a review of DBS in Chapter 2.

Getting Started: How Far In Advance?

Most bridesmaids' gowns take two to four months to special order. If you are getting married in the popular summer months, give yourself a little more time. In general, once you have selected the bridal gown, begin the search for bridesmaids' apparel.

Step-by-step Shopping Strategies

❦ *Step 1:* After buying your bridal gown (and hence deciding on the setting and formality of your wedding), start the search for bridesmaids' gowns. Shopping for bridesmaids' before you find your gown will only distract you.

❧ *Step 2:* Take into account your bridesmaids' ability to pay for the dress. (Traditionally, the bridesmaid pays for her gown plus alterations.) Are your bridesmaids starving college students or corporate lawyers earning $75,000 a year? Obviously, this is a big factor in your decision.

❧ *Step 3:* Given the financial condition of your attendants, start the shopping process. Follow much the same steps as for finding a bridal gown. Look at fabrics, finishes, and styles.

❧ *Step 4:* When you decide on a gown, announce your decision to the bridesmaids. Make sure each bridesmaid is individually measured and receives a written receipt that specifies the manufacturer, style number, size and delivery date.

❧ *Step 5:* Be sure to leave two weeks or more for alterations. Get written cost estimates on the alterations before the order is placed.

Helpful Hint

DON'T GO SHOPPING WITH MORE THAN ONE BRIDESMAID. If you want to make the process of shopping for bridesmaids' gowns go as smooth as possible, just take along one friend. Too many bridesmaids (each with their own opinions and tastes) will only complicate the decision. Make the decision and announce it to the other bridesmaids.

Pitfall to Avoid

CLASHING COLOR MOTIFS.
"I was a bridesmaid in a wedding recently. The bride picked out lovely peach bridesmaids' gowns. Unfortunately, the church was all decorated in bright red—all her pictures looked like 'Night of the Clashing Circus Clowns!' It wasn't pretty."

Be careful when you select the bridesmaids' gowns to take into account the decor of your ceremony site. Many of your wedding pictures will have the ceremony site as a backdrop. Try to pick a color that not only pleases you but also doesn't clash with the decor of your ceremony site.

Reviews of Selected Bridesmaids Designers

Obviously, there are many manufacturers of bridesmaids' gowns. Frankly, most of the bridesmaids' gowns we have seen are hideous. So we are not going to waste your time by writing about the worst. Instead, here are reviews of some of the best and most visible manufacturers. Just like our rating system for bridal gowns, these reviews are based on our personal experience with these gowns. Our opinions reflect hands-on inspections.

So, what's new in the bridesmaid world? Well, the good news is more designers are producing more stylish dresses. Encouraged by the phenomenal success of Watters and Watters, designers are attempting more flash and dash. We've seen floral embroidery, frothy chiffons, and even embossed fabrics. Many designers are showing very short skirts—the jury is still out on whether bridesmaids will flock to these styles. Here's a round up of what's new.

The Ratings

★★★★ EXCELLENT — *our top pick!*
 ★★★ GOOD — *above average quality, prices and creativity*
  ★★ FAIR — *could stand some improvement*
   ★ POOR — *yuck! Could stand major improvement*

Alfred Angelo ★½ Described by one bridal industry veteran as "disposable dresses," Alfred Angelo's bridesmaids' gowns are underwhelming in our opinion. We just aren't impressed with the quality or designs. Perhaps the best thing we can say about Angelo's gowns is that they are widely available. New this year is quick delivery—Angelo has four styles in sizes 4 to 44 that are available for immediate delivery. Prices range from $80 to $240. (800) 528-3589 or (215) 659-8700.

Bill Levkoff ★★½ Considered higher quality than other designers, Bill Levkoff offers good value for the money. Designer Veronica Cifone was trained at Galina and is very plugged in to the latest trends. While some designs are incredibly boring (the "typical bridesmaid" taffeta with puff sleeves), others are more creative. New this year are big and brilliant floral designs, as well as several strapless options. With a look leaning toward evening wear/cocktail dresses, Levkoff is heavy on the use of netting this season. Basically, this line has something for everyone—from two-piece suits to your standard bridesmaids look. Prices range from $102 to $234 with sizes on some styles up to 42 (but no petites). (800) LEV-KOFF.

Currie Bonner ★★★ With four retail stores, in Atlanta, Charlotte, Nashville, and Dallas, Currie Bonner is a custom manufacturer of bridesmaids' dresses. A wide assortment of fabrics are available, from the ordinary (taffeta and satin) to the exotic (linen, velvet, and shantung). Styles are quite impressive, including some drop-waisted designs, several dresses with ruffles, and others with full skirts and fitted bodices. New styles offered this season include cropped jackets and drop-waisted gowns with peplum and bow accents. Prices, which vary depending on the fabric and style chosen, range from $125 for the simplest plain taffeta design to $270 for a silk gown. (214) 739-6477.

Dessy Creations ★★½ This line is designed by Vivian Dessy Diamond, whose hallmark appears to be more wistful designs than her competitors. Of course, "wistful" ain't cheap. Dessy's dresses *start* at $194 and go up to $230. Floral chintz prints are in this year, as are halter-style dresses and navy blue suits (very 1940s). Only sizes 4 to 20 are available. (800) 52-DESSY.

Jordan ★★ Known for their basic, "bread-and-butter" bridesmaids' designs, Jordan's dresses go for $118 to $188. Very basic accents: bow bustles, puff sleeves—you get the idea. The colors are quite conservative, too (rose, teal, royal blue). New this year are several dresses that are knock-offs of Levkoff's designs. If you're in a hurry, Jordan offers "jet service" for quick delivery. Six styles are available for fast shipping, for an additional $6 charge. Sizes up to 42 are offered. Jordan is available nearly everywhere. (212) 921-5560.

Lanz ★★★ This suggestion was called in by a reader of our last edition—she loved Lanz's simple, floral-print dresses that are reasonably priced. In 100% cotton, most Lanz dresses range from $100 to $150. Best of all: Lanz is widely available at most department stores (no messy bridal shops). (800) 421-0731.

New Image ★★½ New Image seems to be suffering from the "conservative" disease this year. Compared to previous seasons, this line seems to be lacking pizzazz. Stripes and check patterns are in, while satin edging on the sleeves seems to be the hip detail.Prices run $150 to $250, sizes 4 to 22. (800) 421-IMAGE.

Watters and Watters ★★★★ This young, Dallas-based designer continues on a roll. Perhaps the hottest bridesmaids' designer in the country, Watters and Watters seems to be working from a simple concept: design a nice-looking dress that doesn't look like a bridesmaid. More like well-tailored suits than cheap polyester dresses, WW gowns still keep a feminine look with beautiful fabrics and colors, plus lace and floral touches. New this year are lots of organza skirts, in purple, copper, and coral colors. The hot fabric this year is an iridescent organza. If we had to complain about anything with Watters and Watters, it would have to be their prices—bridesmaids' are an expensive $200 to $280. Also, their ads make it difficult to see the dresses. On the upside, the designer has expanded their line of informal bridal dresses, which run $284 to $560. Sizes 4 to 24 are available. While we like WW's dresses, their customer service could stand some major improvement. When a chain of Detroit bridal shops declared bankruptcy in 1992, WW treated stranded brides with indifference and was completely irresponsible. We hope they'll learn some better manners as they grow older. (214) 991-6994.

Spotlight: Best Buy #1

Formals Etc. *(318) 640-3766*
Jandi Classics *(800) 342-1544*

Despite the best efforts by the bridal magazines to kill rental companies, two national companies have emerged to offer brides and bridesmaids quality apparel for rental: Jandi Classics and Formals Etc.

Formals Etc. is a fantastic company headquartered in Pineville, Louisiana. With 18 stores in thirteen states and Canada, Formals Etc. has a nice selection of bridal gowns and bridesmaids dresses—all for rent. Bridal gowns by Mary's, Bonny and San Martin that would retail for $800 to $1200, cost just $200 to $275 to rent.

Formals Etc. decided to manufacture their own bridesmaids dresses in order to utilize better fabric and designs. The taffeta gowns in a variety of colors cost only $55 to $75 to rent (which would probably retail for $150 or more). We've seen several pictures of the dresses and found them to be quite stylish. To find the store nearest you, call (318) 640-3766.

Based in Tennessee, Jandi Classics has developed a fantastic line of bridal and bridesmaids rentals. We saw a video of their designs and were impressed. Nothing fancy here—most designs are similar to Jordan, a basic bridesmaids designer. One standout was a two-piece outfit with peplum. Others featured modified bubble skirts with bows at the shoulders. While the tea length dresses were pleasing, some of the floor-length styles missed the mark, however.

Of course, the best news is the rental prices: the bridesmaids dresses (30 styles in 17 colors) rent for $59 to $70. Jandi even has six bridal gowns (basic styles with a little lace trim) that rent for $97 to $150. You can even rent a flower girl dress (with a color-coordinated sash) for $45 to $60.

Jandi Classics are available to rent from over 300 dealers across the country—mostly tuxedo shops and even some bridal stores. Gingiss is even test-marketing Jandi in some stores. For a dealer near you, call (800) 342-1544.

Tuxedos

Nowhere are the wedding etiquette rules sillier than for

men's formal wear. For example, they say you MUST wear a black tux with tails for a formal wedding after six in the evening. If you don't, the vengeful WEDDING GODS will strike you down, ostracize your family and charge obscene amounts of money to your credit cards.

Now if your wedding is before six you can wear grey or white short coats... but not if the moon is full. And, of course, you must follow the omnipotent "formality" rules that dictate proper dress for weddings that are very formal, just plain formal, semi-formal, pseudo-formal and the dreaded para-formal. Just kidding.

We believe all this is nonsense. The grooms and groomsmen should wear whatever they believe is appropriate. Who cares what time of day the wedding is? If your wedding is an informal ceremony in a local civic rose garden, you don't have to wear a tuxedo. We know we might incur the wrath of Emily Post for saying this, but hey do what you want to do. If you look good in a double-breasted tux, wear that. If you don't, look for another style. You get the idea.

What Are You Buying?

Actually, most grooms and groomsmen rent formal wear for weddings. Imagine what would happen if the men had to shell out the same kind of money that bridesmaids spend on those horrendously ugly bridesmaids' gowns. There would be mass revolts and street rioting. Fortunately, for national security's sake, most men's formal wear is rented. Typically, the groomsmen are financially responsible for their tuxedo rentals, so basically you and your fiance's only expense is the groom's tux. Here are the three basic options for men's formal wear:

1 RENT. When you rent a tux, you get just about everything: jacket, pants, cummerbund, shirt, tie, cuff links, and, of course, shirt studs (little jewelry that covers your buttons and makes you look rich). Notice what's missing? If you answered "shoes" give yourself extra points. While most tuxes rent for $50 to $90, the shoes are often $10 to $15 extra. Of course, it's more expensive in LA and New York where tux rentals can top $125 and shoes go for $20. A small deposit ($10 to $20) is required to reserve a tux. There are three types of places to find formal wear rentals:

❧ *Chain stores.* Large formal wear franchised chains (a la McDonald's) are located across the U.S. They basically offer the same styles and brand names. Service can range from helpful to dreadful. Most of these chains don't carry any stock at their stores—a central warehouse is used to dispense the tuxedos. Hence, it's difficult to decide which style is best for you by just looking at the mannequins. To try on a particular style, you must ask the shop for a "trial fitting." For no charge, most shops will bring in a style in your size. The only disadvantage is that this requires a second visit to the shop, rather inconvenient for those of you who lead busy lives.

❦ *Bridal Shops.* More and more bridal shops are now getting into the business of renting tuxes. However, instead of stocking tuxes at their store, they use a service which supplies them with rentals. Hence, the way you pick a tuxedo is to look through a book with pictures of tuxedo-clad soap stars awash in testosterone. Thrilling. Personally, we'd rather look at the mannequins. Anyway, on the up side, the bridal shops may cut you a deal if you buy the bridal and bridesmaids' gowns from them. On the down side, while bridal shop employees may know a lot about bridal gowns, they may know diddly-squat about men's formal wear.

❦ *Independent shops.* Occasionally, we find an independent tuxedo rental shop, one that is not affiliated with a national chain. We often are impressed by the quality of service at these outlets. Furthermore, independent shops may carry a wider selection of styles and designers. You can also find some great deals. For example, Tux Express in Scottsdale, Arizona (602) 991-6655 rents designer-brand tuxes for $29 to $59, far below the prices of the chains.

2 BUY. If you expect to need a tuxedo again for a fancy party or corporate banquet, it may pay to buy. That's because most tuxedos cost $200 to $400 to purchase. Considering rental fees of $50 to $100, it may pay to purchase.

3 GO WITH YOUR OWN SUIT. Especially for less formal weddings, having the groom and groomsmen wear dark suits is perfectly acceptable. There is no law saying you must wear a tuxedo for your wedding.

Spotlight: Best Buy #1

Gingiss Formalwear

Probably our most favorite formal wear chain is Gingiss Formalwear. Perhaps what we like most about Gingiss is the fact you can try on tuxedos right in their store. Hey, what a concept! Most Gingiss stores keeps their stock right in the store, enabling you to try on several styles in your size. You get to see how the tuxedo looks on you, not on a mannequin or a model in a catalog. Furthermore, you don't have to make a second trip back to the store for a trial fitting—you can look at the styles, try on a few top choices, and make your decision all in one shot.

Another plus for Gingiss: their mail-in measurement program for out-of-town groomsmen. With more than 200 stores in 35 states, Gingiss enables out-of-town groomsmen to go to the Gingiss in their city, see the actual tux, and get measured. Sure, other chains have mail-in measurement programs, but Gingiss seems more organized.

Gingiss's prices are moderate, ranging from $50 to $90. There are discounts for group orders; the Gingiss in our town gives the groom's tux rental free with five other rentals. Most tuxedos they carry are well-known brand names such as Christian Dior.

One interesting piece of news from the Gingiss camp in 1991 was their buyout of Tuxedo Junction, a 31-store chain based in Buffalo, New York. Tuxedo Junction manufactures its own line of tuxedos, shirts, and shoes, and Gingiss now plans to market these as their own "in-house" brand. Unfortunately, Gingiss does not plan to pass on the savings from manufacturing its own products to consumers in the form of lower rental rates. Gingiss President Michael Corrao told *Vows Magazine* that "the intent... [is] to provide unique styles, greater selection, a more directed product, without a compromise on price." Hmmm.

Despite this transgression, we still like Gingiss and pick the company as one of the very best formal-wear chains in the U.S.

Our Favorite Tux Designers

Henry Grethel ★★★★ Grethel isn't a big player in the tux market but his designs are top-notch. Contemporary and stylish, Grethel's tuxedos are a breath of fresh air. Perhaps our only complaint is that Henry Grethel's tuxedos aren't as widely available as those of other designers. You're more likely to see a Grethel at independent shops that carry a wider selection of tuxedos than at their chain counterparts.

Lord West ★★ Referring to itself as the "All-American Formalwear," Lord West does very traditional styles. One standout was a white, double-breasted coat with shell collar and black pleated pants. New this year are several "western-style" tuxedos, with bolero-style coats.

Raffinati ★★★ Beyond the traditional styles, Raffinati also goes out on a limb with some stylish, European-inspired looks. Our favorite is the "Seville," a black tuxedo with a white shawl collar and white buttons. Other variations on this theme include the "Passion Grape" in deep purple and "Royal Teal," both that sport black collars.

Our Top Money-Saving Secrets for Tuxedos

1 PACKAGE DISCOUNTS. Almost all tuxedo places offer a free tux rental with the rental of five or six tuxedos. In some cases, tux shops distribute coupons good for $10 or more off each rental. Be sure to ask about group discounts if the shop "forgets" to tell you about them.

2 SKIP THE RENTAL SHOES. Why? Those cheap rental shoes can be awfully uncomfortable. Instead, wear your own black dress shoes if you have them and save $10.

How the Bridal Designers Block

In the last chapter, we talked about how bridal magazines block ads from companies that want to rent bridal and bridesmaids dresses to women. By locking these rental firms out of the only national advertising vehicle that reaches brides, the magazines have worked to shut the door on dress rentals.

But that's not the whole story. Several bridal manufacturers have taken public and not-so-public steps to stop dress rental. Such actions have aroused the attention of the Federal Trade Commission, whose Dallas office has launched an investigation into the practices of certain designers.

Our investigation into the tactics of one of the largest bridal designers, Alfred Angelo, revealed some surprising information. As one of the top three bridal dressmakers, Angelo's designs are available in hundreds of shops. In 1992, Angelo sent a "marketing statement" to each of its dealers, requiring them to agree in writing that they will "not rent Alfred Angelo Dream Maker dresses to consumers." Stores that do face "immediate termination of your account."

We asked the company about this practice. Bernard Toll, Angelo's public relations liaison, told us that "we do this for obvious reasons. Alfred Angelo dresses are not designed to withstand multiple wearings, countless alterations which leave telltale needle marks and legally required cleanings. Each Alfred Angelo dress is produced to make just one bride's dreams become a lovely reality on her wedding day."

Now, this is a curious argument. Angelo is essentially arguing that their dresses are of such poor quality that they won't "withstand repeated wearings." Considering the average bridesmaids dress costs $150, we find this to be appalling. Angelo's arguments seem to give credence to the perception that the industry designs "disposable dresses" of

Getting Started: How Far in Advance?

 Boy, this varies greatly from area to area. In small towns, or for less popular months, you can shop one to two months before the wedding. However, you may need to reserve your tuxedos three to four months before the wedding in larger cities or for popular summer wedding months. If you have out-of-town groomsmen, you may want to leave extra time to get their measurements in.

Helpful Hint

LIE TO THE GROOMSMEN. We got this tip from one frustrated groom who found his groomsmen procrastinated getting measured for their tuxedos. The tardy groomsmen got measured

Rental of Bridesmaids Dresses

such inferior craftsmanship you can't be expected to wear them more than one day.

The bridal industry says that women "don't want to rent dresses. They'd rather buy." However the actions of the magazines and dress designers indicate quite the opposite—they're trying to stifle the consumer demand for a needed service for purely selfish reasons: women buy $500 million worth of bridesmaids dresses each year. Rental of these dresses would half this business and force the designers to make dresses that don't disintegrate after one wearing. By renting bridesmaids dresses alone, women could save $250 million each year.

It is our opinion that designers who block stores from renting dresses are guilty of restraint of trade. We hope the FTC's investigation of these practices reaches a similar conclusion.

On another related issue, we also noted that Angelo promises stores that it will "not sell discontinued merchandise to the large bridal outlet warehouses." However, Angelo operates a separate company called "Bridal Placements of Boca," which sells discontinued merchandise to shops. While the company denies it, insiders say Bridal Placements sells Angelo gowns to bridal warehouses. In fact, we called several bridal warehouses and every one told us they carry Alfred Angelo dresses. While Bernard Toll told us that Angelo "will not knowingly sell to bridal discount warehouses," it's obvious *someone* is supplying these outlets with gowns. One warehouse even told us we could special order a brand new Alfred Angelo dress at a discounted price.

If you disagree with Angelo's policies on rental dresses and discount stores, we urge you to write Alfred Angelo's president, Vincent Piccione, at 601 Davisville Road, Willow Grove, PA 19090.

just days before the wedding, frustrating everyone from the engaged couple to the tux shop. So, he recommended that other grooms lie about when the measurements have to be in. For example, tell them they must get measured two weeks before the wedding even though the real deadline is just one week before. That way the procrastinators won't upset the schedule if they are slightly late.

Trends

❦ *White and black.* In the 1980's, tuxedo designers offered you a choice of three colors: black, black or black. Lately, designers having been adding a new twist: white jackets. In a throwback to the 1950's, white dinner jackets (or completely white tuxes) are reappearing. Color might be creeping into the tuxedo palette this season, with Raffinati's line of deep purple and teal tuxedos.

❦ *Striped trousers and shawl lapels.* Another throwback to "old times."

❦ *"Black Tie Invited" pressure from the bridal shop.* Here's an ominous new trend: a new campaign launched by the formal-wear industry urges bridal shops to "suggest" brides put on their invitations "Black Tie Invited." Of course, when guests get these invitations, they will trot down to their favorite tuxedo rental place and shell out the bucks. What a marketing breakthrough.

 If you have any questions or comments about this chapter, please feel free to call the authors. See the "How to Reach Us" page at the back of this book!

Chapter 4

Ceremony Sites

D id you realize how much rental fees vary from site to site? In this chapter, we'll show you a group of often-overlooked wedding ceremony sites that are extremely affordable—plus we'll give you five important questions to ask a ceremony site coordinator.

Selecting a site for your ceremony first requires a decision on the type of ceremony you want. We basically divide ceremonies into two categories: religious and civil.

1 RELIGIOUS CEREMONIES. Religious ceremonies (75% of all weddings), of course, are most likely held in a house of worship. Requirements for religious ceremonies vary greatly from one denomination to another. Pre-marriage counseling is required by some religions; others forbid interfaith marriages. Often the rules are established by the church or temple's local priest, minister, pastor or rabbi. Call your local house of worship for guidelines and requirements.

2 CIVIL CEREMONIES. About one-fourth of all weddings are civil ceremonies. Legal requirements vary from state to state, but usually a judge or other officiant presides over the ceremony. Customs and traditions vary greatly from region to region of the country. For example, we spoke to one hotel catering manager who worked in both Boston, Massachusetts and Austin, Texas. In Boston, she told us nearly 75% of couples had a civil ceremony on site at the hotel. Just the opposite was true in Texas where most weddings are held in a church with only the reception following at the hotel.

Religious vs. Civil: It's All a Matter of State

Interestingly enough, the split between civil and religious ceremonies varies greatly from state to state. According to federal government statistics, the state with the largest number of religious wedding ceremonies is West Virginia. In that state, a whopping 97% of all weddings are religious ceremonies. On the other end of the spectrum, South Carolina leads the nation in civil ceremonies (54% of all weddings).

So what happened to Nevada, where the large number of Las Vegas weddings probably would rank that state #1 in civil ceremonies? Well, Nevada was omitted from this study for reasons unknown. Other omitted states include Ohio and Iowa (both of which do not record the type of ceremony) and Arkansas, Oklahoma, Texas, New Mexico, Arizona, Washington, and North Dakota.

HERE ARE HOW SOME OF THE OTHER STATES STACK UP:

States with a high number of civil ceremonies: South Carolina (54%), Florida (45%) New Hampshire (40%), Hawaii (36%), New York (35%). Other states with higher than average numbers of civil ceremonies include Maine, Georgia and Virginia.

States with a high number of religious ceremonies: West Virginia (97%), Missouri (91%), Nebraska (84.2%), Michigan (83.9%), Pennsylvania (83.7%), Idaho (83.5%), California (83.1%).

What Are You Buying?

When you book a ceremony site, you not only are purchasing use of the site for the wedding but also for time to set-up and tear-down the decorations. Now we say purchasing because many sites charge fees to use the facilities for a wedding. One bride we spoke to was surprised that the church they belonged to charged her over $600 in fees for her wedding. Of course, these fees often go to reimburse church staff and to pay expenses like utilities, clean-up, etc. Unfortunately, some churches use weddings to subsidize other less-profitable operations. Anyway, the fees vary widely from site to site but the charges tend to be more in larger cities.

What if you are not a member of a church but you want a church wedding? Well, a few churches allow non-members to use their facilities for weddings...but with a few catches. First, the fees are normally higher. Secondly, members get first shot at dates so non-members may not be able to book a wedding until, say, three months in advance. Obviously, this is a roll of the dice.

Sources to Find a Great Ceremony Site

There are several great sources to use to find ceremony sites.

❧ *Local Visitors/Tourism Bureaus.* Many have a guide to local facilities that are available for weddings and receptions.

Losing their religion

Think you're the only one who's frustrated with the seemingly ridiculous policies of your local church? Lisa Olson Kirsch of Salem, Massachusetts sent us a copy of a letter she mailed to the Salem Ministerial Association. She received no reply from the association.

"During recent wedding planning, I have been shocked by local churches' insensitive and self-serving policies. I've heard horror stories about weddings being bumped at the last minute by 'regular' church members, as well as long lists of mandates stipulating where photographers may stand and what types of equipment they and the guests may use. You cannot select your own minster or, for that matter, your own organist. You can indicate your music preferences from a small, pre-approved list of traditional songs, but the final decision is left to their discretion and you can think again if you hope to have meaningful, contemporary music or taped selections.

While churches often emphatically state that their building is their 'home' and 'not for rent,' they all seem to have ready a pre-printed fee schedule with very specific and commercial-like rates. The list goes on and on. I understand the intent of the churches may be to protect their facility and the credibility of the ceremony, but the way they go about it seems less than Christian-like and disregards the unique qualities and contributions that should make each wedding memorable and personalized. It's a disgrace that deserves thoughtful reconsideration by each church and it's members."

Your local Chamber of Commerce or Historical Society office may also have more leads.

❧ *Local parks departments.* Most city and county parks and historical areas are administered by a parks department. Ask them which sites are most popular for wedding ceremonies.

❧ *For historic sites, check out the book* Places *at your local library.* This directory lists historical and other interesting places (many of which are available for rent) across the country. Published by Tenth House Enterprises, call (212) 737-7536 for more information.

Getting Started: How Far in Advance?

Especially for popular wedding months, start your search for a ceremony site as soon as you have selected the date. Prime dates can book up to a year in advance—you know, there are only so many

Saturdays in June. However, be aware that popular months vary by region. For example, in the South, December is a particularly popular month. In Arizona, and many areas of the desert Southwest, the spring months (February, March and April) are more popular than the hot summer months.

Be aware that religious restrictions may rule out certain times of the year. For example, Catholics and Greek Orthodox avoid marrying during Lent in March. Jews don't have weddings during the High Holy Days (usually in September or October).

Top Money-saving Secrets

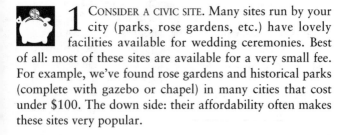

1 CONSIDER A CIVIC SITE. Many sites run by your city (parks, rose gardens, etc.) have lovely facilities available for wedding ceremonies. Best of all: most of these sites are available for a very small fee. For example, we've found rose gardens and historical parks (complete with gazebo or chapel) in many cities that cost under $100. The down side: their affordability often makes these sites very popular.

2 CALL AROUND TO DIFFERENT SITES. You wouldn't believe how widely fees vary from facility to facility.

3 CONSIDER BECOMING A MEMBER. Many churches charge less for weddings of members than non-members. If you are planning to settle down in the town where your wedding is, consider joining the church where you'll be married.

4 ASK ABOUT ANY DISCOUNTS. For example, some churches and synagogues offer discounts on wedding invitations as a fund raiser.

Questions to Ask of a Ceremony Site

1 WHAT ARE THE RESTRICTIONS, SET-UP TIMES AND CLEAN-UP REQUIREMENTS? Boy, this is an important question. Many sites have written rules about this stuff. One local church we know has so many rules and guidelines for weddings that they filled up a 72-page book! Make sure you are fully aware of these details to avoid any surprises.

2 WHO WILL BE MY CONTACT AT THE SITE? In order to prevent miscommunications, make sure you find out who is the wedding coordinator. This person will be an invaluable referral source of other wedding services.

3 WHAT IS THE EXPECTED HONORARIUM, DONATION OR FEE PAID TO THE CHURCH/OFFICIANT? WHEN IS THIS NORMALLY PAID?

4 WHAT KIND OF EQUIPMENT MUST BE RENTED FOR MY WEDDING? Don't assume that something in the sanctuary or at the site is included in your rental of the facility.

5 IS ANY PRE-WEDDING COUNSELING REQUIRED? Some churches require couples to attend pre-wedding counseling. Others require the couple to promise to raise their children in that religion. Before you are asked to make any commitments, ask the site coordinator about this matter.

Call for updates! By calling our special hotline, you'll hear the latest bridal bargains, trends and news! (See inside back cover for price information.)
(900) 988-7295

Chapter 5

Wedding Flowers

Hey, getting flowers for your wedding should be easy, right? Well...maybe. But the average floral bill for a wedding can top $1000—so some of the 15 money-saving tips we discovered for wedding flowers may come in handy. Some may even surprise you! We also cut through the "floral speak" and give you seven floral "best buys."

What Are You Buying?

 Besides the flowers themselves, you are buying a decorating consultant. Not only is the florist's knowledge of flowers important but also their understanding of colors and contrasts. Florists must be able to come up with a floral motif to best complement the bride, the bridal gown, the bridesmaids' colors, the ceremony and the reception. To synthesize these elements and the "feel of the wedding" (a formal sit-down dinner versus an informal bar-becue) takes talent. Lots of it.

Your tastes and desires are key here, and a florist who understands a couple's individuality is the best choice. There are three basic categories of flowers that you are buying:

❧ *Personal Flowers.* The bride's and bridesmaids' bouquets, corsages for the mothers and house party, and boutonnieres for the men.

❧ *Ceremony Site Flowers.* Altar flowers and/or aisle arrange-ments (ribbons, candles, pew markers).

❧ *Reception Site Flowers.* Guest book table, table center-pieces (including a head table, buffet table and individual guests tables) and the cake table. Other floral expense areas may include the rehearsal dinner and any other pre-wedding parties.

AVERAGE TOTAL COSTS: About $750 covers the total floral bill at most weddings, according to industry estimates. In the largest cities (such as New York or LA), the flower budget can easily zoom past $1000 or even $2000 for lavish affairs. Deposits range from nothing (the exception) to as much as 50% of the estimated bill. Many ask for $50 to $100 to reserve the date. The balance is usually due one to two weeks before the wedding (because many florists must order the flowers in advance from their suppliers).

Sources to Find an Affordable Wedding Florist

 Since there are three general types of florists out there, we thought it might be helpful to explain the differences, then detail where to find the one that will work best for you:

1 CASH 'N CARRY. These shops basically specialize in providing an arrangement for Mother's Day, or a friend's birthday. They usually don't do many weddings and may not have as much experience with such a special event.

2 FULL SERVICE. Weddings, funerals, wire service arrangements, special events are within a full service florist's repertoire. A majority of florists fit in this category, although some are better than others at weddings.

3 SPECIALISTS. Some florists specialize in one aspect of the floral business. Obviously, those who specialize in weddings are your best bet. Those that don't may have little incentive to do a good job since they don't target that market anyway. Don't assume that your neighborhood florist, who has done great arrangements for you at Christmas and other times, will be best for your wedding.

Where to Find Florists
Who are Wedding Specialists

❦ *Ceremony site coordinators.* Ask the person who coordinates (or books) weddings at your church, synagogue, etc. for florist recommendations. This is a great source since they often see florists' work up close and personal. They also know the florists who have been late to set up and those who have not provided the freshest flowers or best service. If your ceremony site coordinator doesn't have any recommendations, call around to a few popular churches in your area. Odds are you'll turn up some valuable referrals.

❦ *Photographers.* Many have opinions as to which florists offer the best service and which don't. However, their contact with florists is limited to the final product at the wedding— their opinions could be somewhat biased.

❦ *If you plan to produce your own arrangements* or have a friend do it, look under the Yellow Page heading of "Florists-Wholesale" for options. Some wholesalers refuse to sell to the public while others don't have such restrictions.

Top Money-saving Secrets

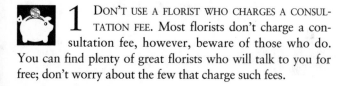

1 DON'T USE A FLORIST WHO CHARGES A CONSULTATION FEE. Most florists don't charge a consultation fee, however, beware of those who do. You can find plenty of great florists who will talk to you for free; don't worry about the few that charge such fees.

2 CHOOSE A WEDDING DATE THAT ISN'T NEAR HOLIDAYS. As you may well realize, all roses are outrageously priced in February thanks to Valentine's Day. So if you want roses, don't plan on a wedding at that time. Also, December is an expensive time to buy fresh flowers since the supply is limited and the demand from Christmas and other events is high.

3 SEASONAL AND REGIONAL FLOWERS CAN BE GREAT BARGAINS. For example, in California, certain orchids and other tropicals grown locally may be available at affordable prices. Also, seasonality often affects floral prices. For example, tulips are abundant from December through February and as such are fairly inexpensive. If you want them in July, however, they will be extremely expensive if they are available at all.

4 AVOID EXOTIC FLOWERS. What is considered an exotic flower may vary from region to region. For example, in the Southwest, lilies of the valley are very expensive and difficult to find. Yet in the northern part of the U.S., where they are common, they may be very reasonable.

5 INSTEAD OF BIG (AND EXPENSIVE) BOUQUETS, CARRY A SINGLE FLOWER. This is extremely elegant especially with long stem varieties like calla lilies and roses. If you want to carry a bouquet, consider having the bridesmaids carry single flowers.

6 CONSIDER USING SILK FLOWERS to replace expensive, fresh varieties. Even dried flowers may be affordable alternatives. All-silk arrangements may not be much less expensive if you have them made by a florist—their charge for labor may be expensive no matter what type of flower they use. However, you can save money doing it yourself or substituting silk exotics (like orchids) for real ones.

7 LIMIT THE NUMBER OF ATTENDANTS. This is just basic math: the more attendants, the more flowers, the higher the final cost.

8 SPEND YOUR MONEY WHERE PEOPLE WILL SEE IT. Most wedding ceremonies are relatively short (about 30 minutes) therefore your guests will be spending most of their time at your reception. We suggest that you spend money on flowers at the reception rather than at the ceremony. You'll be able to enjoy them more at the reception and so will your guests. Typically the ceremony site flowers are your biggest expense, but you see them for the shortest amount of time!

9 IF THERE IS ANOTHER WEDDING SCHEDULED for the same day at your ceremony site, share the floral arrangements with the other bride! Splitting the cost here could be a major savings.

10 BALLOONS CAN BE AN AFFORDABLE OPTION FOR RECEPTION SITE DECORATION. For example, we priced balloon table centerpieces at about $18 each. To get the kind of height and volume that balloons provide, you would need to spend two to three times that amount on fresh flowers. We recommend balloons for reception sites with high ceilings since the height of most balloon arrangements can make small rooms look crowded.

11 RENTING PLANTS AND OTHER GREENERY AS FILLER. A great money-saving option, this may save you from buying tons of flowers for a reception or ceremony site that needs lots of decoration.

12 RE-USE SOME OF THE ARRANGEMENTS AND BOUQUETS. The bridesmaid's bouquets can be used to decorate the cake and guest book tables. Some altar arrangements can be moved to the reception site (although there may be a delivery fee).

13 CONSIDER ARRANGING THE FLOWERS YOURSELF OR HAVING A FRIEND ARRANGE THEM. This option is available only for those who feel confident in their skills at flower arranging. Many wholesale florists can supply all the necessary accessories for flower arranging. Silk flowers are also available from wholesalers in your area and can be arranged by you or a friend. The savings from this option may be as much as 50%.

14 SCALE-DOWN THE PEW DECORATIONS AT THE CEREMONY. Consider using just greenery or bows instead of fresh

flowers. Some brides have eliminated this decoration altogether. Another option: craft stores will teach you how to make the bows yourself.

15 PICK THE GENERAL COLOR SCHEME AND LET YOUR FLORIST BUY THE MOST AFFORDABLE FLOWERS available the week of your wedding. Obviously, you must feel very confident in your florist to go this route. Specifically rule out any flowers you don't want but try to remain flexible. This tip is a money-saver since your florist may be able to purchase certain in-season varieties at substantially lower prices.

Spotlight: Best Buys

For some lovely but affordable flowers that won't bust your budget, we've compiled a short list of flowers that can be used to fill out arrangements. Be aware that certain flowers may be more affordable in various regions of the U.S. Ask your florist for local recommendations. Also, seasonality may affect the prices of certain flowers.

❦ *Gerbera Daisies.* These giant-sized versions of common daisies make wonderful and colorful bridesmaids' bouquets. They also have long stems and can be used successfully in table and altar arrangements. They come in incredible colors from plain white to deep fuchsia. Pastels are also available.

❦ *Alstroemeria Lilies.* These are miniature lilies that come in over 20 different shades. Some flowers are even multi-colored. Because they are small, they look best in bouquets, hairpieces, on wedding cakes or in table arrangements.

❦ *Gladiolus.* These long-stalked flowers are covered in bright blooms. They look especially nice in altar or buffet arrangements to add height. Individual blooms can be used as glamelias (ask your florist for an example). Colors range from white to pink to deep, true red.

❦ *Freesia.* Another small delicate flower with a pleasing scent, freesia can be used as a wonderful substitute for the more expensive stephanotis. They come in white, yellow, pink, orange, lavender, and red.

❦ *Stattice.* A fabulous filler flower for bridal bouquets, these bunches of tiny white or purple blossoms are reasonably-priced options. Other fillers that are inexpensive include Queen Anne's Lace and Stock.

❧ *Carnations.* Ah, the old standby. These are a great pick for altar arrangements since they stand out without great expense. They come in every color variety, but we don't recommend the dyed ones—stick to natural colors. Some varieties are also available as miniatures if you want to add them to table arrangements or bouquets. These are very "heat-hardy" too for those of you in hot climates.

❧ *Chrysanthemums.* More commonly referred to as mums, these flowers are also great filler for altar arrangements. They add oodles of volume to your arrangements without costing a great deal. These flowers are available in a wide range of colors from white to bronze. Some even look like daisies in pinks, yellows and white.

Getting Started: How Far in Advance?

 Book a florist up to six months in advance of your wedding. In larger cities, some florists may even require more time. For most towns, however, many florists consider three to six months notice adequate. Realize that you can put down a small deposit further in advance and then talk specifics at a later date.

Biggest Myths about Wedding Flowers

 Myth #1 *"My mother insists that we have lots and lots of flowers at my wedding. Is this really necessary?"*

Bridal magazines often tell us we should have flowers dripping from the ceiling and crawling along the floor. Some florists feed this perception by suggesting superfluous floral items like "cake knife corsages" (believe it or not, a special flower wrapped with a bow around the knife you cut the cake with), "hairpiece flowers" and arrangements for the gift table. We are not making this stuff up. Does the gift table really need a floral arrangement?

Emily Post even recommends flowers or greenery to decorate the area where your receiving line stands. How silly! Florists must see brides as an endless money pit. We hate to tread on those floral traditionalists but remember that the next day, all those flowers will be dead.

Myth #2 *"I figured on spending only about $100 on my wedding flowers. Given the cost of arrangements I've sent friends, I assume this is a good estimate."*

Most flowers are cheap. Most florists aren't. What you are paying for is the florist's talent, skill and overhead. The manual labor needed to create beautiful bouquets and arrangements (not to mention delivering them) is what costs big money. We should note that some exotic flowers (orchids, etc.) are pricey exceptions: they virtually guarantee an astronomically high floral bill.

Step-by-step Shopping Strategies

 ❦ **Step 1**: First, you must have the time, place and apparel selected before you can get an accurate bid from a florist. The bridal gown is crucial—everything flows from this design element. The colors of the bridesmaids gowns are also important.

❦ **Step 2**: Choose two to three florists from the sources above to visit. Make an appointment with each and leave about one hour's time to discuss the details.

❦ **Step 3**: Be sure to bring swatches of the bridesmaids apparel and a picture of the bridal gown you have selected. A magazine ad or rough sketch will suffice. Give this to the florist so they'll remember what the dress looks like when they actually make the bouquet. Also, it will be helpful to bring any pictures of flowers/designs you like.

❦ **Step 4**: Look through actual photographs of their previous work. Don't settle for FTD design books or floral magazines. Identify flowers and designs that fit your wedding's style. See if the florist attempts to understand your tastes and desires instead of merely telling you what you must have.

❦ **Step 5**: Get a written proposal specifying exact flowers to be used. Each item (brides bouquet, corsages, etc.) should be priced individually.

❦ **Step 6**: Pick your top florist choice and ask to visit one of their weddings during set-up. On your visit, check to see if they are on-time and organized. Also, look to see how fresh the flowers are. Do you find the designs pleasing (keeping in mind that the other bride's taste may be different from your own)?

❦ **Step 7**: If you believe an on-site meeting at your ceremony or reception site is necessary, now is the time. Finalize the details.

❦ **Step 8**: Get a written contract that spells out the date, set-up time, place, and specific flowers and designs to be created. Specific details (if you want open roses, for example) need to be spelled out clearly. As you get closer to your wedding, there may be some modifications (more corsages, etc.). Make sure you have the florist write down any changes—send written notes to verify the alterations.

❦ *Step 9*: If you're having a large or complex wedding, a pre-wedding floral check-up may be necessary. Here you'll meet with the florist about one to two weeks prior to the date to iron out any last minute details/changes, etc.

Questions to Ask a Florist

1 DO YOU HAVE ACTUAL PHOTOGRAPHS OR SAMPLES of your past work? It's important to see the work of your florist, not the airbrushed photos from an FTD book. There is no better way to see if their style complements your tastes and to see just how skilled they are.

2 DO YOU OFFER ANY SILK OR DRIED FLOWER ARRANGEMENTS? This may be important to you if you want to save your bouquet or want an unusual look. Sometimes these two options may be less expensive than fresh flowers, especially for some exotics like orchids.

3 IS THERE A DELIVERY OR SET-UP FEE? Watch out—this can be a substantial extra charge. Most florist will charge you some set-up fee especially if you have either complex flower arrangements or a site that is a long distance from their shop. If the charge is high, consider finding a florist closer to the site or cut back on the complicated decorations.

4 HOW MANY WEDDINGS DO YOU DO IN A DAY? The biggest problem with some florists is that they become "overextended"—trying to do too many weddings in one day. A florist can probably do up to two or three weddings a day if they are held at different times and/or they have plenty of help. If their schedule looks crowded for your wedding date, however, they may arrive late or deliver the wrong flowers. Look for someone focused on your wedding.

5 ARE YOU FAMILIAR WITH MY CEREMONY SITE LOCATION? If not, will you visit it with me? It may be a good idea to get the florist accustomed to the set-up of your ceremony or reception site if they've never seen it. Ask if there is any charge for this on-site visit.

6 WHAT RENTAL ITEMS DO YOU HAVE? How are they priced? Some things you may want to rent include candelabrum,

aisle standards, or urns. We prefer florists who don't over-charge on rentals. One way to find out is to compare prices with a local rental store. A common markup for florists is about 10% for their time to coordinate this detail. If you would prefer to rent the items yourself because you can get a better price, be sure you have the time to take care of it.

7 CAN I ATTEND ONE OF YOUR WEDDINGS DURING SETUP FOR A LOOK AT YOUR DESIGNS? Here is another way to determine how professional and talented your florist is. You'll need to visit during setup and leave before the wedding party arrives. Look for timeliness, freshness and beauty of the flowers and how well the florist and staff work together.

8 WHAT TIME WILL YOU BE AT MY CEREMONY/RECEPTION SITES TO SET-UP MY WEDDING? Confirm this time constantly throughout your planning. Many florists set-up weddings a couple hours in advance. If this is the case with your wedding, be sure the temperature at the site is not too hot for the flowers—you want them to look fresh at wedding time.

9 WILL YOU MERELY DROP OFF MY FLOWERS OR STAY THROUGH THE CEREMONY? The degree of service here differs dramatically from florist to florist. Some just drop off the flowers at the ceremony and leave, while others stay to pin on corsages, make sure nothing is missing, etc. There may be an extra fee ($50) for this service—for large weddings, however, this may be a worthwhile investment.

Helpful Hints

1 PUT YOUR DEPOSIT AND BALANCE ON A CREDIT CARD. We have heard countless stories of couples who hired a florist to do their flowers only to have the wrong flowers delivered. Or worse, the florist went out of business. Although these are rare occurrences, it's best to be safe. Payments on credit cards are protected by special consumer protection laws. See Chapter 2 for more details.

2 KEEP AN OPEN MIND. Instead of setting your heart on a particular design or flower, let your florist come up with some suggestions. Because florists work with flowers so closely, they may be aware of some options that are really terrific. Especially with regard to colors, listen to your florist's ideas and look at some of their past work before you make up your mind. You might be surprised!

Pitfalls to Avoid

Pitfall #1
"FTD COOKIE-CUTTER" WEDDINGS
   "I met with a florist for my wedding and was extremely disappointed. All they showed me were boring FTD design books. The few real photos I saw featured bouquets that all looked the same."

Some florists try to make every wedding fit a "cookie cutter" mold. Instead of keying on the individuality involved, they merely suggest stiff, formulated designs that are uninspired at best and dreadful at worst. We find "cash and carry" florists most guilty of this offense—they simply don't care enough about weddings to try harder.

Pitfall #2
PLASTIC BOUQUET HOLDERS
   "We attended a fancy wedding last weekend and were surprised at the bouquets. The beautiful flowers were stuck in cheap, plastic holders that just looked out of place!"

Plastic bouquet holders have become a crutch for many lazy florists. Instead of hand-tying and hand-wrapping the bouquets, some florists simply stick the flowers into floral foam inside plastic holders. Besides looking cheap, poorly-inserted flowers can actually drop out of the plastic holder!
   Some florists insist plastic holders are necessary since they provide a water source for delicate flowers. If your florist uses plastic holders for this purpose, insist the plastic be covered with green floral tape or pretty ribbon. Better yet, choose a florist that hand ties and hand wraps the bouquets. A small tube of water can be attached to delicate flowers needing moisture.

Pitfall #3
HEAT-SENSITIVE FLOWERS.
   "My friend got married last summer in an outdoor ceremony. Unfortunately, the heat caused many of the flowers to wilt and even turn brown."

If you live where it will be hot during your wedding, watch out for heat-sensitivity. Some flowers with this problem include stephanotis and gardenias. Ask your florist for flowers that can withstand the heat and still look fresh. As a side note, we heard from one florist who uses an "anti-transpirant" spray such as Bloomlife Plastic Wax or Crowning Glory. These products seal in the moisture so flowers don't wilt as fast.

Trends

❦ ***English garden style bouquets.*** These are garden-influenced styles that are very unstructured and free-form. The idea is to have a bouquet that looks like it was fresh picked.

❦ ***More color.*** All-white brides' bouquets are being replaced by bouquets with more color. From the barest blush to the most vibrant jewel tones, color isn't just for bridesmaids anymore.

❦ ***New growing techniques have produced some unique hybrid flowers.*** One neat example of this is the posy calla lily. A much smaller version of the huge white blooms, this one comes in burgundy, electric yellow or white. For the smaller bride who wants to carry calla lilies, here's an option that won't overwhelm.

❦ ***Wedding floral specialists.*** We've noticed an upswing in the number of florists who are concentrating solely on weddings. Some will even come to your home for a consultation or make appointments with you after work.

Unique Ideas

1 ONE OF THE MOST INTERESTING IDEAS WE'VE SEEN FOR RECEPTION SITE DECORATIONS IS BALLOONS. We've seen arches and canopies made of balloons and watched balloon releases as the couple leaves rather than rice throws. Balloons are best suited for high ceilings and can provide an impressive setting as you enter a ballroom or reception hall.

2 CONSIDER USING FRUITS AND VEGETABLES OR DRIED FLOWERS TO DECORATE YOUR RECEPTION TABLES. These will fit themes such as a fall wedding (gourds and pumpkins with fall leaves) or a Victorian style wedding. We've even heard of dessert being used as a centerpiece: piles of strawberries with silver bowls of chocolate sauce and powdered sugar on mirrors. Mmmmm.

Spotlight: Roses

Roses are still by far the most requested flowers in wedding arrangements and bouquets across the U.S. Without exception, every bridal consultant we talked to mentioned roses as popular wedding flowers in their city. With this in mind, you might appreciate a little extra information on roses.

Types of Roses

"Where do florists get roses? Will they look like roses at the grocery store? How can I be sure to get the best quality?"

Florists buy roses from wholesalers. Wholesalers buy them from a variety of sources. California is the largest producer of roses for the U.S., but roses also come from Colombia (Visa roses) and Mexico (Vega roses). Holland and France also export some varieties. Some of the best roses are Vegas, whose blossoms tend to be bigger than California roses and better shaped than Visas. Each florist has his or her own preference on which kind you should buy.

Roses also come in a variety of qualities, similar to eggs at the grocery store. California roses, for example, come in Select (the best), Extra Fancy (middle quality) and Fancy (cheap). Most of what you see in grocery stores are Fancy. Few professional florists sell Fancy roses, but it is difficult to determine yourself which grade your florist buys. If you are concerned about the quality, ask the florist which grade is used. Hopefully, they'll say Select. Select roses will be more expensive, but the quality will be better.

Color Options

"I requested bridal white roses from my florist for my bridal bouquet, but the bouquet I saw on my wedding day looked pinkish rather than white. Was my florist substituting the wrong flowers?"

Definitely not. One thing brides should understand about colors in the floral business is that they can be very deceiving. For example, a red rose isn't actually a true red. And a bridal white rose isn't really all-white. A bridal white rose, one of the most common roses for weddings, is actually a creamy white rose with a pink or peach tinged center. Many bridal white roses together in a bouquet may give the illusion of more pink than you intended. So you see how misleading names can be.

Here are some examples of other popular wedding roses:

❦ *Champaign*
A creamy, antique ivory colored rose.
❦ *Candia*
Creamy white with dark pink edges to the petals. This would be a truly unusual look.

❦ *Darling*

A creamy peach rose suitable for a touch of color in the bride's or bridesmaids' bouquets.

❦ *Bridal Pink*

These are definitely all-pink roses. Many brides assume they will be soft pink, but they are actually quite a bit brighter.

❦ *Delores*

This is a soft pink rose.

❦ *Jacaranda or Purvey*

A hot pink rose; perfect with the jewel tones of brides-maids' dresses.

❦ *Lady Diana*

Named after the Princess of Wales, these are pale peach roses. They are beautiful for bridal work and may even look pinkish rather than peach against a pink background.

❦ *Sonia*

A brighter peach rose with a little more vibrant color than the Lady Di.

❦ *Jacqueline Kennedy*

One of the few true red roses but tends to be rather small.

❦ *Madame Delbard*

This is a French rose with a rich velvety red color. It opens well but can be expensive.

❦ *Sterling Silver*

Also called an *Elizabeth Taylor,* the color is a lovely lavender. It tends to have a small blossom so you may need more of these blooms than you think.

❦ *Ranunculus*

These flowers aren't actually roses, but they do look a lot like a fully open rose. They make a very inexpensive alternative to roses especially since they are available in February and March, the time of year when roses are most expensive. They come in reds, pinks, and yellows.

One interesting final note on roses: colors have little or nothing to do with prices. You might expect more unusual hues (lavender, for example) to cost more but in reality the whole-sale price is often the same.

Spotlight: Do-it-yourself Supplies

Michaels Arts and Crafts Stores
(214) 580-8242

One of the best sources for silk flowers and wedding

supplies in the U.S. has got to be Michaels Arts and Crafts stores. With over 168 stores across the country, Michaels provides not only a large number of attractive, affordable silk flowers, but they also have in-store arrangers who can help put your wedding flowers together.

Michaels sells all the supplies necessary to design your own bouquets and arrangements, but if you prefer to use their staff to help you, they do provide a very reasonable alternative to retail florist shops. For example, when we visited a Michaels store, the floral department told us most bouquets range from $25 to $65. Wow! This is a great savings when compared with the average fresh bouquets from a retail florist—which can range from $75 to $150 and more.

Michaels stores also carry other accessories for do-it-your-self brides. They have supplies with which to make veils and headpieces, wedding cakes, your own favors and other wedding items. They carry accessories ranging from ring pillows to cake knives as well.

We've been big fans of the options available at Michaels Arts and Crafts stores for a long time. Their wide selection of silk flowers, craft supplies and wedding accessories make them a unique and valuable alternative.

Michaels are mainly located in the south, midwest and west coast states.

Leewards
(708) 888-5800

Leewards, a national chain with 90 stores, offers a variety of wedding packages. One store we visited offered a package that included a bride's nosegay, maid of honor's nosegay, groom's boutonniere and best man's boutonniere for less than $60. The package options vary by store, but a floral designer should be available to help customize flowers to fit your budget.

Leewards also offers extra bouquets, flower girl arrangements, extra boutonnieres and corsages at an additional charge. The silk flowers they use are good quality and come in a wide range of colors and types.

The prices for these silk wedding flowers make Leewards an affordable option for brides on a strict budget. Leewards even throws in an extra gift for brides that changes each month.

Michaels/MJDesigns
(214) 929-8595

Michaels/MJDesigns is a wonderful craft store with locations in Dallas/Ft. Worth and the Washington D.C.

metro area. What makes these stores unique is their incredible selection of silk flowers. Shoppers in Dallas, for example, have told us they wouldn't shop anywhere else for floral supplies!

MJDesigns has a huge selection of fine quality silk flowers and supplies for the do-it-yourselfer. If you prefer to have your wedding flowers arranged for you but can't afford the high prices of retail florists, MJDesigns has the answer.

Each store carries a catalog of 10 different designs for brides' and bridesmaids' bouquets. When we looked through the catalog, we noticed all shapes and sizes including natural clutches, nosegays, cascades and crescents. Besides bouquets, there were ten possible corsage designs, and five boutonniere options. We also saw pew bows, hairpieces, flower girl baskets and veils—all at very affordable prices.

For example, bouquets range from a small nosegay for $15 up to a large cascade with Japhet orchids and stephanotis for only $60. Corsages range from $3.50 to $10.50, while boutonnieres are $2. After interviewing over 200 retail florists, we couldn't find any source for flowers (silk or fresh) that's more affordable than MJDesigns.

To order a bouquet from MJDesigns, you first pick a color from the display in each store. Then, you choose a style from their catalog. MJDesigns then sends your order to their main design studio where it takes about seven days to produce.

MJDesigns also provides other wedding accessories, including cake decorating supplies, toasting glasses, cake toppers and veil supplies. Overall, we highly recommend Michaels/MJDesigns.

Other Do-It-Yourself Floral & Wedding Supplies

Do-it-yourself wedding supplies can be a significant source of savings. Here are our picks for the best craft stores in the country:

NATIONAL CHAINS
Fabric Centers/Jo Ann Fabrics
Fabric World
Hancock Fabrics
Leewards
Michaels Arts and Crafts
Petals (800) 431-2464

NORTHEAST
Hills

MIDWEST
Franks Nursery and Crafts

SOUTH
White Rose Crafts and Nursery (also in Canada)

SOUTHWEST
Michaels MJDesigns (Texas and Virginia)
Zaks (Texas and Florida)
Hobby Lobby (Oklahoma, Colorado, and Kansas)
Crafts Etc. (Texas)
Amber's (Texas)

WEST
H & H Crafts (California)
House of Fabric (Northwest)
Sprouse Stores (Northwest)

Dictionary of Flowers

Here are a few flower names and descriptions we found ourselves running into frequently. Hopefully this will help you understand our "lingo."

LILIES
❦ *Calla*
Huge, long white flowers on thick stalks (as in Katherine Hepburn's "...the calla lilies are in bloom.")
❦ *Rubrim*
Star flowers, come in colors from white to peach to deep maroon.
❦ *Lily of the Valley*
Small, white blooms that look like tiny bells. This flower is affordable in the north but quite expensive in other parts of the U.S.

ORCHIDS
❦ *Cymbidium*
Smaller than Japhet orchids with a curly edge only at the center.
❦ *Dendrobium*
Miniature orchids that come in sprays, may be used individually or as trailing pieces.
❦ *Japhet*
Large orchids with a curly edge all over, often have yellow throats.
❦ *Phalaenopsis*
These are round-edged orchids that are white with reddish throats. They don't always wear well.

MISCELLANEOUS

❧ *Stephanotis*
   Small, white flowers with star-like petals and a deep throat
   (we've been told that these can discolor in extreme heat.)
❧ *Anthuriums*
   One of the few "true red" flowers, this has a heart-shaped
   bloom with a large stamen.

If you have any questions or comments about this
chapter, please feel free to call the authors. See the
"How to Reach Us" page at the back of this book!

Chapter 6

Invitations

In this chapter, we'll tell you about a printing process that can save you 50% or more on your invitations. We'll show you the five-step shopping process for finding invitations, and share several unique ideas with you such as edible invitations.

What Are You Buying?

 Buying invitations is a little like buying a meal at an à la carte restaurant. In other words, everything is priced separately: the appetizer, salad, entree, and dessert. With invitations, the entree is the basic invitation design itself (the paper style and the printing). Thankfully, the price does include the envelopes (two for very formal invitations and one for more informal options).

There also are other "accessories" (appetizers, salads, desserts) available but these are priced separately from the original invitation. Here are some options and a short description:

❦ Reception cards announce to the guest the location and time of the actual reception.

❦ Response cards are just as they sound—a card that asks guests to tell you whether or not they can attend. An envelope (with your return address printed) is included with each response card. Response card envelopes must carry the correct postage—this encourages your guests to respond.

❦ Envelope linings add a little flair and color to invitations.

❦ The return address is printed on the back flap of the envelopes.

❦ Informals, used mainly as thank-you notes, usually are blank cards with your names printed on the outside.

❦ Exclusive (or photo) lettering versus regular lettering refers to the style of lettering you choose for your invitation. Most invitation books offer you a choice between styles of script. Some, however also offer two separate lists to choose from called "exclusive (or photo)" and "regular." Exclusive lettering is more expensive than regular lettering but we recommend using exclusive lettering anyway. The difference is that the exclusive options give you more choices than regular lettering. Also, the size of regular lettering cannot be adjusted to fit the size of your invitation and may look awkward. The choice is up to you but the added expense is very small (about $4 or $5 per 100 invitations).

Average Total Costs The average couple pays between $300 and $400 for invitations and other stationery needs. The average deposit is 50% down with the balance due when you pick up your order.

By the way, the wholesale prices of wedding invitations are typically 40% to 50% off the retail price. Since the retail prices of invitations are printed in sample books, some manufacturers give their dealers a choice of mark-ups. Hence, you could see the exact same invitation priced differently at different stores.

Sources to Find an Affordable Stationer

Most wedding invitations are printed by big, national manufacturers. Each manufacturer puts samples of each invitation style they offer into large catalogs. These sample books are sold to local dealers (stationery shops, etc.). Brides choose a design from these sample books and then place an order (through the dealer) with the manufacturer. Hence, the challenge is to find a quality local stationer who offers the styles you want. There are four types of stationers:

1 RETAIL STATIONERS. Anyone who sells stationery from a store front fits in this category. Typically, they also carry cards and some gifts as well.

2 OUT-OF-HOME STATIONERS. Some stationers who work out of their home offer 15% to 20% discounts on many of their stationery lines.

3 DEPARTMENT STORES. A few department stores with bridal registries also offer stationery as a convenience to their customer.

4 PRINTERS. Off-set printers also carry wedding invitations but may not be as knowledgeable about how to word them as other stationery professionals.

5 CHURCHES, SYNAGOGUES AND CORPORATE OPTIONS. Some churches and synagogues offer invitations at discounted prices as a fund-raiser. Even some companies offer invitations as a perk for their employees. One bride who worked at Xerox told us she was able to order invitations through the company at a substantial discount.

Sources to Find Stationers

❦ *Friends* Recently-married couples may be your best resource to find a good stationer.

❦ *Bridal shows* Bridal shows are a great place to find little-known stationery companies. You may be able to look through some of their sample books at a show too.

❦ *Other bridal businesses.* Many other bridal businesses such as photographers, florists and bridal shops may be able to suggest a good local stationer.

❦ *Discount Bridal Service.* Many DBS representatives also offer discounts on invitations as well as on bridal gowns. For a list of their representatives who also discount invitations call (800) 874-8794.

Top Money-saving Secrets

1 CHOOSE THERMOGRAPHED INVITATIONS instead of engraved. Right about now you may be wondering what is thermography. Let's take a quick look at the difference between the two printing processes. Note: we aren't talking about the style of script or the quality of the paper, this is just the actual printing process.

Engraving is the Rolls Royce of embellishments. It has been with us for quite a long time and actually was the only option available for invitations until about ten or 15 years ago. Both engraving and thermography create raised printing. However, with engraving, a copper or steel plate is etched with the type and design. These etchings fill with ink and are forced against a die, lifting the ink out of the plate and creating a raised image on the paper. The paper is left with an impression from the back.

Thermography is often used to simulate engraving. A resinous powder is dusted over the ink while it is still wet. The pieces then are heated where the powder melts, fuses with the ink and swells to create a raised surface. While metal plates may be used, this process is much less expensive (up to 50% or even more!). Thisoption also allows you to use a wide variety of ink colors. Thermography has become extremely popular, thanks to better production processes. Ask for dull thermography (instead of gloss or semigloss) for a more formal look. The process is virtually indistinguishable from engraving except to those snobs out there who feel the backs of invitations.

2 ORDER FROM A PROFESSIONAL STATIONER who discounts. Discount Bridal Service has many representatives around the country who regularly discount invitations 10% to 20%.

3 CHECK THE LOCAL NEWSPAPER FOR SALES. Some professional stationers have periodic sales.

4 DON'T BUY ALL THE EXTRAS. As you've read above, there are quite a few different accessories and extras available to match your wedding invitation. Instead of ordering separate reception cards, consider printing "Reception Following" at the bottom of your actual invitation. This could save about 15% off your bill. Also, skip envelope linings and response cards if you don't see a need for them. To see how all these charges add up, let's look at the sample costs for an invitation with black ink from the popular Carlson Craft line (800)328-1782:

INVITATION PRICING EXAMPLE
Carlson Craft Invitation #WC 298-71
Price for 200 Invitations

BASIC INVITATION	$151.70
RETURN ADDRESS ON FLAP	38.60
RECEPTION CARD	75.10
RESPONSE (RSVP) CARD	91.90
LINED ENVELOPES	32.00
INFORMALS (THANKYOU NOTES)	75.10

TOTAL $464.50

As you can see by this example, the original invitation is much less costly by itself than after you add in all the options.

5 BUY AN EMBOSSER WITH YOUR RETURN ADDRESS instead of paying extra to get this printed on the back flap. The cost of an embosser is about equal to or less than the return address charge in many cases—the advantage here is you can use the embosser again.

6 TO SAVE ON POSTAGE, DON'T BUY AN OVERSIZED INVITATION. Oversized invitations require more postage. Also, an invitation with lots of enclosures (reception cards, response cards, maps, etc.) will be more expensive to mail. Remember that response cards require their own stamp, too.

7 FOR ENGRAVED INVITATIONS, CONSIDER ALTERNATIVES TO CRANE. If you must have engraved invitations but can't afford Crane engraved, there are several affordable alternatives. For example, Carlson Craft engraves invitations on beautiful, 100% cotton paper (similar to Crane). The cost:

$152 for 100 invitations—nearly half the cost of Crane!

Helpful Tip

FOR LARGE ORDERS, ENGRAVED INVITATIONS MAY BE A BETTER BARGAIN. While thermography are generally cheaper than engraving, there is an exception. After you get beyond 300 to 350 invitations, the reverse is often true. For example, we priced 350 thermographed invitations from Carlson Craft for $344. The same number of engraved invitations from Jenner were $339. Also, Jenner will fold, tissue and stuff the invitations for that price—no thermographer offers this service.

Spotlight: Best Buys

Through our research for this book, we have identified a couple "best buys" in wedding invitations. Here are the manufacturers:

The Ratings

★★★★ EXCELLENT — *our top pick!*
   ★★★ GOOD — *above average quality, prices and creativity.*
     ★★ FAIR — *could stand some improvement.*
       ★ POOR — *yuck! Could stand major improvement.*

William Arthur ★★★★ Our pick as the best bet for invitations is Maine-based William Arthur. Their fabulous collection of thermographed invitations offers a more sophisticated and classic look for brides who want an alternative to the plain, traditional invitation. With a variety of unique type styles and card-type designs, Arthur's line runs $189 to $257 per 100 invitations ($286 to $382 for 200 invitations). Included in that price is return address printing, which is nice plus. The customer service is excellent, according to two stationers we interviewed. "They're in a class by themselves," one told us, adding that their shipping (5 business days) is incredibly reliable. One and two day rush service is also available. New this year is an entire book of recycled paper invitations printed with soy ink. (207) 985-6581.

W.A. Beunings ★★½ Here's a good source for engraved invitations. North Carolina-based Beunings has a high quality 100% cotton paper, similar in quality to Crane. We liked the moire fabric linings, as well as some of the traditional style designs decorated with ribbon ties. Prices run $224 to $300 for 100 engraved invitations, which includes stuffing the envelopes (thermography is also available, but our sources liked the prices and quality of the engraved invitations better). Recycled paper invitations are an option, as are heavier weight papers and square format designers. (800) 347-1151. (704) 376-1151.

Chase Paper ★★★ From plain traditional to glitzy contemporary, Chase Paper has a very wide selection of unique papers you just can't find anywhere else. The quality of the thermography is top-notch, says our stationery sources. Prices run $54 to $325 per 100 invitations. Best of all, the lower-priced options are a definite step-up in quality compared to other companies. Shipping takes about three weeks. (508) 366-4441.

Embossed Graphics ★★½ If you're planning a large wedding, Embossed Graphics should be at the top of your invitations shopping list. That's because the company has incredible prices for large quantities of invitations. For example, 400 invitations from Embossed Graphics costs just $200. While the styles and extra options are limited, the heavy paper is high quality. Another incredible buy is their personal stationery album, which has a one-time $17 fee to print your return address on back flaps, regardless of the quality of invitations ordered. The only slight negative: Embossed Graphics customer service department is reportedly understaffed and is slow in responding to requests. (708) 369-0999. (800) 349-2407.

Indelible Ink ★★★ Looking for something different? If whimsical invitations will fit the bill, check out Indelible Ink. This New York-based company offers unconventional wedding invitations with fun wording, heavy paper and nice envelope linings. The price is moderate, running $123 to $183 per 100 thermographed invitations. (800) 448-0870.

Jenner ★★★½ If you like the Crane look but not the Crane price, here's the best alternative: Jenner Invitations. The company gives you two options—engraved invitations on Crane paper or on Rosetone paper (their in-house clone of Crane). Not all of Crane papers are available, but most of the requested styles are in stock. Prices for Jenner engraving on Crane are about 15% cheaper than Crane—for example, 200 engraved invitations run $342. Rosetone is even better: $249.50 per 200 invitations. Best of all, those prices include folding, tissue, and stuffing of invitations into the envelopes. "Jenner is a joy to work with," a stationer told us. "In five years, I've never had a problem with one order." (502) 222-0191.

Getting Started: How Far in Advance?

There are five steps in the shopping process for invitations. Overall, we recommend you order invitations at least three to four months before your wedding.

1 SHOPPING. Take a couple of weeks to visit two or three stationers in your area.

2 ORDERING. This varies greatly by manufacturer. Generally, it can take anywhere from 10 days to two months to order invitations. Most orders take three to four weeks.

3 MISTAKES. We suggest you leave a two week "buffer zone" in case your invitations come in with errors. One stationer told us that one out of every three orders comes in from the manufacturer with errors.

4 ADDRESSING. Considering how busy you probably are with work and wedding planning, leaving four weeks here is prudent. If you choose to hire a local calligrapher, most take between one and three weeks to complete a job.

5 MAILING. Everyone knows how wonderfully efficient the U.S. Postal Service is. Give yourself plenty of time. Mail invitations to out-of-town guests at least six weeks before the wedding. For in-town guests, mail at least four weeks before the event. If your wedding is on a holiday weekend, consider mailing even earlier so your guests will have time to make plans.

Biggest Myths About Invitations

Myth #1 "*My aunt, who is a real stickler for etiquette, says that engraved invitations are the only option to consider. She says the quality of thermographed invitations is awful.*"

Unfortunately, your aunt has been reading too many outdated etiquette books. In reality, thermography technology has improved so much in recent years that even Crane, the number-one seller of engraved invitations, now offers thermography as well. The only visible difference between thermography and engraving is the dent on the back of your invitation—and in your pocketbook.

Myth #2 "*I thought it would take 15 minutes to write up my invitations order at the stationer. Boy was I surprised when it took an hour and a half!*"

That's right! Many folks think writing an invitation is easy—until they actually try it. In reality, finding the right combination of words and type styles that make an aesthetically attractive invitation is challenging. That's why just writing up an invitation order can take an hour or more.

Myth #3 "*I assumed when we ordered our invitations that extra envelopes would be included—is this true?*"

Nope, many printers send the exact compliment of envelopes as invitations ordered. If you want extra envelopes, they must be ordered in advance (there is a small additional cost). Why is this important? Well, if you're addressing your own invitations, it pays to have extra envelopes in case of mistakes. Even calligraphers will request you supply extra envelopes.

Step-by-step Shopping Strategies

❦ *Step 1:* Determine the number of invitations you need. This is not the same number as the guest count, because you send only one invitation per household. The exception: if a guest's child is over 18 and living at home, he or she receives their own invitation. This step, of course, actually involves the groom. You must compile a list of his, yours, theirs (parents' friends) and ours.

❦ *Step 2:* Confirm the place and time of the wedding and reception. Also, verify the spellings of the facilities and names of participants. (We heard one story of a bride who didn't know how to spell her fiance's middle name—the resulting invitation was misspelled! Doing your homework here is obviously helpful.)

❦ *Step 3:* Determine your overall wedding style. For example, an outdoor afternoon wedding followed by a barbecue reception will probably not have a formal, engraved invitation. On the other hand, a formal wedding with a sit-down dinner reception at the Waldorf-Astoria isn't the time for embossed hearts and flowers on parchment paper. The invitation is your guests' clue about what to expect. To decide how formal your wedding is, consider time of day, formality of dress, and reception style. At the same time, you and your fiance's personalities should also be reflected in the wedding invitation.

❦ *Step 4:* Decide on an invitation budget. Prices range from $35 to $900 per 100 invitations, so have some amount in mind.

❦ *Step 5:* Once you find a professional stationer (see the sources above), look at their sample books. First, decide on the paper. Forget the wording, type styles, and ink colors. Instead, look at the paper design and quality. Any style of type, wording and colors can be put on any paper design, so key in on that aspect first. The heavier the paper, the higher the quality. The grades of paper largely determine the price.

❦ *Step 6:* Next, consider the printing. Decide on the ink color, lettering style and printing method (engraving or thermography). Some invitation designs limit choices in these areas.

❧ *Step 7:* Given the paper design and printing that best fits your reception, choose an invitation in your price range. Don't forget to factor in the cost of extras including napkins, place cards and matchbooks if you want them.

❧ *Step 8:* Order at least 25 more invitations than your actual count in case you decide you need more later. Also, order extra envelopes in case of addressing goofs (calligraphers often ask for 10% extra for mistakes). After the order is written proofread very carefully before the order is sent off. This is a critical step to catch any errors.

❧ *Step 9:* When the order comes in, proofread again and count the number of invitations to be sure you received the amount you ordered. Do this before you leave the store. Stationers have only a three to five day window allowed by printers to catch mistakes.

Questions to Ask a Stationer

1 How many different lines do you carry? A wide assortment of styles and manufacturers not only gives you more choices (and price ranges) but also a clue to how serious the stationer is about their business. Since stationers must purchase those sample books (at a cost of $35 to $250 a book), the number they carry indicates their commitment to wedding invitations.

2 Given my wedding and reception, what is your opinion of having response cards? Response cards, an extra expense, request that your guests reply to your invitation. However, in some regions of the country (parts of the South and Southwest) guests often don't send in their response cards because they prefer not to "disappoint" the bride by saying no. In other regions, particularly the Northeast, response cards are considered a must and are routinely returned by guests.

Your stationer should be aware of what is most common in your area. Even if you do choose to send response cards, you may only receive as few as 30% back. We recommend response cards when you are inviting a large number of guests and/or are having a very expensive meal. If you are only planning cake and punch or are having fewer than a hundred guests, response cards may not be needed. Remember that response cards also require their own stamp, raising your expenses accordingly.

3 Can I see some samples of actual invitation orders? This is one way to separate the part-time stationer from the full-time professional. Some part-time stationers may not keep samples while professionals should have samples from

previous orders. Don't look at the style or color of the samples. Instead key in on the wording and the overall composition. Is the overall effect pleasing? Are the lines of type proportionate to the paper size? If the invitation wording looks awkward, you may not want to trust your invitation to this shop.

4 WHO IS RESPONSIBLE FOR ANY ERRORS THAT OCCUR? Some stationers may not offer to fix errors, whether you made them or they did. The true professional will take care of anything that goes wrong regardless of who is responsible. You shouldn't have to deal with the manufacturer to correct mistakes—that's what you pay the stationer for.

5 CAN I SEE A PROOF OF THE INVITATION? Some printers offer this at a very small cost ($20 or less). If you have a large order or complex invitation, this might be a prudent way to go.

Pitfalls to Avoid

Pitfall #1
UNDER-ORDERING OF INVITATIONS.
"When I first ordered invitations, I ordered exactly enough for the people on my list. Later, my mother came up with some long-lost relatives, and I had to go back and reorder another 25. I was shocked at the extra expense!"

If you guess wrong and need more invitations, the set-up charge to reprint will be tremendous. For example, let's look at a sample invitation order. The total for 100 invitations is $204.50. If you decide you really need to order 125 invitations, the total would be $246.20—a $41.70 difference. However, if you order only 100 and find out later you need 25 more, the total cost will be $363.50. Wow! Ordering 125 in the first place would have saved you $117.30! As you can see, ordering extras in your original order is much more cost effective. That's because the set-up charge for additional orders is the same as for the original order. There is no cost savings on invitations if you go back later to order more. Also keep in mind that if you "go back to press" later, the ink color and paper may not match the original order.

Pitfall #2
MAIL-ORDER INVITATIONS.
"I saw an ad in one of the bridal magazines for mail-order invitations. The cost was incredibly cheap so I decided to get the catalog and order a design. When the order came in, I was extremely disappointed."

The price of invitations you order through mail-order houses is definitely tempting. The problem is that the price is lower but, often, so is the quality. Also, don't underestimate the difficulty of writing a wedding invitation. The proper combination of words, type styles and paper design is best left in the hands of a professional. Also remember if you make a mistake in your order, you have to pay the cost to fix it. Truly professional stationers often will absorb the cost of fixing errors. Professional stationers also have more leverage with manufacturers if a dispute develops.

If you go this route, look for mail-order companies with toll-free consultation lines and "unconditional guarantees."

Pitfall #3
WHEN INVITATIONS ARE JUST A SIDELINE.

"My bridal shop offered to order invitations for me at a 10% discount. However, the salesperson who helped me didn't seem to know much more than I did about how to write up the order or word the invitation."

Competition in the invitation business is intense. Many bridal businesses (particularly bridal shops and photographers) now offer invitations as an enticement to order a gown or purchase photography. The discount is usually 10% to 20% off retail. The problem: many of these businesses are inexperienced. Their selection and knowledge of invitation printers is limited and service by low-paid clerks is lackluster. Many also lack the skills to word the invitations correctly.

Pitfall #4
LAST MINUTE CHANGES.

"My church just called to say that we have to move up the time on our ceremony by one hour. The problem is I've already ordered invitations. Can I make a change?"

Not without incurring some big charges. First, understand that most invitations orders are faxed to the printer within 36 hours. Once received by the printer, it is very difficult to locate, change or stop the order. If changes can be made, there is always a charge. For example, one big printer we researched charges $10 per item "per inquiry" and another $10 per change.

Pitfall #5
THE REVENGE OF THE ETIQUETTE POLICE.

"I just got in my invitation order and got a big surprise. With no warning, the printer had changed my order to fix an alleged 'etiquette error' in the wording! This is ridiculous."

Hard to believe, but it is true that some printers will change the wording on invitations to conform to "proper etiquette" as they see it. The only way you can avoid this problem is to tell the stationer that you want the wording (and any capitalization) to be exactly as you specify. This is usually accomplished by checking a box on the order form (or noting it in some other way). That way the printer won't substitute their etiquette rules for your finely-crafted prose.

Pitfall #6
PET POSTAL PEEVES

"My stationer told me the invitations would cost just 29¢ to mail. However, after I added two maps and took the invitations to the post office, they said it would be 52¢. As a result, we have to shell out another $50 in postage. Is that fair?"

This pitfall is why we recommend you take your invitation (and all the enclosures) to the post office and get it weighed *before* you buy all those cute "love" stamps. Start adding maps, response cards or other enclosures and you'll notice the postage bill soars.

Another interesting twist on this scam is a story we heard from Austin, Texas. A mailing service there was advertising an "addressing, stuffing and mailing" service for just $1 per invitation. Sounds great, huh? The problem was the service didn't tell brides they were mailing their invitations *bulk rate*. The post office treats bulk rate mail as a very low priority, to put it charitably. As a result, some of the brides' invitations arrived six weeks after the wedding—others didn't arrive at all. The best advice: always mail invitations first class.

Unique Ideas

For brides with a flair for the unusual and a corresponding pocketbook, there are five companies (most available through local retail stationers) we recommend for unique wedding invitations. One company is *Encore* (800) 526-0497, a very contemporary, elegant invitations company.

In Encore's catalog, we have found some of the most wonderful papers, ranging from elegant taffeta moire to pearlized satins. If you want to match the flowers you'll be using in your wedding, Encore offers incredible embossed lilies, roses and more on textured papers and card stock. All the Encore invitations are thermographed and a wide variety of ink colors is available.

The costs for these one-of-a-kind invitations range from $99 to $824 for 100 invitations. The average order however, falls in the range of $230 to $240. These design may be rather pricey, but they are also popular since they give a contemporary look without compromising elegance.

Another company similar to Encore is *Elite,* (800) 354-8321, owned by the Regency Company. Elite can cost up to $950 per 100 invitations and are equally as unique as Encore. By the way, Elite also offers engraved invitations.

Checkerboard Invitations, (508) 835-2475, by Metropolis feature a wild assortment of designer invitations. We saw styles with splattered ink, mylar prisms, and marbled paper. Funky envelope linings complete the look. Prices range from $39 to $375 per 100 invitations.

If money is truly no option whatsoever (and if so we'd like to meet you!), consider a company called *Creative Intelligence* in Los Angeles. Creative Intelligence custom-designs invitations and can fulfill your wildest invitation fantasy (if you have one!).

Owned by Marc Friedland, Creative Intelligence, (213) 936-9009, has made quite a splash among the Hollywood jet-set. He offers hand-designed invitations for all kinds of events at an average cost of $14 each (not per 100). His prices have even reached as high as $100 *each.* Designs have incorporated western themes, others have included plastic hula dancers and astro turf. Of course, Friedland custom-designs these outrageous invitations for each event, so if you choose to hire him, your invitation will undoubtedly be quite unique (and expensive).

Wouldn't you like to see your actual invitation on a computer screen before you order? Well, Atlanta-based Innovative Icons (800) 929-4266 has created the *"Isabella"* computerized invitation system to let you compare paper, typestyles, ink color and more. The prices are competitive and delivery is fast.

Trends

"Green" marketing has invaded every consumer product imaginable. Today, you can buy recycled toilet paper, biodegradable trash bags, and "environmentally safe" detergents. But what about wedding invitations?

Well, it didn't take stationary printers long to recognize this lucrative trend. Recently, Carlson Craft, (800) 328-1782, rolled out an invitation line printed on recycled paper. The company says the line are for "an elegant wedding and a brighter future."

Green of a different shade also tops other invitation news. Emerald green is a hot color, with several printers debuting envelope linings and matching ink in this "rich jewel-tone shade."

Embossed paper is in vogue, too. One new invitation style we viewed was covered in tiny embossed roses. Other stationers we saw are personalizing wedding stationery by hand-painting designs directly on the invitation. In Denver, Debbie Bodian of Paper Talk, (303) 759-1581, paints mountain scenes on invitations for couples planning nuptials in the Rockies.

Spotlight: Unique Idea

Barbara Logan's Paperworks (800) 458-9143

If you're tired of "traditional" (read: boring) wedding invitations, have we got a company for you. Barbara Logan's Paperworks in Rockville, Maryland has created some of the most unique wedding invitations we've ever seen. And believe us, we've seen a lot.

What makes Barbara's invitations special are handmade papers embedded with dried flowers or sparkling glitter. Matching parchment invitations with raised printing are inserted into the paper for a truly unique look.

The handmade papers are available in one of four styles: floral, glitter, parfait papers with threads and fibers, and earth-colored natural papers. A variety of color choices are available.

So, how much does this cost? Okay, it isn't cheap. The price for 100 invitations (floral or glitter with raised-print parchment insert pages) costs $339.90. That includes your choice of lettering style and ink color. The prices in other styles range up to $840.

Additional extras include tassels, ribbons, envelope linings, return addresses, reception folders or response folders. One bummer: invitations ship unfolded and unassembled. Assembled invitations cost an additional $85 (for 100). Shipping is also extra (UPS charge plus $2 handling). Delivery takes four weeks.

Paperwork's Alina Zygmunt told us that their invitations "combine the best of both worlds—a unique innovative decorative cover with the more traditional invitations insert." And we couldn't agree more.

Spotlight: Best Buys

Alegra's Discount Bridal (512) 499-0421
Invitation Hotline (800) 800-4355

If mail-order prices are attractive but the quality of mail-order invitations is disappointing, consider Alegra's Discount Bridal. This Austin, Texas-based company discounts Elite, Encore and other first-quality invitations by 15%. All brides have to do is call with the name of the book, page number and style number of the invitations. Once you decide on the wording, Alegra's does the rest.

If you decide to order from a mail-order company, Alegra's owner Nancy Owen offers another service which might be helpful: etiquette and proofreading advice. For $7.50 for an invitation (and $12.50 for the invitation, reception and response cards), Owen will help you with any wording challenges. Mail the proposed wording (and a return address) to 3110-B Windsor Rd., Austin, TX 78703, or fax it to (512) 499-0674.

The Invitation Hotline in Manalatan, New Jersey, offers a 25% discount on such famous lines as Carlson Craft, Elite, Encore, StyleArt, and more. Over 25 lines are available and the company does take VISA and MasterCard. Owner Marcy Slachman told us that all brides need to do is call her with the book name and style number. She'll help troubleshoot any etiquette or wording questions.

Spotlight: Wedding Favors

When we decided to write about wedding favors, we thought we should talk to an expert about their origin and popularity. We spoke to a major distributor and wedding-favor manufacturer.

❦ **Where did favors originate?** Popular mainly on the East Coast and in California, wedding favors have had a long, rich history. When we say rich, we really mean royal. In fact, in France during the 16th century, nobility and royalty gave valuable gifts (usually of porcelain) to their wedding guests as mementos of the occasion.

In the middle of the 16th century, almonds came to Italy from the Far East. These almonds were very expensive and became popular to give as favors to guests at royal weddings. To preserve the almonds, a sugar-coating was invented and Jordan almonds were born.

During the 17th century, three almonds, painted in bright colors and wrapped in bridal veiling, were given to guests. The significance of three almonds is this: From the union of two comes three—a baby. The veiling meant that the guests shared the couple's happiness.

❦ **What about favors in the U.S.?** In the U.S., favors are most popular with ethnic communities (particularly Italians). Our source told us that nearly 25% of their orders come from Pennsylvania, New York, and New Jersey. Brides and grooms in these states order more expensive favors, with almonds inside a porcelain swan or champagne glass—these favors can cost as much as $3 to $4 each! In other parts of the country, potpourri is a more popular favor choice. While favors are also common in the Southeast (Georgia, Florida, and North and South Carolina in particular), brides in the Midwest, Northwest, and Southwest rarely give favors to guests.

Our manufacturer sells mostly traditional favors such as

tulle wrapped around potpourri or almonds, and foil-imprinted ribbons are also popular.

❦ *A source for wedding favors:* Favours Internationale, (800) 649-1065 or (617) 383-1065, is a Massachusetts-based company that makes favors. Their showroom in Cohasset features more than 200 items. They can even design a favor from a verbal description. Call for a price quote.

In Favours Internationale's most recent catalog, we noticed a wide variety of options. Prices ranged from $1.69 each for a basic almond favor to $6 to $7 each for porcelain favors. In addition to favors, the company also sells ring bearer pillows, cake servers and porcelain cake tops.

❦ *Another catalog for wedding favors:* Wilton, the company famous for cake tops and various baking supplies, has released a book called "Party Favors" ($5.95). This 40-page guide gives you "how to" advice on assembling your own favors plus a complete catalog of various supplies. Call (708) 963-7100 for more information.

PART II

Your
Reception

Chapter 7

Reception Sites

The reception is certainly the biggest expense area of any wedding. Think you can't save money here? Think again! We'll show you seven money-saving tips that could save you thousands—plus we'll give you the four most common pitfalls with reception sites and how to avoid them! Finally, we'll take a candid look at the real pros and cons of the four most common types of reception sites.

What Are You Buying?

 Basically, you are buying two things here:

❧ *Exclusive use of the facility.* Either you are charged a flat fee for a certain period of time or there is an hourly rate. Obviously, rates vary with the amount of ambiance. A historic restored mansion will cost much more than a local union hall. Most places require a booking deposit, which can be several hundred dollars. A second deposit (to cover any damage or cleanup) may also be required at some sites.

❧ *Catering* (food, liquor, service, and rentals). All reception sites either require you to use their in-house caterer or allow you to bring an off-site caterer. When a site has an in-house caterer, there is often no "room charge"—the facility makes its money from the catering. Unfortunately, some sites not only charge you for the catering but also tack on a facility rental fee. We cover wedding catering in-depth later in this book.

The Big Trade-off: Ambiance vs. Great Food

Brides tell us that they must make a basic trade-off in their search for a reception site: the ambiance versus quality of food. Often, you must decide which is more important—how the site looks versus how the food tastes. Many lovely reception sites have just mediocre offerings for food. Other less attractive sites may have great reputations for sumptuous buffets or sit-down dinners. Of course, the perfect compromise is to find a beautiful site that allows you to bring in an outside caterer. As you will find in our later discussion, these sites are rare indeed.

Sources to Find a Reception Site

Finding the right reception site for your wedding may be the most challenging task you face. That's mainly because of the big bucks involved here—the reception (and, specifically, the catering) is the most expensive part of getting married. Here are some top sources to find affordable sites.

❦ *Wedding coordinators at your ceremony site.* Yes, these folks probably have talked to hundreds of brides over the years. They might be able to give you the "word on the street" for several reception sites.

❦ *Caterers.* Most off-site (or independent) caterers are well aware of the best local wedding reception sites. That's because their livelihood depends on the existence of facilities that let outside caterers come in for receptions. Call around to a few local caterers to find leads.

❦ *Recently-married couples.* Ask your co-workers or friends if they know anyone who was recently married. These couples are often more than willing to share their research and experiences about reception sites.

❦ *Visitors/Tourism bureaus and local parks departments.* If you are looking for a civic site (such as an historic home), your local visitors/tourism bureau (or chamber of commerce) may have some suggestions. Many civic sites (like gardens and parks) are booked by local parks departments.

❦ *Bridal shows.* Yes, bridal shows can be a source for reception sites. Large expos with many vendors are your best bet. Reception sites often set up booths and hand out food samples and menus.

Top Money-saving Secrets

1 CITY SITES. Fortunately, most sites run by cities or municipal governments aren't trying to make a killing on weddings. Hence, city sites are the most affordable reception sites you can find. For example,

in one city we researched, a nice clubhouse in a park that overlooked the skyline was rented by the city for $125 for five hours. That's right, just $125 (you bring a caterer). Another similar-sized facility run by a private company in the same town cost $750 to rent for four hours. Obviously, the ambiance of these city sites (clubhouses, recreations centers, parks, gardens) is different than a downtown hotel, but, hey they are great bargains.

2 CHOOSE A SITE WHERE YOU CAN BRING IN A CATERER. In every city we've researched, there are always a handful of sites where you can rent the facility and then bring in an "off-site" caterer. Often, this is where the big savings are found—see our chapter on catering for more details.

3 CONSIDER AN OFF-PEAK TIME OF THE WEEK OR YEAR. Everyone wants to get married on a Saturday in June. Now, if you pick a time with less competition, you can often negotiate better rental rates. Many sites have stated discounts for Friday or Sunday weddings. In other cases, you may be able to negotiate a lower rental rate for less popular months of the year.

4 HAVE A RECEPTION LUNCH OR BRUNCH INSTEAD OF DINNER. The biggest expense of most receptions is catering, and the most expensive meal to serve is dinner. Wedding lunches or brunches often are much more affordable. Furthermore, a two o'clock wedding with cake, punch and light hors d'oeuvres will be even less expensive. Check the catering chapter for more tips to save money on this big budget item.

5 CONSIDER YOUR CEREMONY SITE. Many houses of worship have attached reception halls. In fact, almost one-quarter of all receptions occur at churches or temples. Perhaps this is because rental rates are particularly affordable. Either you are allowed to bring in a caterer or you are required to use the site's in-house catering.

6 YOUR HOUSE. Hey, the rental is at least cheap. Be aware that you may have to rent chairs, tables, etc. and this might add to the tab. If you plan to pitch a tent in the backyard, the expense can go even higher. Of course, the savings of bringing in a caterer (instead of holding the reception at a pricey hotel) may put you ahead overall. Between 10% and 20% of all receptions are held in private homes.

7 HOW ABOUT A DESSERT RECEPTION? One bride in Chicago called in with this suggestion—she was planning a late evening ceremony (about 9 pm). Figuring the guests would

already have eaten dinner, the couple chose to have a lavish dessert buffet—much less expensive than a full dinner. The total savings for 200 guests was $2000. (To avoid any confusion, it's appropriate to add on your invitation or reception card "Dessert Reception Following.")

8 Restaurant receptions. A Connecticut bride called in this tip: she found a restaurant with a nice banquet room that was perfect for her 50-guest reception. Instead of telling them it was a wedding reception, she said the party was a family reunion. As a result, she was able to get a great price for a complete sit-down luncheon. Two weeks before the reception, she told the restaurant it was actually a wedding—too late for the restaurant to raise the price! Many restaurants have banquet rooms, some that can hold large crowds. These may be a great alternative to pricey hotels or catering halls.

Getting Started: How Far in Advance?

 Don't delay the search for your reception site. As soon as you have confirmed your ceremony site, start the search for a reception facility. Time is of the essence. Most cities have a shortage of great reception sites; prime dates in the spring and summer often go quickly. In the South, December can book up to a year in advance for popular Christmas weddings. Since June is also popular in many areas of the country, booking a site nine months to a year in advance may be necessary.

Step-by-step Shopping Strategies

 ❦ *Step 1:* Figure out how many guests you want to invite. Then look for a site that fits that capacity. Many brides make the mistake of doing this the other way around—picking a site first and then having to adapt their guest list around its capacity.

❦ *Step 2:* Using the above sources, make appointments with three to five of the top prospects. Bring a friend along to help inspect the facilities.

❦ *Step 3:* When you visit a reception site, look carefully at the facility. Can the room really hold all your guests comfortably or does it looked cramped? Is the lighting on a dimmer system? How is the traffic flow pattern?

❦ *Step 4:* Try to meet the catering manager (if the catering is done in-house). Honestly discuss your budget and suggest the manager custom-tailor a menu for your reception. Read the catering chapter to make sure you cover all of those details. Get a detailed price breakdown—in writing—on everything (food, liquor, service, centerpieces, linens, china, etc.).

❧ *Step 5:* Ask to see the site set-up for a wedding. It's sometimes hard to imagine an empty ballroom dressed to the nines for a wedding reception. Here's a good way to get a more realistic impression. Ask to visit just before the reception is to start. Check the traffic flow—for buffets, see if the lay-out of the food stations makes sense. Does the staff seem organized, or are they running around at the last minute like chickens with their heads cut off?

❧ *Step 6:* If the site has in-house catering, ask for a taste-test of the food. The quality of food varies greatly from site to site, so asking for this is a wise precaution. Most sites offer taste tests at no charge.

❧ *Step 7:* After visiting several sites, make your decision and put down as small a deposit as possible. Sign a contract that includes the date, the hours, the rental fee and any other charges and approximate guest count. Be very careful to get any verbal promises by the site ("oh, sure we can decorate that landing with flowers for no charge") in writing in the contract.

❧ *Step 8:* Any subsequent contact with the site from here on out will depend on whether the site is doing the catering or not. In any case, call the site back one month before your wedding to confirm the details of your reception.

Questions to Ask of a Reception Site

1 How many guests can the space accommo-DATE? Typically, the capacity is given in two numbers, one for a buffet/hors d'oeuvres (or standing) reception and one for a sit-down (seated) dinner. Be careful about these figures—sites often fudge capacity numbers or give "approximate" guesses. Don't forget to account for any buffet tables or dance floors—these all take space.

2 How many hours does the rental fee cover? What are the overtime charges? Be sure to ask about whether set-up and clean-up time is included in the stated hours. Some sites don't count this time "on the clock" while others do.

3 Is there an in-house caterer or a list of approved caterers? Or can you bring in any caterer? Obviously, hotels have in-house caterers (that's how they make the big

bucks). But many other sites are also picky about this—after they get burned by a sloppy caterer, a site may restrict brides to a list of "pre-approved" caterers. In case you can't find a caterer on their approved list who meets your specifications, ask if you can bring in another one.

4 ARE THERE ANY COOKING RESTRICTIONS? Are the kitchen facilities adequate? For a site where an outside caterer is brought in, check the kitchen facilities. Some sites restrict caterers from cooking on-site and just allow the warming of food that is prepared elsewhere. Make sure you confirm with your caterer to see if the kitchen facilities are adequate.

5 IS THERE A PIANO AVAILABLE? How about a dance floor? Obviously, bands don't cart around a baby grand with them to every reception, so ask the site coordinator. Don't assume anything is free. Ask the site about any extra charges to prevent surprises.

6 WHAT ELSE IS HAPPENING AT THE SITE THE DAY OF MY WEDDING? This is especially problematic at some hotels. Will you have to compete with a noisy convention of insurance agents that has a 10-piece band in the next room? Press the catering rep to give you exclusivity over the facility. Or at least, insist on a layout of the parties that minimizes overlapping noise.

Pitfalls to Avoid

Pitfall #1
THE NEXT DOOR NEIGHBORS.

"I attended a wedding last weekend in a hotel that was ruined by a loud band in the next ballroom. The band played so loud we could barely hear ourselves talk!"

Ah, this is a common problem at sites that have more than one function going on at the same time. Hotels are often most guilty of this problem, but we've even seen smaller sites try to cram two or more weddings into a facility. Ask the site point blank about this issue. If you don't get a sufficient answer or fear a loud neighboring party, consider another site.

Pitfall #2
UNWRITTEN PROMISES.

"I booked my wedding and reception at an historic home. The wedding coordinator there told me all the wonderful things they would do for my reception at no charge. For example, they said they would decorate the gazebo for no charge if I brought them the fabric. Then, wouldn't you know? My contact person left and the owner of the site

refused to fulfill the promises she made! I was furious! The only problem was I couldn't prove a thing since nothing was written down. Rats!"

Well, this is perhaps the most common complaint we hear about reception sites: unfulfilled promises. To get you to book the site, some unscrupulous site managers will make wild promises they never intend to keep. Or the person you first meet with conveniently leaves the site, which happens more than you think (catering and site mangers hop from job to job like rabbits). A word to the wise: get every last promise and detail in writing in the contract. This protects you from dishonest people or from changes in personnel. If promises are made after the contract is signed, get them to write a note or type a letter putting the promises in black and white.

Pitfall #3
MENU GOOFS.

"My wedding and reception was at a popular hotel in our town. We spent hours going over the menu but what was served at the reception in no way resembled what we ordered. Worse yet, then we couldn't find anyone from the catering department to fix the problem! What happened?"

Sometimes the bloated bureaucracy at hotels and other reception sites can lead to snafus. Perhaps the catering manager "forgot" to inform the kitchen of your menu. Maybe the chef just had an extra 200 Chicken Cordon Bleus left over from a banquet the night before. In any case, you deserve a refund or the site should offer a fair reduction in the bill as compensation for their mistake.

Pitfall #4
KICK-BACKS AND CATERING MANAGERS.

"I picked a band for my reception based on the recommendation of my site's catering coordinator. It was a disaster—the band was a flop! To add insult to injury, I later found out the catering coordinator received a 'commission' from the band!"

One scam we uncovered in this field are catering managers/coordinators who take kick-backs from bands (or other wedding merchants) they recommend. In California, one musician blew the whistle on a site that was charging a $200 fee to get on their "recommended list." We've also encountered this on the East Coast. Protect yourself by thoroughly checking out any of these "recommended" services.

A Look at the Four Most Common Reception Site Types

Hotels

Well, only about 10% of all wedding receptions are held in hotels, but that doesn't mean these sites aren't important. Often, hotels hold the distinction of hosting the biggest and most lavish receptions in many cities. Nevertheless, couples having smaller weddings find the packages offered by some hotels to be attractive. Hotels are especially popular in areas of the country where sit-down dinner receptions are common (i.e., the Northeast). Here are the pros and cons of having your wedding reception at a hotel.

Advantages of Hotel Receptions

1 ALL-INCLUSIVE PACKAGES. When you have a reception at a hotel, all the rentals (tables, chairs, serving pieces, bars, dance floor, etc) are generally included in the price.

2 LARGE WEDDINGS. For large weddings, hotels may be the best choice. That's because a hotel's big ballrooms can accommodate large parties up to or over 1000 guests. Most other sites have peak capacities at about 200 to 300 guests.

3 CLIMATE CONTROL. In areas of the country with harsh weather, hotel climate control systems are a plus.

4 DISCOUNTS ON ROOM RENTALS, HONEYMOON SUITES. Most hotels are willing to negotiate a discounted rate for a block of rooms. If you have many out-of-town relatives, this may be a big plus. Some hotel packages also throw in a honeymoon suite gratis—a nice touch.

5 SPECIAL WEDDING RECEPTION PACKAGES. Many hotels have special catering packages for wedding receptions. Unfortunately, these are sometimes more expensive than their à la carte choices! Why? The extra labor needed for a reception versus other functions might be an answer. Or maybe it's just pure greed (brides are sometimes seen as a money-machine for these guys). Be sure to crunch the numbers for different packages to see which is the best deal. On the other hand, some hotels aggressively pursue weddings by offering many freebees—you'd be surprised at the big difference in costs from one hotel to another.

6 DIETARY RESTRICTIONS. For those couples who need Kosher catering, hotels are often a best bet. Hotels must

meet certain standards before they are certified Kosher. Call a local synagogue or rabbi to get a list.

7 SOME HOTELS CAN ALSO HOST A LOVELY CEREMONY. One West Coast hotel has an outdoor garden and gazebo for ceremonies. The convenience of having everything at one location may be a big plus.

8 ADVICE ON ENTERTAINERS, FLORISTS, BAKERS, ETC. Hotel catering managers often have their pulse on the best wedding bands and entertainers. Use their experience, but be careful of unscrupulous managers who take kick-backs from "recommended" services. (See Pitfall #4 above for more info.)

Disadvantages of Hotel Receptions

1 DRAB INTERIOR DECOR. Some hotels look like they were decorated in Early Eisenhower.

2 HOTELS ARE DARN EXPENSIVE. While hotels offer all-inclusive packages, you definitely pay for this with high-priced food and liquor. Food quality varies greatly from hotel to hotel, so ask for a taste test. At best, hotels have what could be charitably described as a "mixed" reputation for food, making many brides wonder where all their money is going.

3 FROZEN FOOD. Perhaps the biggest problem that plagues many hotels is poor quality food. Hotels often buy frozen food that can be quickly prepared. Ever seen those mini-quiches at a hotel wedding reception? Hotels can buy these and other popular buffet items in bulk from suppliers. Unfortunately, frozen hors d'oeuvres that are quickly warmed simply don't compare to freshly-prepared foods.

4 BUREAUCRACY OF HOTEL CATERING DEPARTMENTS. From busboys to waiters to captains to catering assistants to managers, the multi-layer management of catering departments can be vexing. Ask if the catering manager (or the contact person whom you have dealt with) will be at your reception.

5 WEDDINGS CAN BE LOW ON THE PRIORITY LIST. Especially in December, hotels are distracted with corporate Christmas parties on large budgets. Competition with convention and reunion business can also be a headache.

6 REMEMBER THE CATERING REPRESENTATIVES ARE ON COMMISSION. The more money you spend, the more money they make. Hence, we find many hotel caterers pushing exotic

(and expensive) foods such as shrimp to jack up the tab. Many hotels also "suggest" expensive wines and other liquor.

7 OVERPRICED LIQUOR. Here's one example: One moderately-priced hotel we researched had a $22 retail price on a specific bottle of wine. That same bottle wholesales at $4—and that wine was the most "affordable" option the hotel offered!

8 BE CAREFUL OF NICKLE-AND-DIME CHARGES. Never assume that anything is free. Extra charges could include valet parking, special table skirting, ice carvings, a dance floor, corking fees, cake cutting charge (see catering chapter), food station attendants, and any audio equipment (a microphone for toasts, for example). Also, silk table centerpieces and special linens or china may be extra. Compare the estimate on centerpieces with your florist's bid to get the best deal.

What Does a Hotel Reception Cost?

Reception packages vary widely. Hotels in downtown areas tend to be the most expensive (and also expect to pay extra for valet parking). In suburban areas, rates are somewhat less and these hotels tend to be more aggressive in their competition for wedding business (since they can't rely on downtown convention traffic). In our research, we've found hotel packages that start as low as $10 per person for a buffet at an Oklahoma hotel and go up to $125 per person for a complete sit-down dinner at a posh downtown Boston hotel. In general, most hotels are in the $20 to $50 per person range for basic receptions (not counting liquor). In the biggest cities (New York, LA, Chicago, Philadelphia), you can expect to pay twice to three times more. Add in a big liquor tab and you can expect your total costs to soar at any hotel.

Consumer Tip

Be aware that hotels sometimes lie to prospective customers. One catering manager at a California hotel told us they regularly told inquiring brides, with small to medium-size receptions, that a room was booked for their date. Was it booked? No.

Why would they do this? Well, the folks in this business are always looking for the big fish (i.e., a big convention or large wedding). If they can't fill the room to capacity, they lose money (so they claim). What if that big fish doesn't arrive? As the date approaches, nervous managers will then book a smaller function just to make some revenue.

STRATEGY TO AVOID THIS PROBLEM: When you first contact the hotel, lie about the size of your function if it isn't very large. Inflate the guest list count by 50% to 75%. After you find out the room is available, scale back your estimate when you talk about menu particulars. While this is somewhat deceptive, it may take such drastic tactics to get a prime reception site in large metro areas.

Private and Country Clubs

Think you have to be a member of those fancy country clubs and private clubs to hold a wedding reception in their facilities? Not always. In fact, many clubs welcome non-members with open arms! That's because weddings often bring in badly-needed revenue to clubs. We define private and country clubs as any site that has membership requirements or restrictions. While you may have to be a member at some sites, others just require a "member-sponsor." Still others don't have any requirements at all.

Types of Clubs

1 BUSINESS CLUBS. Often downtown on top of skyscrapers, some business clubs have a restaurant open for lunch each day and host meetings and receptions. Various professional organizations (i.e., Engineer's Clubs, Doctor's Clubs) may own and operate these facilities. Such sites vary widely in appeal (we saw one Engineer's Club that looked like it was decorated by, well, engineers) but are generally more open to wedding receptions. Mostly likely, you must use the club's in-house catering.

2 COUNTRY CLUBS. These sites normally have a golf course and several acres of grounds. Here, the clubhouse is the focal point for receptions. Some of these sites can be quite stuffy, with the snob appeal often spread rather thick. Nonetheless, lush grounds can make more beautiful backdrops for photos. These sites may be the most restrictive, as most require a member (who can be a friend or just an acquaintance) to at least "sponsor" the reception. Many times, this sponsorship is just a token technicality where the member assumes responsibility in case you don't pay the bill and move to Peru. In most cases, you must use the country club's in-house catering.

3 CIVIC/SOCIAL CLUBS. Elk's Clubs, Garden Clubs, Federation of Women's clubs, Junior Leagues, Junior Forums—each of these clubs may have facilities they rent for receptions. Often, you must bring in an outside caterer. Prices and quality are all over the board: Elks Clubs and Veterans of Foreign Wars (VFW) Posts, for example, are often quite affordable but offer rather Spartan decor. Other clubs are located in historic buildings that are beautiful but also carry a

hefty price tag. Membership requirements are often nonexistent.

Advantages of Private Clubs

1 MORE PERSONAL SERVICE. Many of these sites don't have the bloated bureaucracy that hampers hotels. Less bureaucracy often means improved service.

2 NICER SITES. Unlike the drab and sterile decor of many hotels, country and private clubs are often set on beautiful sites. In the South, many are surrounded by lush grounds with golf courses. In many metro downtowns, clubs may occupy the top floor of skyscrapers—offering spectacular views of the skyline.

3 SOME CLUBS PERMIT OUTSIDE CATERERS. While business and country clubs usually have in-house (read: expensive) catering, some clubs let you bring in a caterer of your choice—this can be a fantastic savings (see Chapter 8).

Disadvantages of Private Clubs

1 SOMETIMES YOU MUST BE A MEMBER. Frequently this depends on "supply and demand" of the local economy. Hence, if the club is in need of funds, they may let non-members in to boost a sagging financial situation. However, if the club is flush with members (and hence revenue), they will limit the use of the club to members only.

2 IF YOU AREN'T A MEMBER, SOME CLUBS REQUIRE YOU TO HAVE A MEMBER-SPONSOR. Here, a member of the club must "sponsor" your reception, agreeing to attend the event and pay for it if you skip town. If you have a friend who is a member, great. If you don't, some clubs may negotiate around this point—perhaps by requesting a larger deposit. We know one club that will find you a sponsor if you don't know one!

3 FOOD QUALITY CAN VARY WIDELY. Some clubs have gourmet chefs on staff who create wonderful dishes. Other clubs may not be as lucky and their food quality is, at best, as good as that in the average hotel. Ask for a taste test to confirm food quality.

4 EXPENSIVE RECEPTIONS. Some clubs can be on par with or even more expensive than hotels. Overpricing of liquor is a common problem. Just like with hotels, club catering managers receive commissions based on the total amount you spend—giving them an incentive to inflate the tab. Many clubs also add on a high gratuity, similar to hotels.

What Does it Cost?

Well, it depends. Fancy country clubs may be just as expensive as the prices we quoted above for hotels. Other clubs, that don't have in-house catering, just charge a rental fee for the facility.

Civic Sites

A "civic" site is any reception facility that is owned and administered by a city or municipal agency. Almost always, you must bring in your own caterer. Some civic sites have a recommended list of caterers that you may have to choose from. Be aware that some sites may have time and beverage restrictions (no liquor) and others require you to hire security officers. Civic sites are usually the best bargains. Why? Subsidized by taxpayers, these sites aren't out to make a quick buck like private facilities.

Types of Civic Sites

1 PARKS, GARDENS, AMPHITHEATERS. Often quite affordable, these sites are usually administered by city parks departments. Some sites even have clubhouses. If you decide to have an outdoor ceremony or reception, make sure you have a backup plan in case of inclement weather.

2 RECREATION CENTERS, CIVIC CENTERS, TOWN HALLS, CONFERENCE CENTERS. Quality varies greatly with these sites (some are spectacular while others are dumps), but they are often quite affordable.

3 SITES OWNED BY UNIVERSITIES OR COLLEGES. These sites include faculty clubs, chapels, etc. Some of these facilities can be expensive.

4 MUSEUMS. Rare but available in some cities, these sites may be quite expensive and even require you to be a "museum patron" (i.e. a hefty donation).

Advantages of Civic Sites

1 LOW COST.
Most of these sites are very affordable.

2 BRING IN AN OUTSIDE CATERER. Off-site caterers can save oodles of money and offer creative, delicious menu options.

3 UNIQUE ONE-OF-A-KIND LOCATIONS.

Disadvantages of Civic Sites

1 VERY POPULAR SITES BOOK UP QUICKLY. Since civic sites are so affordable, they are also very popular. Many book months in advance.

2 EQUIPMENT RENTAL EXPENSE CAN BE HIGH. Some of these sites might require you to bring in rentals (tables, chairs, serving pieces, etc.). This could be a significant expense.

3 MAKE SURE THE CATERER IS VERY FAMILIAR WITH THE SITE. Some brides find hiring and dealing with an outside caterer challenging—increasing the complexity of the event by adding another person in the loop. On the plus side, the savings here can be tremendous. Kitchen facilities may also affect a caterer's flexibility.

Catering Halls, Restaurants, Restored Mansions, Laundromats, Etc.

Yes, you can have a wedding reception just about anywhere. Smiley's Laundromat, in Denver, Colorado has hosted weddings and receptions where brides and grooms have exchanged rings between the spin and rinse cycles. Catering halls are most common on the East Coast, while the South (particularly Atlanta) has several stunning restored mansions available for receptions. Other possibilities include theaters, ranches, private estates, chartered boats and yachts, bed and breakfast inns, and so on. Anything goes!

What's the message here? Don't think you must have your reception in a hotel or club just because all your friends did that. Every city has many romantic and beautiful settings for receptions—it may just take a little creative searching.

In fact, that's perhaps the biggest challenge to using a "non-traditional" site—finding one! (Perhaps the second biggest challenge is convincing parents and relatives that the site is better than the traditional options!) To find a non-traditional site, look in bridal editions of local newspapers and other local wedding advertising publications. Ask local caterers for suggestions. Don't overlook even the national bridal magazines—each has "regional" advertising sections that are full of ads from local sites.

Often you must bring in your own caterer (the exceptions, of course, are restaurants and catering halls). As a side note, more receptions are held at restaurants and catering halls than any other type of site. Nearly half of all receptions are held in this type of facility.

CAUTION: Many of these sites (private homes and estates, for example) can be quite expensive. Some have "all-inclusive" packages (catering, flowers, cakes, etc.) that provide dubious value.

Chapter 8

Catating

I f you read just one chapter in this book, make it this one. That's because we give you 10 little-known money-saving tips that could save you hundreds if not thousands on your wedding catering. Also, you'll learn the inside scoop on catering with 17 questions to ask any caterer and 3 pitfalls to avoid with wedding catering.

What Are You Buying?

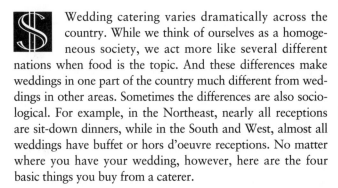 Wedding catering varies dramatically across the country. While we think of ourselves as a homogeneous society, we act more like several different nations when food is the topic. And these differences make weddings in one part of the country much different from weddings in other areas. Sometimes the differences are also sociological. For example, in the Northeast, nearly all receptions are sit-down dinners, while in the South and West, almost all weddings have buffet or hors d'oeuvre receptions. No matter where you have your wedding, however, here are the four basic things you buy from a caterer.

❦ *The food.* This includes everything from hors d'oeuvres to dessert. Sometimes caterers will also offer to do the wedding cake (and the groom's cake, a Southern tradition). The typical method of calculating costs of wedding catering is based on a figure per guest. Cost can range from $4 to $6 per guest for a simple "cake, punch, and mints" reception to over $100 per person for a full sit-down dinner with open bar at a posh hotel.

❦ *The beverages.* Whether your reception will just have punch and coffee or a full open bar with premium well brands, the cost of beverages can be a significant part of the catering budget. For a hors d'oeuvre reception at a posh hotel with a full open bar serving premium liquor, the total bar tab for 400 guests was $6500—almost half the $14,000 total cost of the evening! Of course, the charge for beverages depends on what you serve and how the reception site accounts for this.

Open vs. Cash Bars

One big controversy in the world of wedding etiquette is whether bars should be open or cash. In the latter case, guests pay for their drinks. As you can imagine, etiquette gurus wildly flail their arms at the suggestion that guests pay for their drinks, reasoning that you are in a sense charging them to attend the reception. For couples on a fixed budget, however, the debate is moot—they simply don't have the funds to stock an open bar for several hours. Adding to the debate is the nation's recent trend toward sobriety—people are drinking less alcohol. Some couples compromise by having an open bar for an hour at the beginning of the reception and a cash bar for the rest of the evening. This also discourages guests from getting smashed toward the end of the evening when they might get behind the wheel. The liability issue is also forcing many couples (and reception sites) to rethink serving alcohol.

☙ *Labor.* Hey, don't forget those folks who actually serve the food. Of course, most sites won't let you forget to pay the staff—they impose a mandatory gratuity of 15% to 20%. This applies to the food and sometimes the liquor served at the reception. If you serve a buffet that costs $3000, you must pay as much as $600 extra for the servers, bus boys, etc. Frankly, we think a percentage gratuity is slightly deceptive—most sites don't pay their staff anywhere near the amount of money they collect for "service." They pocket the difference as pure profit. For example, in the above case, let's assume the reception was for 150 guests. Using an industry rule of thumb of one server for 25 guests at a buffet reception, we would need six servers. Hence, each server would theoretically receive $100 of the $600 service charge for the evening. If the reception lasts four hours, do you really think the site is paying the servers a wage that totals $25 per hour? In most cities, we wouldn't bet on it.

Perhaps a more equitable way of paying for service is a method adopted by some independent caterers. This involves paying a flat per hour fee per waiter at the event—usually $10 to $20 per hour per server. No matter what the total tab of your function, you pay only for the number of people actually serving your guests.

☙ *Rentals.* Certain reception sites may lack tables, chairs, silverware, china, glassware, table linens, etc. All these items must be rented separately and brought to the site. Some caterers have an in-house supply of rentals while others arrange the needed rentals through an outside rental company. Charges for this service vary greatly—sometimes the caterer will charge you what the rental company charges them. Other caterers may tack on an extra fee of 5% to 10% of the rental bill to cover the administrative expense of dealing with the rental company. Some caterers (who charge this fee) also absorb any charges for broken or missing rental items. However, in some cases, you may be responsible for any breakage or damage.

❧ *Coordination of the reception.* In the past few years, many caterers have added a new service: coordination of the entire reception. This can range from simply referring names of good florists or entertainers to actually booking and negotiating with other services. Some caterers offer such coordination as a free customer service; others charge fees that are similar to that of a professional wedding consultant. The degree you will want your caterer to coordinate your reception will depend on how much you trust them.

❧ *Average catering costs.* Catering prices vary greatly from city to city. That's because a caterer's overhead is vastly different in, say, Minot, North Dakota than in San Francisco, California. The exact menu that costs $15 per person in Albuquerque could be as much as $60 in Chicago. For example, one bride told us she had to move her reception from Dallas, Texas to Washington D.C. In Dallas, she priced her reception at $24 per person. A very similar menu at a comparable hotel in Washington D.C. cost $56 per person!

Most caterers require a deposit that is as much as 50% of the total bill to hold a date. The balance is customarily due a week or two weeks before the date.

Sources to Find an Affordable Caterer

 ❧ *Ask friends and other recently married couples for suggestions.* Finding a good, affordable caterer is by far the biggest challenge faced by engaged couples. The best caterers work strictly by word of mouth and hence, don't do much high-profile advertising.

❧ *Reception sites that don't have in-house caterers.* Most will have a list of local caterers they recommend. This will be an invaluable time-saver. Ask them for their opinions as to which caterer offers the best service or most affordable prices. Also, we have found some photographers who have recommendations on catering (they usually sneak a taste during receptions!).

❧ *Don't look in the phone book.* Unlike some other categories, the best caterers do not have the biggest Yellow Pages ads.

Types of Caterers

1 IN-HOUSE OR ON-PREMISE CATERERS. These are catering operations that exclusively provide the catering for a site. Examples are hotels and many country clubs. Unless they're really desperate, most of these sites won't allow outside or "off-premise" caterers.

2 OFF-PREMISE CATERERS. These caterers bring in food to an existing site. The caterer's services can be limited to just providing the food or include the coordination of the entire event. Here, caterers become more like party planners or wedding consultants—either providing or contracting out for services like decorators (table centerpieces, table skirting, for example) and entertainers.

No matter which type of caterer you choose, the following information will be crucial.

Top Money-Saving Secrets

1 FIND A SITE WHERE YOU CAN BRING IN AN OUTSIDE CATERER. Outside caterers are not only more affordable but many times offer higher quality than caterers at hotels or other sites. The big savings come in lower overhead. Outside caterers may let you buy liquor at wholesale, provide rentals at cost and basically provide more food for the dollar. Best of all: outside caterers usually don't have lots of "nickel-and-dime" charges.

2 HOLD THE RECEPTION IN MID-AFTERNOON. For example, a wedding reception at one or two in the afternoon will be much less expensive than evening affairs. Why? Because guests will probably have already had lunch, they won't be expecting a six-course, sit-down meal.

3 CONSIDER A WEDDING BRUNCH OR LUNCHEON. These meals will also be less-expensive than dinner. One new idea a Chicago bride suggested to us was a dessert reception. She planned a late evening ceremony (9 pm) and threw a reception for 200 guests that featured a lavish buffet of desserts afterward. Since there wasn't a full meal served, she saved $2000. (To avoid any confusion, it's appropriate to add on your invitation or reception card "Dessert Reception Following.")

4 AVOID SATURDAYS. Some on-premise caterers have reduced rate-packages for Fridays and Sundays. You may be able to negotiate a better deal.

5 AVOID "BUDGET-BUSTING" MENU ITEMS. Certain food items are extremely expensive and can bust your budget.

Two common examples are shrimp and beef tenderloin. An universally-affordable item is chicken.

6 CHOOSE ITEMS THAT AREN'T "LABOR INTENSIVE." Certain hors d'oeuvres may be made of simple ingredients but require painstaking labor to assemble. For example, hors d'oeuvres like "Boursin cheese piped into Chinese pea pods" take a long time to prepare since the cheese has to be hand-piped into the pea pod. Caterers pass along that labor cost to you.

7 FOR BUFFET AND HORS D'OEUVRES RECEPTIONS, HAVE THE CATERER'S STAFF SERVE THE ITEMS instead of letting the guests serve themselves. This will control the amount of food served (and hence, cost). When guests serve themselves, the food always seems to go much quicker (wonder why!)! Also, having the catering staff serve the food may keep you from running out.

8 BUY YOUR OWN LIQUOR, IF POSSIBLE. The savings of buying liquor at or near wholesale prices will be tremendous (perhaps a 50% to 70% savings). Ask the caterer if they will refer you to a good wholesaler in your area. When you buy by the case load, you can normally negotiate lower prices than retail. Some liquor suppliers may even let you return unopened bottles for full credit. One note of caution: the liquor must be chilled down prior to the reception, so plan ahead.

9 PROVIDE YOUR OWN BAR SERVICE. In some cases, "freelance" bartenders are cheaper than the caterers' own staff. If the caterer allows you to have your own bar service, do a cost comparison between the two options. On the other hand, some caterers may not allow free-lance bartenders because of liability concerns.

10 DON'T MOVE THOSE HORS D'OEUVRES! Having hors d'oeuvres passed on silver trays may look elegant but watch out! One Florida wedding planner told us sites there charge exorbitant prices for "passed hors d'oeuvres." The more affordable alternative is to keep them stationary—scattered about the room at "stations" in chafing dishes.

Spotlight: Best Buys

Affordable Wines and Champagnes

Liquor prices vary greatly. For hotels, there is often a killer markup. The house brands are often the most affordable bet (but do a taste test, first.) If the choice of wines and champagnes is up to you, here are some recommendations that are not only tasty but also affordable:

Wines

❦ *Glen-Ellen Chardonnay.* 750 milliliter bottle. Retail price: $4.99. Best price we found: $4.50. A nice California Chardonnay that's very affordable.

❦ *Moreau Blanc.* 1.5 liter bottle. Retail price: $5.99. Best price we found: $5.30. This French white wine is packaged in affordable, big bottles.

❦ *Sebastiani White Zinfandel.* 1.5 liter bottle. Retail price: $6.99. Best price we found: $5.69. Popular California blush wine that also is also a best buy.

❦ *Kendall-Jackson Vintners Reserve Chardonnay.* 750 milliliter bottle. Retail price: $10.99. Best price we found: $8.50. Very popular California wine.

Champagnes

❦ *Valdivieso Brut Champagne.* Retail price: $5.99. Best price we found: $4.99. Good, affordable champagne from Chile.

❦ *Codorniu Blanc de Blanc.* Retail price: $8.99. Best price we found: $7.20. Excellent champagne from Spain.

❦ *Chardon Brut or Blanc De Noir.* Retail price: $14.49. Best price we found: $11.99. Very dry California champagne in both white and blush.

Remember, the taste of wines is not often related to the price. We've tasted some very expensive wines that weren't winners.

Getting Started: How Far in Advance?

 Book your caterer as soon as you confirm your reception site. Many book up far in advance (as long as a year) for popular summer wedding weekends. Also, December is an extremely busy time for caterers because of Christmas parties.

Biggest Myths about Catering

 Myth #1 *"If I invite fewer guests, I assume my catering bill will go down dramatically."*

Well, yes and no. Obviously, fewer mouths to feed will have an impact on your total bill. However, if you invite fewer guests, the price per person may go up. Why? That's

Deals at Wholesale Clubs and Gourmet Supermarkets

Liquor prices too much for you to swallow? Full-service catering charges too high to stomach? Consider two new alternatives that offer great deals: wholesale clubs and gourmet supermarkets.

Popping up in most major cities, wholesale clubs like Sam's, Pace and Price Club offer cut-rate prices on everything from electronics to groceries. Best of all, some of the clubs have fully stocked liquor departments where you can buy in case quantity at fantastic discounts. We visited a Price Club and found prices 15% to 30% below regular liquor stores. Name brands of wine, beer and spirits were available in big quantities. If you're hiring a caterer who will let you purchase your own liquor, be sure to get a quote from a local wholesale club.

While many wholesale clubs have been adding liquor and groceries, many supermarkets have remade themselves into "gourmet markets" with full-service catering departments. The quality has also improved. We've spoken to brides who've found affordable catering options for small at-home receptions at a local gourmet supermarket—and they found the quality to be excellent. Many markets also have pastry chefs on staff that can whip up a respectable wedding cake. With full-service floral departments as well, some markets offer an affordable one-stop shopping service. Prices for catering, cakes and flowers tend to be about 10% to 20% below retail.

because a large part of the per-person price caterers quote you is "fixed." Fixed costs include office expenses, the caterer's time, etc. No matter how many guests you invite, caterers still have to pay these administrative expenses. Hence, you're paying for more than just the food. In a sense, most caterers have an unwritten base price or minimum that engaged couples must pay—no matter how many guests they want to invite.

Myth #2 *"Given the expensive prices caterers charge, you get the feeling these guys make big, fat profits off weddings."*

Gosh, it may be hard to believe, but most don't. Profits only range from 8% to 15% of the total bill. In the past few years, food and insurance costs have soared for most caterers. Don't shed too many tears for them, though. Since the average business only earns a 5% profit on sales, caterers' profits aren't all that bad. Different caterers make more money in different areas. For off-premise caterers, the biggest revenue area is the food. For on-site or in-house caterers (like hotels), the biggest money-maker is the liquor.

Myth #3 *"We're having a buffet reception. Isn't using plastic plates and glasses more affordable?"*

Nope. In many cases, the cost of renting glass is actually almost as affordable as using plastic! Besides looking nicer, glass also doesn't have the negative environmental impact caused by throwing away plastics. Ask your caterer to do a cost comparison between plastic and glass.

Step-by-step Shopping Strategies

 ❦ ***Step 1:*** Using the sources above, set up appointments with at least three recommended caterers. When you call for an appointment, notice how promptly the caterer returns your call. Within the business day is good—if it takes them more than a day, that's not good. Prompt attention is your first clue to the caterer's commitment to service. Before your meeting, discuss with your fiance your likes and dislikes for catering.

❦ ***Step 2:*** Ask to see photographs of their previous work. Look for a colorful and creative presentation of food. Is it artfully arranged with flowers and garnishes or just piled up on mirrored trays?

❦ ***Step 3:*** Ask for sample menus. These may list some popular hors d'oeuvre choices or sit-down options. Hopefully, their prices will be listed to give you a better idea of costs. While most caterers customize menus for each reception, they should be willing to give you basic cost parameters for certain items.

❦ ***Step 4:*** Be honest about your budget. If you're not sure, give them a range of costs per guest that you feel comfortable with. What one caterer will offer you for $20 per person may be vastly different from what another may propose. Also, be specific about your menu likes and dislikes as well as any dietary restrictions.

❦ ***Step 5:*** Ask for a proposal that details possible menu options. Also, the proposal should clearly identify costs for liquor, rentals, and labor. Call the caterer back and ask them to clarify any part of the proposal that isn't clear. One bad sign: caterers who promise to send you a proposal and then fail to do so.

❦ ***Step 6:*** Given the different proposals from each caterer, pick the one you most like and ask to visit one of their weddings during the set-up. Look for how organized they are and how the staff is dressed. Just observe.

❧ *Step 7:* Ask for a taste test. Better yet, get a taste of the proposed menu items. Most likely you are planning to spend several thousands of dollars on catering, so this is the least caterers can do. You may be able to combine the taste test with the visit to one of their weddings.

❧ *Step 8:* Once you select a caterer, get everything in writing—down to the very last detail. Food, labor, liquor, and rentals (if necessary) should be clearly stated in a written contract.

Questions to Ask a Caterer

1 CAN WE HAVE A TASTE TEST OF THE FOODS ON OUR MENU? We positively loath caterers that expect you to pay thousands of dollars for food on faith. Equally reprehensible are caterers that say "why do you need to taste such basic items? Hors d'oeuvres are hors d'oeuvres." We suggest you find another caterer if you get this line.

2 CAN WE SEE ONE OF YOUR WEDDINGS DURING SET-UP? A truly organized and professional catering company should have nothing to hide.

3 DO YOU PROVIDE A WRITTEN ESTIMATE AND CONTRACT? Verbal agreements are a prescription for disaster. Make sure every last promise and detail is in black and white.

4 ARE YOU LICENSED? Almost all municipalities (or counties) require caterers to be licensed. Local standards will stress clean and adequate facilities for food preparation and storage. Liability insurance on liquor and food may also be part of the requirements. Ask the caterer about insurance. Operating a catering business out of a home or residence is often illegal.

5 DO YOU SPECIALIZE IN CERTAIN CUISINES OR TYPES OF MENUS? Caterers often do one or two types of wedding receptions best. Although they may claim to handle all types of weddings, caterers often specialize in certain types of receptions (smaller versus larger, finger hors d'oeuvres versus full sit-down dinners). Some caterers may have chefs who specialize in certain cuisines (Continental, Greek, Southwestern, Indian, etc.)

6 WHERE IS THE FOOD PREPARED? Will you need additional kitchen facilities at my site? Make sure these details are confirmed by the caterer to prevent any last minute surprises.

7 WHEN IS THE MENU "SET IN STONE?" How close to the wedding can we get and still make changes in the menu? Trust us, there will be changes. Different family members, friends and relatives will add in their two cents on the perfect wedding menu.

8 HOW IS YOUR WAIT STAFF DRESSED? The key here is professional attire. Don't assume the wait staff will be wearing tuxedos (the exception is hotels who always have uniformed servers).

9 FOR COCKTAIL OR BUFFET RECEPTIONS, HOW OFTEN WILL THE FOOD BE REPLENISHED? Will the servings per guest be limited? Who makes the decision on when to stop serving?

10 GIVEN THE STYLE OF MY RECEPTION, HOW MANY WAITERS DO WE NEED? For seated receptions, one waiter per eight to 10 guests is adequate. For buffet or cocktail receptions, one waiter per 25 guests is standard.

11 HOW IS THE CHARGE FOR LABOR FIGURED? Is the clean-up (dish-washing, etc) extra?

12 HOW MUCH DOES A DESSERT TABLE COST? Is the wedding cake price included in the package? Dessert or Viennese tables are popular in the Midwest and in parts of the Northeast. Be sure the costs of a dessert table are clearly identified.

13 WHAT ARE YOUR CANCELLATION/POSTPONEMENT POLICIES? Since catering is the biggest expense area, confirming this aspect would be prudent.

14 DO YOU HAVE A LIQUOR LICENSE? How is the cost of the beverages calculated? What brands of liquor will be served? Most caterers offer both "premium" and generic or house brands. If you plan to serve alcohol, you'll want the caterer to carefully explain what brands you are buying and how the cost is calculated. Per drink charges are often the most expensive, although per bottle charges can be just as costly.

15 ARE YOU FAMILIAR WITH MY RECEPTION SITE? If not, will you visit it with me? For off-premise caterers, don't assume they know your facility. Confirming details such as the kitchen facilities and the clean-up rules are very important if you want to get your security/damage/cleaning deposit back from the reception site. The site will hold you responsible for any damage or rule violations by your caterer.

16 DO YOU RECEIVE ANY COMMISSIONS FROM SERVICES YOU RECOMMEND? Caterers may recommend bakers, florists or

musicians, but watch out! Some take "commissions" (kick-backs) from the businesses they recommend. Don't just take their word— thoroughly check out any services before contracting with them.

17 WILL YOU GUARANTEE THESE PRICE ESTIMATES? Many caterers raise their prices at the beginning of the year. Since we urge you to plan in advance in this chapter, your reception may be several months away. Our advice: Negotiate a price guarantee in writing (or at least a cap on future increases). Most caterers will be willing to do this to get your business. One couple we interviewed in Colorado found this out the hard way—the site they booked raised their prices 15% just weeks before their event. Their wedding budget was thrown into complete disarray.

Helpful Hints

1 MAKE SURE THE CATERING REPRESENTATIVE WHO PLANNED YOUR WEDDING WILL BE THERE THE NIGHT OF THE WEDDING. Hotel catering staffs are frequently guilty of not showing up to make sure everything is right. If you contract with a smaller, off-premise caterer, make sure the owner is there. Obviously, the owner may not be able to be at your wedding reception every minute, but there should be a clear chain of command in case a problem arises.

2 HAVE THE CATERER PREPARE YOU A GOING-AWAY PACKAGE. Believe it or not, you probably won't get to taste any of the food at your reception. You'll be too busy shaking hands, giving hugs, posing for pictures, etc. Considering the amount of money you're spending, ask the caterer to prepare a going-away package with a sample of the evening's menu (don't forget to include the cake!). You and your fiance will probably be starved when you leave the reception!

3 TIPS ON TIPPING. We always get many questions on tipping from brides and grooms. Whom do you tip? How much? First, understand that most wedding receptions have a mandatory gratuity added into the final tab. (The same goes for most limousine companies.) As a result, you don't *have* to tip anyone. However, if you believe an individual staffer has gone "above and beyond the call of duty," it may be nice if you slipped him or her an extra $20 or more. A server who tracks down a missing special dietary meal for a relative, a limousine driver who makes a special return trip to your house to retrieve an errant bridesmaid, a head server who works miracles with a cake that's collapsed—these are examples of extraordinary service that you may want to reward with an extra tip. You may also give a tip to the band or disc jockey if they turn in a stellar performance.

Pitfalls to Avoid

Pitfall #1
FROZEN FOOD.

"We went to a friend's reception last weekend at a hotel. I know the bride spent a lot of money on the buffet, but the food was just so-so."

In our opinion, too many sites like hotels rely too much on frozen food. Bought in bulk, frozen versions of mini-egg rolls and mini-quiche are mainstays on some reception site menus. Obviously, its cheaper (and hence more profitable) to buy these items frozen and quickly warm them in chafing dishes than to painstakingly make the same items from scratch. The problem? Besides obviously tasting "frozen," caterers who use frozen food often aren't any less expensive than those caterers who hand-make food from scratch ingredients. If the food at your reception is one of your high priorities, shop carefully for a caterer who doesn't use shortcuts.

Pitfall #2
THE INFAMOUS CAKE-CUTTING FEE.

"Boy am I steamed! The reception site I chose for my wedding said they would charge me $1 per person to cut my wedding cake. After spending thousands of dollars on food and liquor, I think they're trying to wring every last nickel from me!"

WE COULDN'T AGREE MORE! Boy, this is our #1 pet-peeve with caterers and reception sites. Some of these guys have the audacity to charge you a ridiculously high fee to cut your wedding cake. Ranging anywhere from 50 cents to $3 per guest, this "fee" supposedly covers the labor involved to cut the cake, as well as the plates, forks, etc. The real reason some reception sites charge this fee is to penalize you for bringing in a cake from an outside baker (instead of having the site bake you one). Even more amazing are some sites that don't even bake wedding cakes themselves but still charge cake-cutting fees! Talk about abusive—these fees are pure greed! We say if you are spending hundreds or thousands of dollars on food and liquor, the caterer or reception site should NOT tack on $100 to $400 more just for the privilege of cutting and serving the wedding cake! First of all, you are already paying a mandatory service gratuity to have a staff present at the reception. Hence, the cake cutting fee is often double-charging. Secondly, do you really think they pay the cake-cutter $100 to $400 for fifteen minutes of work? We suggest you try to negotiate away this charge—don't forget that everything is always negotiable.

(Note: some caterers or sites try to sneak in the cost of serving coffee into the cake-cutting fee. We suggest you tell

the caterer to forget the cake-cutting fee and just price the coffee out separately.)

Another inflated price we've discovered: the cost of punch. One hotel in the West charges brides and grooms a whopping $35 per gallon of punch! Since a half gallon of Minute Maid Fruit Punch goes for $1 to $2 at grocery stores, you can see how outrageous this stuff can get.

Pitfall #3
CORKING FEES AND THE LIQUOR THAT RUNNETH OVER

"My friend had her reception at a country club that seemed to push liquor on the guests. Every five minutes, they went around to the guests and pitched more drinks. I also understand they charged the couple for every bottle that was opened! Isn't this a bit excessive?"

It's not only excessive but also quite expensive. When couples are charged based on the number of $20 bottles of wine or champagne that are opened, one mad staffer with a corkscrew can inflict heavy financial damage. Such charges (called corking fees) are perhaps one of the biggest cost pitfalls of any wedding reception. That's because you must pay for any opened bottles whether or not they were poured! Think you can just re-cork the bottles and bring them home? Think again—most sites prohibit the removal of liquor from the premises.

In a different twist on the same problem, some sites push drinks on guests when the bar is "open" (i.e., the engaged couple pays for each drink). Why would sites or caterers do this? BIG PROFITS! Liquor is the biggest profit area for most sites and caterers and hence the temptation to push booze or open unneeded bottles is too great for the greedy. The solution to the corking-fee pitfall is to give the caterer or reception site a limit on the number of bottles they can open. Tell them to confer with you before they go beyond that limit.

Another version of this scam surfaced in California. We spoke with a former employee of a catering company who admitted they brought empty bottles to receptions. Since the liquor charges were based on the number of empty bottles at the end of the evening, the caterer was able to make a killing. We recommend you count the bottles at the beginning of the evening and again at the end. If there are 100 full bottles at the start, there better not be 125 bottles (80 empty and 45 full) at the end.

Pitfall #4
GRATUITOUS GRATUITIES

"On the final bill for our reception, the facility charged us a 'gratuity fee' on everything including the room charge! Is this fair?"

Many facilities look at the gratuity as "extra profit," not something that is paid to the staff. One bride in California called in the above story, where the facility was charging an 18% gratuity on the *room rental fee*, of all things (this worked out to an extra $300). In our opinion, the gratuity should only be charged on the food and liquor. (We should note in some states it is illegal to charge a mandatory gratuity on the liquor tab—as an alternative to the gratuity, facilities often charge "bartender or bar set-up fees.") Placing a gratuity on other charges (like room rental, valet parking, coat check) is price gouging.

Another similar rip-off is the "double-charging" of labor. In Denver, Colorado, for example, many caterers charge both a gratuity and a "labor fee." While the staff generally gets the gratuity, the owners usually pocket the labor charge, which, by the way, is illegal in the state of Colorado. As a result of this double-charging, couples are being socked with an effective 25% gratuity rate on receptions—an outrage in our opinion.

Trends

❦ *Food Stations.* Instead of one long buffet line, individual food stations are quite popular today. Food stations offer guests several varieties of pasta, seafood, Mexican food, etc. Improved traffic flow is another plus.

❦ *Less booze.* The nation's neo-sobriety is reflected in the "drying out" of wedding receptions. Open bars featuring hard liquor are becoming an endangered species in many parts of the country. Couples are replacing mixed drinks with bars that serve several varieties of wine, beer, and champagne. In some cases, booze is replaced totally with non-alcoholic beverages like punch and sparkling waters.

❦ *Ethnic foods.* Regional specialties (Crawfish or anything Cajun in New Orleans to lobster in the Northeast to Mexican Fiestas in South Texas) are also quite popular.

❦ *Lighter entrees.* Pasta is in, heavy dishes with cream sauces are out. As the country becomes more "cholesterol conscious," some meat dishes have lost popularity (except in the Midwest and other "meat and potatoes" areas). Chicken remains a perennial favorite that is often a safe choice all guests will enjoy. Prime rib, once the staple of sit-down dinners in the 1950's and 60's, has been replaced by fish, chicken and even veal.

❦ *Theme receptions.* Anything goes here. One interesting new trend is "high tea" receptions held in late afternoon. Guests are treated to a variety of teas, scones and other pastries.

The Wisconsin Pig Scandal

Here's a true story about a catering rip-off that zapped a Wisconsin couple, as reported by the couple's videographer. "I was videotaping a wedding last year that had a Hawaiian theme to it. The bride contracted with a hotel to have the reception and wanted a menu with a roast pig, to be cooked on site. The hotel said yes, promising the roast pig.

"The bride had a list of 'must haves' for her video, which included a shot of the pig coming out of the oven. When I approached the kitchen to video it, the cook and the manager came out to read me the riot act about coming in the kitchen. They quoted me chapter and verse from the Wisconsin Food Preparation Act, which states in so many words that if you're not doing the cooking, you're not allowed in the kitchen.

"I was trying to figure out how I was going to get a shot of the pig when a busboy told me the real reason I wasn't allowed in the kitchen: The hotel was unable to roast the pig on site; they had to send it out to be cooked!

"Well, I was going to get that pig on video because the bride was the type of person that if she didn't get EXACTLY what she wanted, she wouldn't pay on the rest of the video bill. Armed with the information from the busboy, I went back to the cook and manager and I read *them* the riot act. I told them I had found out about the deception and unless I got a video of the pig coming out of the oven, I was going to inform the bride about the pig scandal (why should I take the fall for them when I'm only getting $1500 and she's spending $9500 on the hotel—it was the hotel that broke their end of the bargain).

"Surprise...the manager let me into the kitchen (it was amazing how quickly they forgot the Wisconsin Food Preparation Act). I told them I wanted a shot of a pig coming out of an oven, so I set my camera up in a way that the oven looked larger than it really was. When the pig arrived (which was, of course, late) they put part of the pig into the oven (it was a clean oven, so they dirtied it just for me—weren't they nice!). I got the shot of the pig and they got to keep their $9500. The moral of the story is: Make sure you get what you pay for at the reception, because some sites will say anything to get your business if you spend enough money."

Chapter 9

Photography

E ver hire a professional photographer before? Probably not—that's why this chapter will be invaluable. This country has over 27,000 wedding and portrait photographers, making this a daunting task to find the perfect one for you. From key questions to important pitfalls to avoid, this chapter will give you a clear and concise guide to finding a great photographer at an affordable price.

What Are You Buying?

 When you hire a professional wedding photographer, there are three main areas where your money goes:

1 CANDIDS: These are the pictures taken at the wedding and reception which are assembled into an album for you (the bride and groom). Photographers often assemble candid packages for the parents (referred to as parents' albums) and gifts for attendants (usually 2 or 4 pictures in a gift folio). Note that parents' albums (usually 20 to 60 pictures) and gift folios are extra and are not included in our "average" photography tab.

2 ALBUMS: Most photographers offer a wide selection of albums to hold the candids. The best are Art Leather, Leather Craftsman and Capri. Unfortunately, they also are the most expensive and are sold only by professional photographers. Art Leather albums (which include the less-expensive Aristohyde and super-expensive leather brands) are guaranteed for a life-time. With Capri or Leather Craftsman albums, the pictures are mounted to the pages, which are permanently bound in the album. Some photographers skimp by using cheap, vinyl albums with plastic-covered pages. We'll explain later why these cheaper albums can damage your pictures.

3 PORTRAITS: Pictures taken prior to the wedding day fall into this category. A bridal portrait is a formal portrait

of the bride in her wedding gown. Particularly popular in the Southern U.S., bridal portraits are taken in an indoor studio or "on location" typically four to six weeks before the wedding. An "engagement portrait" is a more informal picture of you and your fiance. This portrait is often used to announce your engagement in the local paper. Two expenses are involved with portraits: the sitting fee and the portrait itself. "Sitting fees" are a charge for the photographer's time and range from $50 to several hundreds of dollars. The most popular print size is 16x20 and this can cost $100 to $500 depending on the photographer and city.

Photography customs and traditions vary greatly across the U.S. For example, in Sacramento, California, many couples have a formal portrait taken after the reception at one of the area's many parks. In the South, a formal portrait of the bride taken a month before the wedding is often framed and displayed at the reception. Several Colorado photographers bring studio-quality lighting systems to the wedding in order to do portraits of the bride and groom before the ceremony.

AVERAGE TOTAL COSTS: In most U.S. cities, the average tab for professional wedding photography—you might want to sit down— is $1000 to $2000. So what does that buy you? That figure just covers your album of candid coverage at your wedding and reception. Keep in mind that certain "celebrity" photographers in larger metropolitan areas charge several times more than the average. Meanwhile, competent photographers in smaller cities can be hired for $500 or less.

No matter where you are, however, the process of selecting pictures is relatively the same. We should note that photographers don't usually talk in plain English, so here are three typical terms you will come across and their simple translations:

❦ *Exposures:* Basically this is defined by every time the camera goes "click." At least 150 to 200 exposures are taken at the typical wedding and four-hour reception. Be careful of packages that limit the number of exposures below that level.

❦ *Proofs:* Exposures are developed into proofs.The proofs are often 5x5 pictures from which you choose the final prints that will appear in your album. Un-retouched, the proofs chronicle all the pictures that the photographer took at your wedding. Photographers often have packages that guarantee the selection from a certain number of proofs. This can range from 80 proofs for small packages to over 200 for the largest.

❦ *Prints:* The proofs are enlarged into final prints. For photographers who use medium format cameras (we'll explain this later), popular enlargement sizes are 5x7, 8x8, 8x10, and 10x10. The final prints are assembled into the album.

Okay, so now you know the basics of what you're buying. But how do you find a competent, yet affordable, professional wedding photographer in the first place?

Sources for Finding a Photographer

 Photographers generally fall into two categories: commercial and portrait. While commercial photographers do work for advertising agencies and other industrial clients, portrait photographers concentrate on weddings, special occasions, and (as you might guess) portraits. The best wedding photographers are those who specialize in just weddings and portraits. Here are three sources to find the very best wedding photographers.

❦ *Recently married couples.* Yep, word-of-mouth referrals from friends are your best bet for finding the best photographers. Ask friends how happy they were with the photographer and final prints. Was there anything they would change?

❦ *Wedding coordinators at ceremony and reception sites.* What an incredible resource! These people have seen hundreds of wedding photographers come through their door. Ask them whom they thought were the best. Of course, their impressions are limited to the photographer's behavior at their particular site. Site coordinators rarely see the final photo album. Nevertheless, their opinions are valuable.

❦ *Bridal shows.* These shows (sponsored by local bridal shops and reception sites) often have several exhibits by local photographers. Be aware that these shows may feature young or new photographers who are looking to build their business. Unfortunately, these shows also tend to feature large photography studios whose quality can vary greatly from associate to associate (we'll discuss these studios later). Keep your eye on the local paper for shows in your area.

Where not to look. Unfortunately, the phone book is not a good source for wedding photographers. Many of the best wedding photographers do not invest heavily in this type of advertising. In fact, many don't advertise at all, working exclusively by word-of-mouth referral. Some photographers will also put a book of their work in local bridal shops. However, whose work is displayed has more to do with politics than with merit. Another place to avoid looking is wedding advertising publications—most good photographers shun these like the plague.

Understanding Wedding Photographers: Some Basics

As you shop for a good wedding photographer, there are three key areas that you must always keep in mind:

1 EQUIPMENT. Obviously, the quality of equipment the photographer uses is directly related to how good your wedding pictures will look. No matter how talented and personable the photographer is, the resulting pictures will be a disappointment if he or she uses an inferior camera.

"I visited a wedding photography studio yesterday that said they use 35 millimeter cameras. They claimed the pictures look just as good as others shot with more expensive cameras. Is this true?"

No, that isn't true. To understand why, let's look at the two types of cameras mainly used for wedding photography: 35 millimeter and medium format cameras.

❦ *35 millimeter cameras:* Most of us are familiar with these widely-available cameras. Unfortunately, 35mm cameras do not produce the best wedding photographs because of their small negative size. Since most wedding photos are blown up to 5x7 or 8x10, this negative produces pictures that are "grainy." 35mm pictures also look "flat" and the colors can be inconsistent at best.

❦ *Medium-format cameras:* The main distinction between medium format cameras and 35mm is their negative size: a medium format's square negative is $2\frac{1}{4}$" wide and $2\frac{1}{4}$" long. This provides much clearer photos when prints are enlarged. Medium-format cameras produce pictures that have richer depth, warmer colors and sharper contrasts than 35mm cameras. (To be technical, the "warmth" of a photograph is determined by the amount of flash light. However, medium-format cameras deliver pictures with more "color saturation" than 35mm. Color saturation relates to the richness of color in the print). The "Hassleblad" is apparently the BMW of medium format cameras. The Hassleblad (which was the one NASA used on the moon for astronaut snapshots) is incredibly popular among the best wedding photographers, apparently for the beautiful pictures it takes. Another popular medium-format camera is the Bronica.

We should note in passing that there are also several larger-format cameras that produce even bigger negatives (and hence, greater color saturation) than standard medium-format. Cameras, such as the Mamiya RB67, are considered the "ultimate" camera in this category. That camera takes a negative that's 6cm by 7cm.

"If medium format cameras are clearly superior to 35 millimeter cameras, why would any wedding photographer use 35mm?"

The main reason is money. 35mm cameras suitable for wedding photography cost several hundred dollars. Medium format cameras cost several thousand dollars—each. For example, a completely-outfitted Hassleblad can cost up to $7500. Obviously, amateur photographers opt for the cheaper 35mm when they are starting out. What's most disgusting, however, are large studios who use 35mm cameras in order to cut corners. While the studio makes a few extra bucks of profit, engaged couples are left with inferior-looking photographs.

We should note that one famous wedding photographer, Denis Reggie, does use 35mm (but only for a small percentage of his photos). In fact, most photo-journalists use 35mm for its versatility and flexibility. Apparently, its easier to use the smaller 35mm for many spontaneous candids than the bulkier Hassleblad. However, we believe the best bet for wedding photography remains the medium-format camera.

Just as important as the camera is the lighting equipment. Lighting equipment and techniques often separate the amateurs from the pros. Amateurs will use only a flash mounted on the camera—the resulting pictures are flat and of poor quality. Professional wedding photographers will use a powerful flash placed about 45 degrees to the subject. The resulting light provides shadows and depth. Some photographers will add one or more flashes aimed at the background. Photographer Mark Spencer of Mountain View, California told us he even puts light behind posed groups and dancing couples to give his pictures additional depth.

Who holds all these extra flashes? Usually it's an assistant. Pros usually have one at their side the entire day. Not only does the assistant hold the additional flashes, but also makes sure the photographer doesn't miss any detail. In Dallas, Texas, we found one expert photographer who brings *two* assistants to each and every wedding.

2 SKILL: Equally as important as having a medium-format camera is knowing how to use it. Photographing a wedding takes a tremendous amount of skill. This is not some-

thing that can be taught in a classroom. Only by actually going out there and clicking the camera can anyone learn how to be a good wedding photographer.

Skill involves not only knowing where to stand to get the best shot of the couple as they are showered with rice (or birdseed!), but also how to coax a reticent flower girl into that perfect pose. The best wedding photographers learn how to work around adverse lighting conditions and, perhaps, adverse relatives.

The only way to tell a wedding photographer's skill is by looking at many albums of their work. After seeing hundreds of wedding albums, we are convinced that you can tell the skilled pros from the unskilled amateurs. One key: posing. Does the photographer creatively pose his or her subjects or are they lined up against a blank wall (like police mug-shots).

One last caution about skill: don't believe studios that tell you that "every one of their associates is trained in the same style." This has to be the biggest lie told by wedding photographers. True, studios may have a professed quality standard that they strive for but what matters most is the talent and skill of the individual photographer who will actually photograph your wedding. Despite the smooth sales pitch, quality can vary widely from associate to associate.

Many photographers attempt to craft an "ideal utopia" studio from which all that flows is quality photography—no matter who is behind the camera. Ha! don't believe it! (See "Pitfalls to avoid" later in this chapter for a solution to this problem).

3 PERSONALITY: Beside professional equipment and the skill to use it, great wedding photographers also must have great people skills. This isn't nature photography where the photographer patiently sits out in a field for six hours waiting for that perfect photo of the yellow-finned butterfly. Wedding photography involves real people.

Obviously, this doesn't come as a surprise to you, but apparently this is news to some wedding photographers. Communication is key. Besides a sixth sense for good pictures, photographers must be persistent in getting the shots the engaged couple requests. Controlling large crowds of unruly bridesmaids and groomsmen for a group shot can be trying on even the best of nerves. Wedding photographers walk a fine line between being gentle conductors (telling a group how to pose) and absolute dictators. In the latter case, some fall victim to "director's disease:" barking orders at the bride and groom and turning the wedding and reception into a military exercise.

Remember that you will spend more time with your wedding photographer than any other service you will hire. For example, you won't see your florist or baker during or after the wedding.

Not only do you meet with the photographer prior to the wedding, he or she will follow you around the entire wedding day. Then, you may spend several more hours with them viewing proofs and ordering prints. Make sure you like this person. We mean you need to really like this person. If anything makes you the slightest bit uncomfortable, consider hiring someone else.

Top Money-saving Secrets

1 GET MARRIED ANY TIME OTHER THAN SATURDAY EVENING. Many photographers offer discounted packages for weddings held during Saturday afternoon or any other time of the week. Savings typically range from 10% to 20%. For example, a 15% discount off a $1000 package would bring the price down to $850. Total savings = $150. (As a side note: some photographers charge extra to work on Sundays for family reasons.)

2 HIRE A PHOTOGRAPHER WHO WORKS OUT OF HIS OR HER HOME. When you walk into a photography studio in a fancy office complex and see all that plush carpeting and furniture, who do you think pays for all that? That's right, you do. No one has ever explained to us how designer wallpaper translates into great wedding photography. Our advice: seek out a photographer who works out of his or her home. Quite simply, the lower overhead of a home studio/office is often passed along in more affordable prices. Believe it or not, after visiting with 200 wedding photographers, we found some of the best wedding photography comes from home-based photographers rather than those who have plush offices. Savings here can range from 20% to 40% off our photography average. Total savings = $300 to $600.

3 SKIP THE EXTRA FRILLS. Forget about the extras that photographers will suggest you buy. Gift folios (suggested as the "perfect gift" for wedding party members) are fluff. Bridal and engagement portraits are expensive extras. Instead, if you really want a portrait, take a candid from the reception and have it enlarged to a 16x20. You'll save the sitting fee (anywhere from $50 to $300) and the print is often less expensive too. Forget about ordering a frame from the photographer; many are grossly overpriced. Instead, go to your favorite framing store. Sample savings: $30 each for two gift folios, $100 for a sitting fee, $300 for a 16x20 portrait. Total savings = $460.

4 HIRE A PROFESSIONAL FOR THE CEREMONY ONLY. Then let your guests capture the reception candids with their own cameras. Provide a basket of film at the sign-in table to encourage the shutterbugs. Many engaged couples don't realize pho-

tographers offer a ceremony-only (two hours or less) package for "small weddings." Of course, there is no law that says engaged couples must have a small wedding to use this package. To see how the savings can stack up, here's one example: a photographer we met in Houston, Texas offered a one-hour, ceremony-only package for $300—significantly less than his $930 full-coverage plan. That's a savings of almost 70%! Obviously, prices will vary depending on the city you are in, but you can expect a savings of anywhere from 40% to 70%. Using our $1500 average cost of wedding photography, these packages would be in the $450 to $900 range. Total savings = $600 to $1100. (Note: beware of studios that might assign less-experienced photographers to shoot the ceremony-only packages.)

5 BUY THE ALBUM SOMEWHERE ELSE. Chances are you will get a photo album as a gift. If your budget is tight, forget the fancy leather album. If the photographer includes the cost of the album in the package, ask him or her what the discount would be for an album-less package. Art Leather albums cost (at wholesale prices) $75 for the cover and $5 for each page. Hence, the total wholesale cost (the price the photographer pays) for the typical package is about $140. Retail prices of albums range from $150 to $350 when they are priced separately. Hence, total savings = $150 to $350.

6 CONSOLIDATE YOUR ORDERS TO TAKE ADVANTAGE OF QUANTITY DISCOUNTS. Okay, you've decided which pictures you want but, hold it, now your parents want a few extra prints. And Aunt Bea wants an 8x10 of you and your fiance exchanging vows. By consolidating several small orders into one large one, you may be able to take advantage of quantity discounts offered by your photographer. Also, you'll be able to avoid "service charges" some photographers slap on orders after the bride and groom's album is delivered. One photographer charges an extra 20% "service fee" on such re-orders. In addition, we found several photographers who offer discounts if you turn in your order within a certain number of days after the wedding. Read the fine print.

Spotlight: Best Buys

Flexible Packages. The most affordable professional photographers offer flexible packages that include a certain number of prints in a leather album. The coverage should be at least four hours (except for small weddings) and should include a specified number of proofs to choose from.

Home-based Photographers.   As mentioned above, these photographers often offer good value because they have lower expenses. Instead of investing in fancy furniture, the photographers invest in their equipment and expertise. It shows.

A la Carte Plans (sometimes). Occasionally, an "a la carte" plan can be a best buy. Here you choose the number of prints and album from a price list. What you don't need, you don't have to buy. However, be aware of hidden charges like travel fees, overtime costs, etc. Also, many photographers will work up a custom package to fit your needs.

Getting Started: How Far in Advance?

 Obviously, photographers can only be at one place at one time. Hence this "limited capacity" to do weddings makes the competition among brides for good photographers intense. Once you book the ceremony site (and therefore confirm your date), consider shopping for a photographer. While some photographers can be had on short notice (a few weeks to a couple of months), booking nine to 12 months in advance of your date is prudent. That way you won't have to settle on a third or fourth choice. During the "wedding season" in your town, prime dates will go quickly.

Biggest Myths About Wedding Photography

 Myth #1   *"A photographer I visited told me he has won several awards for his portraits. If he has won all these awards, that makes him a pretty good wedding photographer, right?"*

Not necessarily. To understand why, let's look at how photographers "win" these contests. According to a recent article in a professional photography magazine, some photographers hire models to pose for these portraits and then take hundreds of exposures to get just the right pose. Then, an army of "professional retouching and airbrushing artists" are used to enhance the image into an award-winner. "The final work presented before the judging panel [bares] little resemblance to the original print or negative," the article stated, adding that many "award-winning" photographers "create exceptional prints specifically for competitions, while exerting little effort toward producing the same caliber of images for customers."

Myth #2   *"I always see those photography specials advertised by big department stores. You know, the ones for $19.95 that includes several dozen prints. Shouldn't wedding photographers be similar in price?"*

Sorry to say, but that isn't true. Stores that set up these portrait specials hire an amateur to shoot 35 mm pictures in a high-volume operation. Unfortunately, professional wedding photography ain't cheap. The time involved in shooting a wedding is one big factor. Weddings take hours of time, shooting on location with expensive professional equipment.

Myth #3 *"I heard that the best bridal portraits are those that are mounted on canvas."*

Not necessarily. Studios like to pitch canvas-mounted portraits as "top-of-the-line," but there is a catch. In fact, a bride in Alexandria, Virginia alerted us to this rip-off. She spoke with a professor of photography who does not recommend canvas-mounted portraits for a couple of reasons. First, in order to be mounted on the canvas, the print must first be peeled. Hence, the portrait may crack and reveal the canvas beneath. Second, canvas-mounted portraits must be oiled periodically to preserve the print. And guess who pockets these hefty "re-oiling" fees? You guessed it, the photographer. All in all, the extra expense of canvas may not be worth the hassle.

Step-by-step Shopping Strategies

 ❦ *Step 1:* Once you have booked your ceremony site (and, hence, confirmed the wedding date), contact three to five wedding photographers you have identified by using the sources we listed above. Make an appointment with each studio and be sure to request to meet the actual photographer who will be available on your wedding day.

❦ *Step 2:* On your visit, view as many pictures as you can from the photographer's past work. Be sure that you are looking at the photographer's own work, not a compilation of the studio's "greatest hits." If possible, ask to see a proof book from a recent wedding.

❦ *Step 3:* While looking at the work, decide if the pictures strike an emotional chord with you. Is the posing natural or do the subjects look uncomfortable? Are the pictures in-focus and well-framed? Check for any over or underexposed prints—a common problem among amateur photographers. Look to see icing details in wedding cakes and delicate lace in bridal gowns—if these subjects look "washed out" then the pictures are overexposed.

❦ *Step 4:* Ask the photographer the questions we list later in this chapter. Make sure you get a good reading on the photographer's style and personality.

❦ *Step 5:* After visiting with several photographers, pick the one you think offers the best quality for the most affordable price. Be sure to compare prices on an "apples to apples" basis, accounting for differences in package sizes and prices. Don't let any photographer pressure you into a quick decision.

❦ *Step 6:* Once you make your decision, sign a contract with the photographer which specifies:

- ❦ The name of the actual photographer who will be at your wedding.
- ❦ When the photographer will arrive and how long he or she will stay.
- ❦ A minimum number of proofs the photographer will provide you to choose from.
- ❦ The exact number of prints and the type of album.
- ❦ The exact dates the proofs will be ready and the final album will be delivered.
- ❦ Provisions in case the photographer gets sick or can't make the wedding.

❦ *Step 7:* A few weeks before the wedding, set up another meeting with the photographer to go over details. Discuss your expectations of the photography and clearly state the types of pictures you want. Identify on a written list any special friends or relatives that you want photographed. The more explicit your instructions to the photographer, the better the odds your wedding photography will meet your high expectations. Frankly, you're paying a ton of money to this person so they better do as you say. Bring a copy of this list with you to the reception. After taking all the time to make this list, you want to be prepared in case the photographer forgets his or her copy.

Questions to Ask a Photographer

1 WHO EXACTLY WILL BE PHOTOGRAPHING MY WEDDING? This is perhaps the most important question to ask. Don't settle for vague answers like "one of our expertly-trained associates will do your wedding." Avoid wasting time by making sure your appointment is with the actual photographer, not the studio's "marketing representative" or "wedding consultant."

2 CAN I SEE A COMPLETE ALBUM FROM ONE WEDDING YOU PHOTOGRAPHED? By seeing a complete album from one wedding, you can see how the photographer tells a story from beginning to end. Try to look at several albums.

3 CAN I ALSO SEE A PROOF BOOK FROM A RECENT WEDDING? This is the best way to see what you are buying. Proof

books are an unedited and uncensored look at what you might receive after your wedding. Good wedding photographers probably have at least one proof book that is waiting to be picked up—ask to see it.

4 DESCRIBE TO ME YOUR PHILOSOPHY AND APPROACH TO WEDDING PHOTOGRAPHY. Ooo, this is a good question. Sit back and listen to what they say. How active a role do they take in the direction of the day's events? Obviously, some photographers may have a canned speech for this question, but you can shake them up by asking good follow-up questions.

5 WHAT IS YOUR SHOOTING SCHEDULE DURING A WEDDING? When do you arrive and what is your general order of shots? How long do the traditional pictures after the ceremony take? This is a real controversial area of wedding photography. See the side bar "The Great Before or After Controversy."

6 WHAT IS THE BALANCE BETWEEN POSED AND CANDID SHOTS? Some photographers prefer to stage most pictures by formally posing the subjects. Ask the photographer's opinion about whether pictures should be posed or candid. A new trend in wedding photography is "photo-journalism." Here the photographer documents the wedding as it happens without any formal posing.

7 HOW MANY EXPOSURES WILL YOU TAKE AT MY WEDDING? IS THERE A LIMIT ON THE NUMBER OF EXPOSURES OR YOUR TIME? Be careful of photographers who limit the number of exposures or time. Too many times we have seen weddings shift into "fast forward" because the photographer's clock was running out. Limiting the number of exposures is also a problem since it restricts the possible choices for your album. About 150 to 200 exposures should be taken to provide enough choices for an album with 60 to 80 prints (our recommendation to adequately cover the day's events).

8 DO YOU BRING ANY BACKUP EQUIPMENT? What will you do if you are sick and unable to shoot the wedding? Cameras (even expensive medium-format ones) are just machines. Sometimes they break down. Good photographers should have backup cameras and lighting systems ready in case of a mechanical problem. Having an associate on call in case of emergencies is also prudent.

9 CAN I SEE THE ACTUAL ALBUM THAT COMES WITH MY PACKAGE? A favorite trick of wedding photographers is to show you their past work lovingly bound into leather albums. Then they "forget" to mention to you their packages

come with cheaper vinyl albums with plastic-covered pages. And, oh yes, after the wedding, the photographer slips in that "the leather albums are available at an extra fee." Besides the deceptive nature of this practice, vinyl albums with plastic pages are also problematic since the chemicals in the plastic can damage the prints over time. Insist on seeing the actual album that is mentioned in the package before you sign the contract.

10 DESCRIBE TO ME THE MOST DIFFICULT WEDDING YOU EVER PHOTOGRAPHED. How did you handle it? Ooo, this is another good question! It can be fascinating to see what the photographer defines as "difficult."

Helpful Hints

1 PHOTOGRAPHERS' PRICING METHODS MAY BE AS EASY TO UNDERSTAND AS THE FEDERAL INCOME TAX CODE. We are not quite sure why this is. One possible explanation is that photographers want to give you maximum flexibility in choosing prints, albums and portraits. The only problem is that every photographer approaches pricing with a different philosophy that ends up confusing you, the consumer.

Another, more Machiavellian explanation is that photographers want to make comparison shopping more difficult. The lack of a pricing standard makes it very difficult to compare "apples to apples." Instead you have one photographer who offers a complete package with an album of 50 8x10's for $800 and another has an a la carte system. The only way for you to make sense of this is to try to equalize the prices, in the same way the grocery stores often display the price per ounce of certain products. We do this by asking ourselves "So how much does a four-hour package with 50 5x5's and 20 8x10's in an Art Leather album cost?" This package provides adequate coverage for most weddings.

2 SOME OF THE BEST WEDDING PHOTOGRAPHERS ARE WOMEN. Sadly, wedding photography was once (and some say still is) a profession dominated by men. In many cities, men are the majority of professional photographers. The only women at studios are secretaries or the wives of photographers who come along as assistants. Fortunately, today more and more women are actually behind the camera. This is especially a great development for brides and grooms.

Why? That's because weddings are filled with emotions. In our opinion, professional photographers who are best at capturing those emotions are often women. Too often, we see male photographers who seem preoccupied with the technical aspects of photography. Obviously, you need a professional photographer who has a firm grasp on the technical end. However, no one benefits when the photographer worries more about F-stops than getting an intimate moment between the bride and her parents.

Unfortunately, sexism in photography is rampant. For example, we have seen evidence that some male photographers (who control photography guilds) have attempted to block women photographers from the wedding market. Some argue that the women are too inexperienced to shoot an event as complex as a wedding. As a result, many women photographers have to work twice as hard to enjoy the same level of reputation as their male counterparts.

Frankly, good wedding photography is not dependent on the sex of the photographer. Just remember not to let outdated sexist attitudes influence the important decision of choosing a wedding photographer.

The Great Before or After Controversy

Ever attended a wedding where it seemed like the bride and groom took forever to make it to the reception? Where are they? Was their limo hijacked by a group of terrorists? More than likely the bride and groom were hijacked by a wedding photographer who took an amount of time equivalent to the Creation of heaven and earth to do the "after-ceremony pictures."

So what exactly are the "after-ceremony pictures?" Basically, these are pictures of the bride and groom with the officiant at the altar, with the bridesmaids, with the groomsmen, with the whole bridal party, with their various relatives, etc. Also, since some churches restrict photography during the actual ceremony, several events from the ceremony (exchanging rings, lighting of the unity candle, the kiss, etc.) may be restaged for posterity. All told, we are talking quite a few pictures here.

Photographers often lie about how long this process takes. Sometimes photographers sound like a cartoonish version of "Name that Tune." (Yes, Bob, I can take those after-ceremony pictures in 20 minutes. Well, Bob, I can do those same pictures in 15 minutes.) In reality, we have known several couples who took one to two hours to make it to their reception thanks to the after-ceremony session.

Of course, some bright person recently came up with a solution to this problem. Hey, why not do all those pictures before the ceremony? The only problem: this would require the bride and groom to see each other before the ceremony on the wedding day. O H N O ! The screams of wedding etiquette gurus could be heard miles away! "How can you break such a sacred superstition?" they screeched.

Well, let's take a closer look at the prohibition of seeing each other before the ceremony. As far as we can tell, this started back in the year 1008 A.D. when all marriages were arranged and brides and grooms didn't see each other until the wedding day. Keeping the bride and groom separate was intended to prevent Thor the Viking (the groom) from running away in case Freya the Bride was not the beautiful Viking goddess he was promised. Or vice versa.

Today, brides and grooms not only know each other before the wedding, they also probably share the same tube of toothpaste. It seems a little silly that you wouldn't' see your fiance the day of the wedding when you were just sharing the same pint of Ben & Jerry's 24 hours earlier.

Furthermore, brides today are taught to believe that the groom stands at the end of the aisle and looks down toward his beautiful bride, all the while thinking "Wow! Isn't she beautiful? Aren't I lucky?" In reality, most grooms are thinking "Thank god she's here. Now we can get this over with."

We're not trying to take away from this special moment but there are several advantages to doing the "after-ceremony" pictures before the wedding (i.e., seeing each other before the ceremony):

❦ *Everything is perfect:* Hair and makeup are fresh prior to the ceremony and hence those important pictures will capture you at your best. After the ceremony, all the hugging and crying can alter that perfect make-over, etc.

❦ *You can leave immediately after the ceremony for the reception:* You can have more time seeing relatives and enjoying the party you spent so much time (and money) planning.

HERE'S OUR RECOMMENDATION: Get to the ceremony site two hours before the wedding. After everyone is dressed, clear out the church with just the groom at the head of the aisle. Then, with appropriate music playing, the bride emerges and walks down the aisle. After this initial meeting, all the formal group pictures are taken before the guests arrive.

Or here's another variation: in a private room at the ceremony site, have the bride and groom meet prior to the ceremony. Here, you and your fiance can exchange gifts, marvel at each other's dapper appearance, gaze at the gown, etc. What's especially nice about this approach is that you actually get 15 minutes alone, just you and your fiance. For the rest of the day you'll be surrounded by friends, relatives, and that ever-present photographer. On a day that's supposed to celebrate your relationship, it's ironic that most brides and grooms have their first private moment in the car leaving the reception—after the whole shebang is over.

Pitfalls to Avoid

Pitfall #1
BAIT AND SWITCH AT LARGE PHOTOGRAPHY STUDIOS AND "CELEBRITY" PHOTOGRAPHERS

"My friend who recently got married contracted with a well-known, large studio to do her wedding. Everyone was shocked when the photographer arrived—the studio had sent out a person who had never shot a wedding before! The pictures were a disaster! How can I prevent this from happening to me?"

A practice we call "bait and switch" is definitely the #1 problem we hear about photography studios. Unfortunately, some large studios "bait" engaged couples with a great reputation only to "switch" them by delivering less than great wedding photography. How does this happen? Basically, some studios "farm out" their weddings to poorly-trained associates or (even worse) "stringers." Stringers are free-lance photographers who are often amateurs working on the weekend for a few extra bucks. The work of these photographers can be far inferior to professional wedding photographers.

"A famous photographer in our town has taken many pictures of celebrities. Since the studio also does weddings, I assume my fiance and I will get the same high quality photography."

Don't bet on it. Here's how it works in this case: every city in the U.S. probably has at least one "celebrity photographer" who attracts engaged couples to their studio based on their famous name. So who does the wedding photography? Instead of the famous photographer, weddings are often assigned to a no-name associate or a stringer. Hence, couples are "baited" into the studio by the famous photographer and then "switched" to a less-famous associate. While an associate may do good work, this is obviously deceptive since couples are duped into paying a hefty premium for "celebrity photography," then often get much less.

SOLUTION: You can prevent these problems by doing one simple thing: make sure the name of the actual photographer who will shoot your wedding is specified in the contract. Most importantly, before you sign the contract, meet with the actual photographer who will do your wedding and view several albums of his or her work. Don't let the studio show you a few slick sample albums and feed you the line "all our associates are trained in the same great style." Remember your wedding pictures are dependent on who is behind that camera, not any fancy name that's embossed in gold on the studio's stationery.

Pitfall #2
HIDDEN CHARGES.

"I was generally pleased with my wedding photographer. However, when I went to pick up my proofs, the studio gave me a big sales pitch to buy an Art Leather album. I thought my package came with an Art Leather album but apparently it doesn't. What happened?

Basically, the photographer has hidden his extra charge for an album, which is terribly unethical. The most common trick here is to show you sample work clad in an Art Leather album. Then, when you pick up the proofs, you find out that your album is actually a cheap vinyl album with plastic-coated pages. Surprise! An Art Leather album is available for an extra $100 or $200!

You can prevent this problem by asking to see the album that comes with the package you select before you sign the contract. Besides albums, photographers sometimes have hidden charges for travel time, over-time, special handling, etc. Be careful to read the fine print in the photographer's price list and contract.

Pitfall #3
SMALL PACKAGES AND HEAVY SALES PRESSURE.

"I contracted with a photographer for one of his small wedding packages that had 20 8x10s in an album. After the wedding, the studio tried to pressure me into buying more prints than the original package—-at those high reprint prices! My only problem—I never realized how many more pictures I would want for my album! Help!"

Ah, this is a popular deceptive practice by wedding photographers. Here, the studio attracts wedding business with low package prices like "just $495 for complete coverage and an album with 20 8x10s." Sounds like a great deal? No, it isn't. That's because most weddings generate dozens of great pictures—photographers often snap 40 to 50 pictures even before the ceremony!

The result is that most albums need at least 60 to 80 prints to adequately tell the story of an "average" wedding. Of course, photographers are well aware of this and realize those couples will order many more pictures than those packages with just 20 prints. The result is that the $500 package ends up costing $1000, $1500, or even $2000 by the time the total order is placed. We have talked to photographers who admit this deceptive practice is commonplace. Some studios even make matters worse by adding some heavy sales pressure after the wedding to increase the size of the order.

The most blatant example of this practice was one studio we visited that offered a package for $995 which included just 40 5x7s. The price list then went on to say that "brides and grooms may purchase additional 5x7s or 8x10s to create a more complete story." Those "additional prints" cost $12 for a 5x7 and $20 for an 8x10.

You can prevent this practice by selecting a package that offers the amount of coverage that will realistically tell the story of your wedding. For small weddings (under 100 guests with a short reception), this might just be 40 to 60 prints. Most will require 60 to 80 and some large weddings (with big bridal parties and long receptions) may require 100 plus prints. Be realistic and don't get hooked by low-price packages that only give you a miniscule amount of actual prints.

Pitfall #4
UNREASONABLE TIME LIMITS.

"I recently attended a wedding where it seemed like the reception moved at the speed of light. Apparently, the photographer was in quite a hurry."

We can't tell you how many weddings we've seen where the reception looked like a sped-up film because the photographer's clock was ticking. After researching this book we now know why: photographers often sell packages with unreasonable time limits.

For example, we interviewed one photographer whose main package had only two and half hours coverage. Since most photographers start their coverage one hour before the ceremony and since the ceremony itself can take up to one hour (including those pesky after-ceremony pictures), this would leave just 30 minutes to cover all the reception activities! No wonder why the bride and groom seemed in a frantic rush to cut the cake, throw the bouquet, toss the garter, and so on! Instead of enjoying the reception, the couple was racing to get everything on film before the photographer's clock expired.

You can prevent this from happening to you by selecting a package with reasonable time limits, or better yet, no time limits at all. In the latter case, the photographer stays at the reception until both of you leave. However, some photographers argue their time is precious and want to impose some time limit. In that case, select a package with at least four hours coverage for an "average wedding." You'll need more coverage (perhaps five or six hours) if you have a long ceremony (Catholic mass) or a large wedding party (all those pictures take more time).

Of course, it shouldn't come as a surprise to you that those same photographers who have those unreasonable time limits also offer overtime at a pricey charge per hour!

We should note that a close kin to this pitfall are photographers who limit the number of exposures they take at a wedding. Ask the photographer about any such limits before you sign a contract.

Pitfall #5
GREATEST HITS ALBUMS.

"I visited a photographer who only showed me an album with pictures from several weddings in it. Shouldn't this person have shown me more work?"

Yes. This problem is what we call the "Greatest Hits Album." Even lousy photographers can occasionally take good pictures. In order to convince you of their "excellence," these photographers compile all those "greatest hits" into one album. Obviously, you are only getting a tiny glimpse of their work.

When you visit a potential photographer, try to see as much work as possible. The best photographers should have a sample album that chronicles one wedding from beginning to end. This allows you to see how the photographer will tell the story of your wedding. Another helpful album to look at is a proof book. Typically, good photographers may have a proof book in the studio that is about to be delivered to a customer. Proof books give the most accurate picture you can get about the photographer's skill since that's exactly what you will use to select your prints later. Unedited and uncensored, you really see what the photographer can (and can't) do well.

Pitfall #6
FRIENDS AND RELATIVES.

"A friend of mine decided to let her uncle, who is a shutterbug, photograph her wedding. What a disaster! His flash didn't work for half the pictures and the other half weren't that exciting anyway."

As you realize, having friends and relatives do various part of your wedding can save you a tremendous amount of money. While you might have a talented aunt who can help alter your gown and a helpful friend who bakes great cakes, you may want to draw the line at the photographs.

Photography is typically high on everyone's priority list and its no wonder—the pictures are all you have left after the wedding. Investing the money in professional photography is a wise choice. Trying to save money here is tempting but we say resist the urge. Well-meaning friends and relatives who are amateur photographers often bite off more than they can chew when they shoot a wedding. Adverse lighting conditions and other technical challenges can vex even the most talented amateurs.

Unless your budget absolutely forbids it, we recommend going with a professional, which we define as a full-time photographer who has photographed over 50 weddings in the past three years. When friends and relatives offer to do your pictures, simply say you have put down a non-refundable deposit on another photographer.

Also be aware that many photographers' contracts specify that they must be the only photographer at the ceremony. They claim that friends and relatives who snap pictures of the bride and groom compete with their work and equipment (their flashes may set off the photographer's flash prematurely). Ask your photographer about any such prohibitions.

Pitfall #7
"YOU GET THE FILM" PACKAGES.

"I met a photographer at a bridal show who told me that he can save me money by giving me all the film after the wedding. Then I go and get the pictures developed. Is this a good deal? What's the catch?"

The catch is that you have to develop the film, which is much more complicated that it sounds. Unlike 35mm film (which you drop off at Kmart and then a few days later—POOF! You have pictures!), medium format negatives must be developed by professional labs. These labs produce negatives that must be "cropped and masked" to produce final prints. We won't go into more detail on cropping and masking, but we can say that we did this for some publicity pictures and it was quite challenging.

The other main problem is dealing with the lab. As a consumer, you may not know the "photography-speak" that photographers use to communicate with the lab. For example, many labs offer less-expensive machine prints and also custom prints, which include touch-ups and artwork. We found communicating with the lab that did our publicity pictures difficult. Furthermore, you have little leverage over the lab in case the developed pictures have quality problems.

Most professional photographers do not sell their negatives. Also, what incentive does the photographer have to correct any problems if the last you see of him (or her) is when he gives you the film at the reception? Unless you have an intimate knowledge of professional photography development, you may want to steer clear of these "get the film" packages.

Trends

❦ *More candids, fewer posed shots:* Perhaps the biggest trend in wedding photography is a move away from posed shots and a larger emphasis on candids. Obviously, the best wedding albums feature a mix of both candids and posed pictures. However, traditional photographers who pose every shot seem to be falling out of favor.

❦ *Black and white photography:* Yes, it's back. Some couples are rediscovering the contrast and beauty of black and white photography. We've seen several truly striking albums that mix black and white and color photography—à la *The Wizard of Oz.*

❦ *Computerized processing and the "merger" of photo and video:* Computer technology has even invaded the staid field of photography. Some studios use computers to do electronic "touch-ups" on negatives. Others have done away with "proofs" and instead show you computerized previews of portraits within minutes (instead of days.) Perhaps the most intriguing trend is the coming of video cameras that will take high-quality stills. These could be conceivably printed out on souped-up color laser printers. It's quite possible that by the late 1990's, photography and video will merge into one—a video/photographer will use one device to take photo stills and live action video. Stay tuned.

Special Touches to Make Your Wedding Photography Unique:

1 ADD A MEMORY PAGE TO YOUR ALBUM. This is a page at the front of the album with a copy of your invitation. We've seen couples add a few of the dried flowers from the bride's bouquet and some lace from the bridal gown to this page.

2 PERSONALIZE YOUR WEDDING PHOTOGRAPHY. Instead of an engagement portrait in a studio with a boring blue background, have the picture taken at a special location. Perhaps the place you first met or had your first date. If this isn't practical, a romantic picture in a favorite park at sunset is nice. Obviously, photographers will charge a little more to go on location (perhaps $50 to $100) but it is a nice way to personalize the photography.

3 CHRONICLE YOUR ENGAGEMENT WITH PICTURES. With your own camera, document the wedding process (trying on gowns, tasting cakes, visiting various reception sites) from the proposal to the big day. Undoubtedly, you will receive a photography album as a gift, so here's a use for it. Add your honeymoon pictures in the back to complete the album.

Chapter 10

Wedding Cakes

With the four surprising sources discussed in this chapter, we show you how to find an affordable wedding cake that looks as good as it tastes. We'll tell you the biggest myth about wedding cakes and five questions to ask any baker. In short, you will learn how to have your cake and eat it, too!

What Are You Buying?

Wedding cakes are no longer the typical white or yellow cake frosted with white icing! Across the country we have found a great many regional variations (see the Chapter 8 for more details). No matter where your wedding is, however, here are the four basic elements.

❦ *The cake, itself.* Traditionally, wedding cakes are vanilla-flavored confections. However, today anything goes. Some of the unusual flavors of wedding cake we've found include Mississippi mud, pina colada rum, white chocolate mousse, and mocha chip.

❦ *The filling.* In addition to cake flavor possibilities, many bakers also offer a variety of fillings. Fillings used to be fruit jams or butter-cream icing, but have expanded today to include liqueurs, fresh fruit, custards, and mousses. The traditional wedding cake has two layers of cake with one layer of filling in each tier. Lately, we've seen more European torte-style cakes: confections with four or five layers of cake and filling. This torte-style cake tends to be much richer and moister than an American-style cake.

❦ *The frosting and decorations.* As for the outside of wedding cakes, two key elements are involved. The actual composition of the icing can vary in a wide variety of ways. Some opt for the traditional butter-cream icing (to which liqueurs are often added) while rolled fondant or marzipan is also popular (for a more Victorian look). Whipped cream icings and meringue icings are other possibilities available from some bakeries. No longer are you limited to the typical white icing; many brides want their cakes tinted to match the bridal party colors or merely prefer the antique look of an off-white icing.

The second element, decoration, has also changed dramatically. Wedding cakes used to be decorated with icing swags and maybe a few frosting flowers. Today's wedding cakes feature delicate detailing that even copies the lace motif of the bride's dress. Basket weaves are also extremely popular and provide an attractive, contemporary look.

Rather than relying on the standard plastic bride and groom to decorate their cake tops, many brides are using fresh flowers as decoration. Also silk flowers or hard sugar (gum paste) designs are available. The cost of these decorations may be included in the price of the cake or may be extra.

❦ *Delivery and set-up.* Another element you are buying is the delivery and set-up of your cake. This means the actual engineering of the cake with its several layers, possible separations (or stacking if you prefer the tiers to sit one on top of the other) and decoration if you want flowers and greenery. Rental items like the columns and plates for separating tiers are another cost. Some bakers have actually made a special stand for their cakes which they rent to couples for the day.

AVERAGE TOTAL COSTS. Cake prices range from $1 to $4 per serving (this is the typical way cake is priced), but may range up to as much as $8 per serving in places like Manhattan. There is a controversy over how big a serving is; we'll address this question later in the chapter. Deposits range from $50 up to 50% of the total bill. The balance is due usually a week or so before the wedding.

Sources to Find an Affordable Baker

We'd first like to describe the three types of wedding cake bakeries out in the market:

1 CAKE FACTORIES. Better know as commercial bakeries these folks bake and deliver over 10 cakes per Saturday. These businesses may be less personalized than the other two types of bakers. Grocery stores fall into this category, too.

2 RECEPTION SITES AND/OR CATERERS. Quality is sometimes great, sometimes not.

3 OUT-OF-HOME/SMALL BAKERS. These are the hardest to find, but often the best and most creative of these possibilities.

Here are our sources for finding great bakeries:

❦ *Florists.* Because they often work with bakers to help coordinate the floral decorations, florists may have the most contact with bakeries.

❦ *Photographers.* Since they attend many receptions, photographers see the best and worst creations of local bakeries. They also often hear praise or complaints about the cakes while they are working.

❦ *Reception sites.* Besides helping set up the cakes, as well as serving them, catering managers notice whether guests like the cake or not.

❦ *Bridal shows.* Bakeries often offer samples of their cakes at bridal shows, so here's a great opportunity to taste some without any pressure to buy.

Top Money-saving Secrets

1 ORDER LESS CAKE THAN THE NUMBER OF PEOPLE. If you have a sweets table or groom's cake, consider fewer servings. Also if you will be eating a heavy sit-down meal or have a crowd that doesn't eat a lot of sweets, consider cutting back.

2 CHOOSE AN INDEPENDENT OR OUT-OF-HOME BAKER. This could mean as much as $1 to $2 difference in cost per serving. Out-of-home bakeries often have lower overhead which they pass on to brides. Caution: Local health laws may prohibit bakers from operating out of their home. Each city is different, so you may want to check with your local health department.

3 SKIP THE ANNIVERSARY CAKE TOP (SEE PITFALLS).

4 IF YOU WANT THE LOOK OF A LARGE CAKE WITHOUT THE COST, CONSIDER USING FROSTED STYROFOAM "DUMMY" CAKES to make your cake look larger. This may cost as little as $25 extra.

Getting Started: How Far in Advance?

Because bakeries can make more than one cake on a Saturday, brides may only need two to four months to plan. With some of the large commercial bakeries, you may even need less time (as little as a week's notice). Popular bakeries and popular dates may require more advance planning (between three and six months) and you may want to do this part early anyway to get it out of the way. You will need to know how formal the wedding will be and have a general idea of the number of guests you will have. You can finalize this number later, when the guest count becomes more concrete.

Biggest Myth of Wedding Cakes

 Myth #1 *"At every wedding I've ever been to, the wedding cake was tasteless and dry. It's impossible to find a good-tasting cake."*

Wrong. This fallacy is based on all those tasteless white cakes with Crisco-based icings that we remember from the 1970's. Nowadays, with the variety of flavors and choices among bakeries, brides have the ability to serve a beautiful and delicious cake!

Step-by-step Shopping Strategies

 ❦ Step 1: Before visiting a baker, you will need to have a general idea of the number of guests invited. Final exact numbers won't be required until a week or two before the wedding date; this will allow you to get a basic price for a cake. Also, knowing your wedding colors will help guide the baker.

❦ Step 2: Given the resources above, identify two to three bakers who have skill levels and style ideas to fit your needs. Make an appointment with them and ask if you can have a taste test. Time the appointment to make it easier for the baker to give you a sample (like Friday while they are baking cakes for Saturday weddings).

❦ Step 3: At the baker's shop, be sure to look at real photos of their cake designs. Some bakeries use Wilton cake books and tell brides they can make anything from these books. We have found cases, however, where bakeries have promised this and been unable to deliver. It is preferable to see actual photos of what they can do!

❦ Step 4: Given the size of your reception, ask the baker for a proposal or estimate of the cost of a cake based on one or two of their styles. Also ask for suggestions on how much cake to buy. The amount of cake to order will depend on several factors: if you will be having a groom's cake or sweets table; how much other food you will be serving (sit-down dinner vs hors d'oeuvres); the time of day; and the size of the slices (paper thin or birthday cake size).

❦ *Step 5:* Make sure you taste a sample of their cake. There is no substitute for having actually tasted it before buying. If a baker doesn't offer taste tests, you should be very cautious. You may have to buy a small six-inch cake from the baker in order to get a taste, but we prefer bakeries who offer free samples—these are usually the best.

❦ *Step 6:* Compare the bakers you have visited and choose the best.

❦ *Step 7:* Ask the baker for a signed proposal detailing the design, flavors of both cake and filling, any rentals (like columns or stands), delivery and set-up fees, and deposit information. Don't forget to have the date, place and delivery time clearly written on the proposal. If you are planning far in advance, you may have to adjust the number of servings you will need—find out the last possible moment when you can change numbers.

❦ *Step 8:* Confirm any last-minute details and pay the balance on the cake a week or two before the wedding.

Questions to Ask a Baker

1 DO YOU HAVE ANY PHOTOS OF PREVIOUS DESIGNS? The idea is to see the bakery's actual work, not to look through Wilton cake books with designs the bakery may or may not have ever baked.

2 CAN WE HAVE A TASTE TEST? You may have to wait for a day when they are making cakes, but the best bakeries will offer you a free taste test.

3 ARE THERE ANY EXTRA CHARGES? Some bakeries prefer to break down the charges for almost everything. These items may include: fillings, complex decorations, silk or fresh flowers, delivery, set-up, cake plates and columns, and more. Find out exactly what these items will cost and get a written proposal.

4 WHO WILL DECORATE THE CAKE WITH FRESH OR SILK FLOWERS? If you prefer this type of decoration on your cake, you will need to find out how the flowers will be provided and who will decorate the cake. Some bakers can purchase the flowers and decorate it themselves. Others will get the flowers from your florist. Still other bakers are willing to allow the florist to decorate the cake.

5   How far in advance is the cake prepared? This may be a delicate question to ask, but you will want to know how fresh the cake is that you are buying. Some high-volume bakeries will make up cakes ahead of time and freeze them until a day or so before your event. We don't recommend these bakeries since we believe fresh cakes are usually more tasty.

Pitfalls to Avoid

Pitfall #1
ANNIVERSARY CAKE TOPS
"The baker I visited told me that 'of course you will want to save the top tier of the cake for your first anniversary.' This sounds like a silly tradition!"

Yes, we agree. A common tradition in many areas of the country, you're supposed to save the top of your wedding cake to eat on your first anniversary. This entails having mom or someone else remember to take the top home, wrap it very carefully, and put it in your freezer. Even supposing you have room in your freezer, the taste of the cake after 12 months may leave much to be desired. In fact, if you serve the cake at your wedding instead, you may be able to save 10% to 20% off your bakery bill—a much better deal than a stale year-old cake! If you want to follow this tradition, we recommend calling up your baker in a year and buying a small, freshly-made cake to celebrate with on your first anniversary.

Pitfall #2
MYSTERIOUS WHITE ICING.
"We attended a wedding last weekend that had a beautiful wedding cake. But, when we tasted the cake, there was this terrible, greasy aftertaste. Yuck! What causes this problem?"

So what makes a cake's icing white? Well, a key ingredient in icing is butter—which creates a problem for bakers. Most American butter is yellow, which gives icing an off-white or ivory color. To get white icing, bakers must use expensive white butter (imported from Europe). Unfortunately, some bakers use a less expensive short-cut to get white "butter-cream" icing—they add white shortening like Crisco. Yuck! That's why some cake icing has a greasy aftertaste. If you want white icing, you might ask your baker how they make their icing white. Another solution may be to go with an ivory cake.

Pitfall #3
WELL-MEANING FRIENDS AND RELATIVES.
"My aunt has offered to bake my wedding cake. She's

good at baking birthday cakes but isn't a wedding cake much more complicated?"

That's right. Offers like this are made with the best possible intentions but, if accepted, can be disastrous. Baking a wedding cake is far more complex than baking a birthday cake from a Betty Crocker mix. The engineering skills required to stack a cake and keep it from falling or leaning are incredible. Unless you have a friend or relative who is a professional baker, politely refuse their offer. Consider telling them you've already contracted with a baker to make your cake if you don't want to offend them.

Pitfall #4
EARLY DELIVERY AND COLLAPSING CAKES.

"My baker delivered my cake nearly five hours before my reception. In the interim, someone or something knocked the cake over and destroyed it! How could I have prevented this?"

This is a problem that often occurs with large bakeries that have many deliveries. The cake is dropped off (and set-up) hours before the reception and left unattended. As you can guess, Murphy's Law says that an unattended wedding cake is a collapsed wedding cake. No one at the reception site may admit to knocking it over but you can imagine how "things happen" during a wedding reception set-up. Prevent this problem by insisting the baker deliver the cake within two hours prior to the reception. You may want to coordinate with the catering staff to limit any scheduling snafus.

Trends

❧ *Cakes that actually taste good.* As we mentioned above, brides don't have to settle for tasteless white cake and frosting. Now the choices are uncountable! Hurray!

❧ *Chocolate wedding cakes.* In the South, chocolate groom's cakes are very popular and are served on the wedding day with the bride's cake. In areas where groom's cakes are unknown, some brides opt for a white-frosted chocolate cake as the centerpiece of their wedding reception. Some brides add chocolate cakes or truffles to their sweet tables in other areas of the country to satisfy the tastes of those chocoholics out there.

❧ *New flavors.* Other flavors are also coming into vogue, ranging from well-known favorites like carrot or spice cake to exotics like Amaretto mousse cake and mocha chip. Fillings are also becoming a popular addition for many cakes and include fresh fruits, custards and liqueurs.

🍃 *New decorations.* Instead of traditional columns, we've seen more stacked cake designs, such as a basket weaves (à la Martha Stewart's *Wedding Book*). Among other trends are Victorian cakes with smooth marzipan icing and delicate ribbon decorations. Even art-deco is also becoming a popular motif for cake decorating—one cake we saw was covered in edible gold leaf!

As you can see, cakes are now a personal statement, instead of uniform white creations that look the same from wedding to wedding.

Unique Ideas

1 ETHNIC TRADITIONS. Many couples incorporate ethnic traditions into their wedding cake. For example, the French wedding cake is actually a cone-shaped cake made up of cream-filled pastry puffs stuck together with carmelized sugar. Guests serve themselves by merely grabbing a cream puff from the cone! Another ethnic cake is the Kransekai (as the Norwegians call it) or Mandelringstarta (as the Swedes refer to it). Popular among the Scandinavians in Minnesota, this cake is made of almond cake arranged in graduated rings. You may be aware of other ethnic cakes that will adapt well to your wedding.

2 DIFFERENT FLAVORS IN DIFFERENT TIERS. For couples who like variety, some cakes feature different flavors in different tiers—sort of the Neapolitan ice cream idea. Or you can make each tier a different flavor.

3 CHEESECAKE. Ah, here's an unique idea we are particularly fond of: cheesecake wedding cakes. Available in many different flavors, cheesecakes can be frosted with cream cheese icing or left plain and decorated with fresh fruit or flowers. Yum!

Spotlight: Home Bakers

One home baker we know describes her business as the "hobby that got out of hand." Lucky for brides-to-be that this hobby did evolve into a business! Home bakers are often the most talented bakers in a city because their cakes are individually hand-crafted—unlike commercial bakeries that churn out copy-cat cakes. We've found home bakers are more willing to try something unusual—like a new flavor or design. Low price is, of course, another big advantage: home bakers may be less expensive than commercial bakeries because of lower overhead.

A disadvantage of home bakers, however, is their popularity. Because they can only make and deliver a few cakes on a Saturday, some bakers may be booked up far in advance. If you are considering a home baker, contact him or her three to six months before the wedding to set up a visit. You may even have to plan further in advance! With one baker, we had to make an appointment 10 months prior to the wedding date! But it was worth it!

Another problem may occur with the health department regulations in your area. Many cities and counties have legal restrictions on food preparation companies operated out of a home or residence. Therefore, some home bakers operate illegally—ask if you have any doubts.

If you are looking for a home baker, a good source is area caterers. Also ask reception sites and other wedding businesses like photographers and florists. Friends are a good way to to find a talented in-home baker, too, so ask any recently married couples you know.

If you have any questions or comments about this chapter, please feel free to call the authors. See the "How to Reach Us" page at the back of this book!

Chapter 11

Wedding Videos

Lights! Camera! Money! Wedding videos are an expensive newcomer to the wedding market. In this chapter, we cut through the technical mumbo-jumbo to give you a practical guide to finding an affordable yet talented videographer.

What Are You Buying?

 Basically, there are two things you are buying when you hire a videographer: the cameraperson's time, and the video itself.

❦ *The cameraperson's time.* Many videographers will charge you for their time first and foremost. Most offer packages with a time limit of three, four, five or more hours. Overtime is charged on an hourly basis. Some other videographers will charge a flat fee for the whole wedding and reception.

Besides hiring a cameraperson for a certain amount of time, you are also buying his talent and personality. As with photographers, it is very important to find a videographer who is not only skilled at camera work but who also is compatible with your personality. You will be working with him or her as much as with the photographer. Of course, the videographer's investment in equipment is important—we'll discuss this later.

❦ *The final product.* The most important item you're buying is the videotape. There are several types of tapes available:

RAW FOOTAGE. This is a tape that simply starts at the beginning of your ceremony and runs, uninterrupted, to the end of your reception. There is no editing or post-production graphics. Raw footage videos should be the least expensive option.

EDITED "IN CAMERA." This type of video also does not have post-editing or added graphics. However, the videographer edits your video "in-camera." This means the cameraperson shuts off the camera during any uninteresting moments or rewinds and tapes over any unnecessary footage. If done by a professional, this option can work very well. It will usually be moderately priced in comparison with other types of tapes.

POST-EDITED. This type of tape is usually the most expensive because the videographer spends the most time on it. Videographers "post-edit" a tape after the wedding and reception. During this production, the videographer will take raw footage, cut out the boring parts (if there are any!), smooth the transitions, and add in titles and music. Some videographers add still photos (baby pictures, honeymoon photos) to give the tape a truly personal feel. We've even seen tapes with special effects similar to those seen on television newscasts. Many videographers charge an additional hourly fee for post-editing, while others may have packages which include editing and special effects.

Most wedding video packages include one copy of the video tape. Extra copies often cost more; however some videographers have packages that include copies for parents.

AVERAGE TOTAL COSTS: The average wedding video costs about $850. This price may vary from as little as $200 in small towns to over $4000 in the largest cities. The more editing you require, the more expensive the video will be.

Sources to Find a Videographer

 Wedding videos are a relative newcomer to the wedding market. Only in the 1980's did the video-taping of weddings really take off. As a result, most of the companies that videotape weddings are new themselves and may be hard to find. Unlike photographers, videographers are not always listed in the Yellow Pages. Here are some of the best sources to find a good videographer.

❧ *Recently-married couples.* These folks can give some of the best advice about videographers. You may even be able to look at their own video of their wedding to decide if you like their videography choice.

❧ *Television stations.* Many camerapersons at TV stations moonlight on weekends shooting wedding receptions. They may have access to high-tech editing and special effects computers. In Ft. Worth, Texas, for example, one of the most popular videographers for weddings is the chief photographer for the NBC affiliate.

❦ *Wedding photographers.* This may be one of the best sources. Photographers will be able to recommend good videographers they've seen at other weddings. Occasionally, photographers and videographers have conflicts at weddings. You can avoid this by choosing two people who have worked together before. Don't, however, feel obliged to use a photographer's suggestion without checking out the videographer carefully to see if he or she fits your needs.

❦ *Ceremony site coordinators.* These folks often have first-hand knowledge about videographers since they are responsible for reciting the rules to them and determining where they can stand. Site coordinators can recommend people familiar with the site who are also easy to work with. And they may also hear back from brides about how good (or bad) the finished video is.

❦ *Bridal shows.* These shows (sponsored by local bridal shops and reception sites) usually have a few local videographers among the exhibitors. At these shows, videographers will show a demonstration tape at their booth. This lets you see some work without making an appointment. Remember, though that this might be a "greatest hits" tape and that you will still need to see some other samples before you book with them.

Understanding Videographers: Some Basics

When shopping for a professional wedding videographer, there are several elements to remember as you look at their work and talk about their options.

1 LIGHTING As with photography, lighting is key to a good video. Often, existing room light is not bright enough to get a good picture. In fact, one of the biggest fears couples used to have about videographers was their use of bright lights. In the past, videographers would need to flood a room with light in order to get good video.

Well, we have good news for those of you out there who are hesitating about wedding videos. Advancements in technology have led to new professional video cameras that are sensitive enough for use with only available room light. If they do require any extra light, videographers can use smaller, "low wattage" lights that are less distracting and still get good video.

2 SOUND Especially during your once-in-a-lifetime wedding ceremony, it is vital to get perfect sound on your video. Thanks to high technology, great video sound is possible in a number of ways.

There are basically three ways to capture sound at the ceremony. The least effective is through a "boom" microphone. This is attached to the video camera and often picks up every sound in the room, including your vows. If you don't want to hear your seven year old cousin Joey squirming around in his seat and fidgeting, the boom microphone is not for you.

The next option is the "hard-wired" microphone. This type of microphone has a wire which connects it to the camera. The other end is usually attached to the groom, the official, the podium or the kneeling bench. This may not be ideal for some people, especially if there is a lot of movement during the ceremony. The sound quality is usually average to good.

The final option is a "wireless" microphone. This microphone sends sound to the camera via a radio transmitter attached to the groom's waist. Wireless microphones that are not "high band" may pick up interference from police radios or other radio equipment. High band microphones, on the other hand, can weed out most interference and produce a clean, clear "I do" on your tape.

Remember that audio is as important as video. When looking at sample tapes, listen for rough transitions or conversations that are cut off. Sloppy audio can keep you from following the sequence of events on the tape.

3 EQUIPMENT *"All this video camera stuff is so bewildering—I hear there are 8mm cameras, VHS, Super-VHS...I'm so confused! I can't even program my VCR! Help!"*

Well, you're on your own with the VCR. But we can help you to understand the different cameras used for wedding videography.

We've extensively interviewed videographers across the country, so here's the scoop. There are three broad categories of cameras: consumer, professional and industrial. Also, there are two tape formats most used by videographers: VHS and Super VHS (we've encountered very few videographers who shoot on 8-mm). In the next section, we'll explain more about videotape itself.

As for consumer-type cameras, you are probably familiar with their tape quality. Frankly, they aren't the best, clearest pictures we've ever seen.

In contrast, professional-grade cameras (called "prosumer" in the trade) provide much clearer pictures and brighter colors. These professional cameras (one such brand is the Panasonic ProLine) use advanced computer technology to produce better video.

The best professional cameras use "three-chip" technology—a separate computer chip to process red, blue and green colors. Unfortunately, these cameras are also quite expensive ($5000 to $15,000 in price!). As a result, only 10% to 15% of videographers use them. The balance use "one-chip" cameras.

Is it bad for videographers to use single-chip cameras? No, many combine single-chip cameras with Super-VHS tape to provide very crisp video. Are you confused yet? Well, in the next section, we'll try to explain why Super-VHS has become so popular.

What about industrial cameras? This category includes broadcast-quality cameras used by TV stations. These ultra-high priced cameras need bright light to produce good video and, hence, are rarely used by videographers who shoot weddings. Perhaps they're just overkill.

So, what does this all mean? Well, don't get bogged down in this technical mumbo-jumbo. What makes this even more challenging is the fact that video technology (cameras and formats) changes so quickly. The key is to look at the final product—the camera skills of the videographer are just as crucial as the type of equipment he or she uses.

4 THE VIDEOTAPE *"My maid of honor and bridesmaids are planning to give us a VCR as a wedding present from themselves and their spouses. They wanted to know whether we want a VHS tape player or a Super VHS player. What difference does it make and will the videographer be able to provide the right kind of tape?"*

Basically, the difference between VHS and Super-VHS machines is that the Super-VHS format provides more lines of resolution. Translated into English, this means the picture is even sharper for Super VHS tapes than for regular VHS tapes. The technology is moving toward Super-VHS, therefore you may want to get a machine that will play these tapes.

Many videographers are capable of producing either type of videotape. If you have to have Super VHS, check with the videographer before you make an appointment—some companies still shoot with regular VHS cameras.

What if the videographer shoots with a Super-VHS camera and all you have is a regular VHS player? Well, the Super-VHS tapes can be dubbed down to plain VHS.

5 CAMERA ANGLE *"Some sample videos I've viewed show the bride and groom only from the back or from strange angles in the church. Is there any way I can avoid such problems?"*

Some of the responsibility for these strange angles and shots belongs to the church or synagogue you choose. Many don't allow the videographer to move once the bride begins her walk down the aisle. They may also assign the cameraperson to a particular part of the sanctuary (like the back balcony!). This is why it is important to check with the policies of your ceremony site.

Also, it is just as important to have your videographer visit the ceremony site (even attending the rehearsal) to see where he or she will be setting up. This advanced preparation may help avoid those camera angle problems. Be aware that some videographers will scout out the ceremony site for free—others charge a fee.

Top Money-saving Secrets

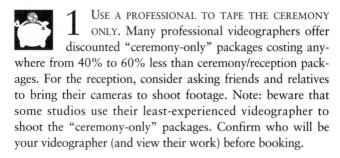 1 USE A PROFESSIONAL TO TAPE THE CEREMONY ONLY. Many professional videographers offer discounted "ceremony-only" packages costing anywhere from 40% to 60% less than ceremony/reception packages. For the reception, consider asking friends and relatives to bring their cameras to shoot footage. Note: beware that some studios use their least-experienced videographer to shoot the "ceremony-only" packages. Confirm who will be your videographer (and view their work) before booking.

2 HAVE A FRIEND TAPE YOUR WEDDING. *ONLY AS A LAST RESORT!* If you choose to go this route, make sure your friend or relative has a tripod (to avoid those wobbly shots) and plenty of extra batteries. We don't really recommend this strategy since the quality of consumer-type cameras is less than professional-grade equipment. Also, your guests may enjoy your wedding more if they aren't stuck behind a camera.

3 MAKE YOUR OWN COPIES. Instead of spending between $20 and $80 per copy for extra tapes from a professional videographer, copy it yourself with two VCRs. The quality will suffer dramatically, but the savings may be worth it. Or consider having a duplication service copy the tape for you. These firms charge about $12 to $15 per tape. Look in the phone book under "Audio/Visual Production Services."

4 NEGOTIATE LOWER RATES for less-popular wedding days/months.

5 ASK THE VIDEOGRAPHER IF THEY WILL DO A SCALED-BACK PACKAGE FOR LESS MONEY. Less bells and whistles (post-editing, fewer special effects) means less time for the videographer. Ask them if they can work out a "special package" that meets your budget.

6 REQUEST A VOLUME-DISCOUNT FOR TAPE COPIES. If you need several copies, the video company should be able to offer you a volume discount off their normal prices.

Getting Started: How Far in Advance?

 As with photographers, good professional videographers can book months ahead of the date. Popular summer months are often spoken for by January or February in many major metropolitan areas. In New York City, videographers are commonly booked up to two years in advance! We recommend you hire your videographer six to nine months in advance (as soon as you book a photographer).

Biggest Myths About Wedding Videography?

 Myth #1 *"We didn't think we wanted to hire a videographer for our wedding because the lights they use are so bright and obnoxious. Is there any other way to have a video done?"*

As we mentioned above, the newest technology in professional wedding videos are low-light cameras. These cameras use existing light or small spotlights to capture everything clearly on tape. One way to tell if a videographer uses overly harsh lights is to see how guests in sample tapes react when the camera is on them. Do they turn away from it? Do they squint into the camera? These observations and some questions about his or her equipment will calm any fears.

By the way, when videographers do use lights, they can avoid irritating your eyes by bouncing the lights off the ceiling. This is just one technique that separates professionals from amateurs.

Myth #2 *"I watched my friend's wedding video and found myself straining to hear the couple say their vows. We're writing our own vows and we really want to be able to hear what we say to one another on our video. Is it true that it's impossible to get clear sound on a video?"*

Sound quality depends heavily on the type of microphone. We recommend the use of a high-band wireless microphone attached to the groom's lapel. This type of microphone will overcome the disadvantages discussed earlier that come with boom microphones and hard-wired microphones. If you can't find anyone with a wireless high-band microphone, listen carefully to the sound quality on sample tapes and decide which offers the best sound.

Myth #3 *"I saw one sample tape that had interviews of the guests on it. I thought the interviews were kind of embarrassing and the guests seemed uncomfortable. Do I have to have interviews on my tape?"*

The answer is an obvious "no." We've seen several tapes where the best friend had too much to drink and related a sick joke. In another case, a guest suddenly has a microphone shoved into her face and makes a few comments that don't need to be saved for posterity.

Well this doesn't have to happen in your video. First, if you don't want any interviews, be specific with the videographer—especially if he or she has these segments on sample tapes. But if you do want interviews, choose a package that will allow you to edit out any embarrassing comments made by your guests. And don't forget to specify what kind of interviews you want. One couple we talked to asked their videographer to only interview relatives. Another couple only wanted guests who really wanted to speak on the tape. These precautions should help you avoid the "video from hell."

Step-by-step Shopping Strategies

 ❦ *Step 1:* Using the sources discussed above, make appointments with two to three video companies. Ask to see a demonstration tape or a tape of a recent wedding. If you contact a studio with several associates, make sure you will be meeting with the person who will videotape your wedding. As with photographers, each person's style is different, so meeting the actual cameraperson is key.

❦ *Step 2:* See the sample or demo tape of each company. Avoid looking at "highlight" tapes and instead view a complete wedding. Even better, ask if they can show you any wedding videos shot at your ceremony/reception site. Don't let the videographer fast-forward through any parts of the tape you want to see or hear.

❦ *Step 3:* Check for sound quality, harsh lighting or uncomfortable-looking guests. Make sure you can hear the vows. This is the most important aspect of the video—the part you want to capture. If the lighting is extremely bright, guests may squint or turn away. You want everyone to feel comfortable so watch this aspect carefully.

❦ *Step 4:* If this is an edited tape, ask yourself if the editing is smooth and professional. Does the tape have a home-movie feel or a raw-footage quality? Or is it seamlessly edited with a smooth flow? Is the video enjoyable or boring? Decide if the special effects (if any) add or detract from the video.

❦ *Step 5:* Make sure the personality of the cameraperson is pleasant. If you don't feel comfortable with this person, shop for another company.

❧ *Step 6:* Get references from previous customers. Ask these recent brides if they were satisfied with their tapes. Did they meet their expectations? If they had to do it over again, would they choose that same company? Checking references here is especially important since many video companies are young and some lack professional track records.

❧ *Step 7:* Once you have decided on a videographer, get a signed contract. Specify the date, time, place, editing and other special points. Make sure they note any preferences too: will there be any interviews, for example.

❧ *Step 8:* Meet with your videographer again closer to the wedding date to discuss any special people you'd like on your tape. It may even be a good idea to draw up a list of names. Also go over the sequence of events and talk about any changes or additions.

Questions to Ask a Videographer

1 WILL YOU ATTEND THE REHEARSAL? Are you familiar with my ceremony/reception site? These are critical questions since the videographer must determine the best angle, lighting options and sound needs for your wedding and reception. Many ceremony sites have specific rules about where the videographer can set up. Some sites may also present sound or lighting challenges—the more familiar he or she is with the site the better.

2 EXACTLY WHAT WILL THE FINAL PRODUCT LOOK LIKE? Find out how long the tape will be, what type of editing or graphics will be done or any additional touches that may be added. Often we've seen demo tapes with music synced to the action, fancy cursive graphics and even dissolves or other effects. Then we've been informed that all those options are extra on top of the package price. Watch out for these tactics.

3 WHO EXACTLY WILL BE SHOOTING MY VIDEO? Again, remember that some companies, especially in busy summer months, may send out unskilled amateurs to some of their weddings. Meet the actual videographer and see their work before booking. Unfortunately, some studios only assign their best camerapeople to the highest-priced packages.

4 ARE THERE ANY PHOTOGRAPHERS IN TOWN THAT YOU HAVE HAD DIFFICULTY WORKING WITH? The fit between photographer and videographer is critical—if they don't work together as a team, the scene may get ugly. Obviously, it may be dif-

ficult to get a truthful answer here since many videographers don't want to offend you or bad-mouth local photographers.

5 EXPLAIN YOUR GENERAL WEDDING SHOOTING SCHEDULE. This way you can find out what they do before the ceremony, whether they do interviews or not and how they expect the evening to run. All this helps you find the best videographer for your wedding.

6 WILL I GET THE MASTER TAPE AND HOW MANY COPIES COME WITH THE PACKAGE? The master tape is the original tape. Some videographers keep this and give you copies just as photographers keep your negatives. If you want the master, shop for a videographer with a different policy. As for tape copies, they are usually extra. Plan ahead for this additional expense. The cost per copy could range from $20 to $80.

7 DO YOU OWN YOUR OWN EQUIPMENT? Do you edit your own work? Do you have back-up equipment? If not, what plans do you have in case problems (equipment failure) arise? Do you offer a guarantee? All these questions will reveal how professional the videographer is.

8 WILL YOU TAKE A LITTLE TIME TO EDUCATE ME ABOUT VIDEO PRODUCTION? This is a trick question suggested to us by Bill Kronemyer, a New Jersey videographer. Bill told us you're not looking for a technical lecture but insights into the videographer's philosophy. The videographer should acknowledge that each wedding is different—and be honest about the shortcomings of his or her work. "Beware of the person who doesn't or can't explain things to you. Or one who thinks he's the greatest on earth. Deep down, he is probably insecure. Picking a down-to-earth 'realist' is often a better bet than a 'braggart.'"

Helpful Hints

1 CHOOSE A PACKAGE WITH ENOUGH TIME TO COVER THE EVENT. A four to six hour package should provide enough time to capture a typical wedding (allow more time for sit-down dinners or receiving lines). If you think your reception will go over, ask about overtime availability and charges. Some packages end when the cake is cut while others stay to the reception's end. Ask when overtime kicks in—if the cake is cut an hour late? What if the bride gets to the church 45 minutes late? Confirming the exact conditions that lead to overtime charges is important.

❧ Many uncontrollable factors can affect the quality of your video. For example, church P.A. systems can interfere with low-band wireless microphones. Another problem may be caused by your officiant or site coordinator. At one wedding we attended, the priest requested the videographer stand in a certain spot. The videographer thought she would have a good view of the couple's faces. However, the priest then decided to hold the entire ceremony with the couple facing the congregation. This left the videographer taping their backs for the entire wedding!

We feel its best to try to keep a sense of humor about these uncontrollable events. Most wedding videos are wonderful, and we highly recommend that couples consider having their weddings videotaped.

Pitfalls to Avoid

Pitfall #1
"DIRECTOR'S DISEASE"

"I was a bridesmaid in a friend's wedding recently and I was very shocked at the behavior of the videographer. He kept ordering everyone around, telling us what to do. Is there a way to avoid this problem at my own wedding?"

Occasionally, we've run into an inexperienced wedding videographer who suffers from that strange malady known as "director's disease." These camerapeople tend to expect weddings and receptions to conform to some sort of script for an all-star movie production. Instead of simply capturing the day as it happens, they try to direct the actors (bride and groom) in a performance (the wedding).

In many ways, however, a wedding is a videographer's nightmare—unscripted and unrehearsed, things often happen spontaneously. Experienced videographers will have discovered this fact and (hopefully) will adapt to each fun, yet frantic event on your wedding day. If you check references carefully and ask former brides about this aspect, you can avoid a videographer infected with "director's disease."

Pitfall #2
MISSING KEY EVENTS

"One of my friends complained that her wedding video was missing one of the events of the evening she thought was most important: her brother giving the toast. I don't want anything to be missed at my wedding. How can I prevent this?"

The bouquet toss, garter throw, toast and cake cutting among other things, are of paramount importance to most brides and grooms. Your videographer should at least be around for these events at your wedding. Amateurs and unseasoned professionals have been known to miss these events—be sure to check with references.

When you hire a professional, you should also meet with him or her prior to the wedding to discuss those things you want in your video. Be specific and have him write your preferences down. Also bring him a list of important people you want in your video.

Pitfall #3
AMATEURS WITH LOUSY CAMERAS

No need to beat a dead horse! Just avoid amateurs with lousy camera skills, trying to pass themselves off as full-price professionals.

Pitfall #4
BIG SCREEN TVs.
"My wedding video doesn't look very good on my parent's big-screen TV. It looked fine on our 19" TV—what's the problem?"

The problem with big screen TV is that it uses a projection process to get the picture onto the screen. Unfortunately, this process causes a video's resolution to suffer. In other words, most videos (including movies) may look fuzzy on a big-screen TV. Don't blame the videographer for this problem!

Pitfall #5
PERFECT DEMO TAPES WITH EXCELLENT ANGLES.
"In one sample video we saw, the bride and groom were perfectly visible throughout the entire ceremony. But in my friends' videos they were sometimes barely visible. What accounts for these differences?"

Beware of demo tapes that seem so perfect. For example, a video where the bride and groom are visible face-on throughout the entire ceremony is probably not realistic. Unless the videographer is real lucky, this seldom happens. Rarely does the angle and lighting work out perfectly every time. We suggest you ask to see a recent wedding video that the videographer hasn't returned to the couple yet. This way, you may be able to see a "real" version of a video, complete with any small imperfections.

Pitfall #6
NICKEL AND DIME CHARGES
"One video company in my area advertises a super-low price for wedding coverage. When I met with them, howev-

er, there were several 'additional charges' that inflated the package price."

We've heard this complaint from several of our readers. In Wisconsin, for example, we discovered a video company that charges extra for each microphone ($50 a pop). And, wouldn't you guess it, the videographer recommends *lots* of microphones. Other additional charges could include exorbitant fees for editing, music, graphics, special effects and tape copies. The best tip to avoid this is to get an "apples to apples" bid from several companies. Don't be fooled by super-low prices that seem too good to be true.

Trends

❦ *Splashier graphics and slick editing.* These new and constantly improving techniques make tapes less like home movies and more like Hollywood productions. Some unique additions we've noticed include dissolves and fades and even a technique called posterization (which freezes the picture and "colorizes" it). Adding still photos of your childhood at the tape's beginning and snapshots of your honeymoon at the end provides a complete video "album" feel to your tape. Of course, all these goodies tend to push up the price of packages.

❦ *Multi-camera shoots.* Having more than one camera at the ceremony may help the videographer catch different angles. When expertly edited, the effect reminds us of a slick TV production. The cost, however, naturally increases with each additional camera.

❦ *Combination photo/video studios.* Some photography studios have the attitude "if you can't beat 'em, join 'em" when it comes to video—many are adding "video divisions." Whether this involves sub-contracting out to another video company or actually having a "staff videographer," photographers have seized on the video trend as a lucrative side-line. Of course, just because the studio offers excellent photography doesn't mean they know beans about video. Be skeptical. Shop for each service as if they were separate companies.

Call for updates! By calling our special hotline, you'll hear the latest bridal bargains, trends and news! (See inside back cover for price information.)
(900) 988-7295

Chapter 12

Entertainment

From harpists to dance bands, choosing music for your wedding and reception can be challenging. In this chapter, you'll learn ingenious ways to find your city's best musicians. We'll also take an in depth look at the controversy between bands and disc jockeys as reception entertainment.

What Are You Buying?

 ❦ *Ceremony Music.* From royal weddings to simple civil ceremonies, music has been an integral part of wedding ceremonies for hundreds of years. However, the role music plays varies from religion to religion. The main issue is the difference between liturgical and secular music. Basically, liturgical music features sacred words from the bible while secular music does not. Policies about what is and what is not appropriate will vary from site to site.

Nevertheless, most churches have a staff organist or music coordinator who will help you with selections. Organists charge a fee based on the amount of time needed to rehearse, learn new pieces, etc. Other musicians (such as soloists, pianists, harpists) may also be employed for the ceremony. Ceremony music can generally be broken down into three categories:

1 THE PRELUDE. Typically 20 to 40 minutes prior to the ceremony, prelude music sets the mood. Even if you don't have specific pieces in mind for the prelude, you can tell the organist/musicians your preferences for happy, upbeat music or perhaps more somber, quiet pieces. Sometimes an eclectic mix of different tempos and musical styles is a nice compromise.

2 PROCESSIONAL/RECESSIONAL. Processional music heralds the arrival of the bridesmaids and, later, the bride to the wedding ceremony. At the end of the ceremony, recessional music is basically the music everyone walks out to. Typically, the slower processional has a more regal and majestic feel than the quicker-paced recessional music. Sometimes, different

musical selections are played for the entrances of the brides-maids and the bride. Or the same piece can be played at a different tempo as the bride enters the ceremony site.

3 MUSIC DURING THE CEREMONY. Soloists or the congregation's choir are often used during this part of the ceremony.

AVERAGE TOTAL COSTS: So, how much does this all cost? Most ceremony musicians charge $50 to $150 per musician per hour. Some may have two to three hour minimums. When you hire ceremony musicians, the only thing you may need to supply is sheet music for unfamiliar pieces. If you're having a string quartet, don't forget to provide chairs without arms so they can bow!

❦ *Reception Music.* Ah, now the party starts! Whether you plan to have only soft background music for listening or a raucous rock and roll bash, there are several aspects to what you're buying. For listening music (a harpist or string quartet), you may simply want to employ the same musicians who played at your ceremony. If dancing is preferred, you have two basic choices:

1 BANDS. When you hire a live band to play at your reception, you are contracting for a particular set of musicians to play a specified period of time. Most bands require periodic breaks throughout the evening and union rules may mandate break times. Bands provide everything (from instruments to the amplification system), but your reception site may need to provide a piano. Sometimes bands throw in a free hour of light cocktail music while guests dine. A specific repertoire of music is often implied in the contract—the best reception bands play a wide variety of music to please everyone's preferences.

So how much does a band cost? The price for four hours on a Saturday night can range from $500 to $5000. The key variable is the number of musicians and the popularity of the band. The majority of four-piece bands in major metropolitan cities charge $1000 to $2000 for a four-hour reception. Deposits for a band can range from nothing (which is rare) to one-third down.

2 DISC JOCKEYS. When you contract with a DJ, you basically get one DJ (plus, perhaps, an assistant), an entire sound system and a wide variety of music on albums, tapes or compact discs. Some DJs will add specialized lighting (colored spots that pulse to the music, for example) for an extra charge. Also extra may be rare or unusual song requests (such as ethnic music).

DJs are much less expensive than bands since, quite simply, DJs require less manpower. The average price for a professional DJ for four hours on a Saturday night can range from $200 to $1000. Most DJs in metropolitan areas charge $300 to $500 for a typical reception. Less experienced DJs may charge only $100 to $200, while in-demand club or radio DJs command higher fees than average. Deposits roughly average $100.

AVERAGE TOTAL COSTS: Overall, couples spend about $1000 on the average for music at the ceremony and reception.

Sources to Find a Good Entertainer

 Every major metropolitan area probably has a plethora of good wedding entertainers. The only problem is finding them. Ceremony musicians, reception bands and DJs typically keep a very low profile, choosing to work by word-of-mouth referral. Many of the most successful bands don't advertise their services. So how can you find these people?

❦ *Ceremony/reception site coordinators.* For ceremony music, the wedding coordinator at your ceremony site may be able to suggest a few names of harpists, soloists, trumpeters, etc. Music directors are also another source since they have worked in close contact with local musicians. For reception music, the catering manager at your site will undoubtedly have heard a wide variety of bands and DJs. Ask who really kept the crowd hopping. See our pitfalls section for a disadvantage to using this source.

❦ *Independent caterers.* If you are having your reception at a site where you are bringing in a caterer, you may ask that caterer for entertainment suggestions. Caterers often are reliable sources.

❦ *Wedding announcements in the local paper.* Here's a sneaky way of finding good entertainers. Some local newspapers print wedding announcements that often list the names of the musicians that played at the ceremony or reception. Call the ceremony or reception site to find out how to contact the musicians.

❦ *Music schools at local universities/colleges.* Many students who are talented musicians pick up extra bucks by performing at weddings and receptions. A nice plus: most are more affordable than "professional" musicians. Be sure to get a contract from them, however. Also make sure the student will be dressed appropriately.

❦ *Municipal symphony organizations.* Most symphony musicians moonlight by playing at weddings and receptions. Call your local symphony for any leads.

❦ *The union directory of local musicians.* Most cities have musicians' guilds or unions that publish a directory of members. If you know a musician who is a member, this directory may be a good source. However, in some parts of the country (like California), musicians that specialize in weddings are often not members of the local union.

❦ *Agents.* Last but not least, many bands and some DJs are booked through agents. Larger agents may book a wide variety of entertainers that specialize in weddings and receptions. In some cities dominated by unions, agents may be the only way to book a band. There are several advantages and disadvantages to using agents, which we will discuss later in this chapter in our spotlight "Agents: Helping Hand or Scum of the Earth?"

Top Money-saving Secrets

1 GET MARRIED ANY OTHER NIGHT THAN SATURDAY. Okay, we realize that this is not a popular alternative but few people realize bands/ DJs often give a 10% to 20% discount for Friday or Sunday weddings. Given the average entertainment cost of $1000, this could lower the music tab to $800. Total savings = $200.

2 GET MARRIED DURING THE "NON-PEAK" WEDDING SEASON. Obviously, this varies from region to region, but generally entertainers offer discounts for particularly slow months like January. Entertainers that would normally sit idle during these slow times might be willing to knock 5% to 10% off their regular rates. Ask and ye shall receive. Total savings = $50 to $100.

3 DON'T GET MARRIED IN DECEMBER. This is an absolute no-no. Corporate and private Christmas/New Year's Eve parties push up the demand for entertainers and (surprise!) up go the prices. One popular band we interviewed regularly charges $1450 for a typical reception. However, dates in November and December go for $2500 and (are you sitting down?) New Year's Eve goes for a whopping $4500. Enough said.

4 HIRE A DJ INSTEAD OF A BAND. DJs charge an average of 60% less than most live bands. If your parents can't stand the thought of recorded music at your wedding, a possible compromise could involve incorporating live music at the ceremony and then a DJ at the reception. We'll examine the

pros and cons of bands and DJs later in this chapter. If you go with a DJ, however, the total savings = $600.

5 IF YOU'RE ON A REALLY TIGHT BUDGET, MAKE TAPES TO PLAY AT THE RECEPTION. Many reception sites already have a sound system. By using your own stereo equipment and record collection (or borrowing from friends and relatives), you can record an evening's worth of entertainment for pennies. Besides your time, the only costs are for the tapes. Total savings = Who knows? Certainly mucho dinero.

6 SELECT A BAND WITH FEWER MUSICIANS. Prices for bands are often scaled to the number of musicians. Fortunately, today's technology enables a four-piece band to sound like an orchestra (or at least a larger band). That's because many synthesizers and drum machines can add a string section to a ballad, a horn section to a Glenn Miller tune or even Latin percussion to a particularly hot salsa song. We met one pianist who uses a computer and keyboard to simulate a several piece band for receptions. Another band we interviewed augments a live drummer with a drum machine to add a complex percussion track to current dance songs. Fortunately, couples today don't have to pay for an extra percussionist or horn section to get the same sound. Remember that every extra musician costs $75 to $150 per hour. For example, choosing a four-piece instead of a six-piece band could save $800 or more on a four-hour reception.

7 CONSIDER HIRING STUDENT MUSICIANS FROM A LOCAL UNIVERSITY OR COLLEGE. Many charge 20% to 30% less than so-called professional musicians. If you go this route, be careful to audition the musicians before signing a contract.

8 IF THE DJ DOESN'T HAVE THE ETHNIC MUSIC YOU WANT, BORROW IT FROM THE PUBLIC LIBRARY. Many public libraries have an extensive collection of music (from polkas to Madonna) all available to the public on loan. This is a cost-effective way of getting the music you want at a price you can afford.

Getting Started: How Far in Advance?

 Don't leave the music for your wedding and reception to the last minute. For ceremony music, you must give the organist time to learn and practice a special request. Meeting with the organist a month or two in advance will smooth the process.

For reception music, many of the best bands and DJs book up months in advance. In general, three to six months is enough time to book an entertainer in smaller towns and for the "off-peak" wedding months. In the largest metropolitan areas, popular dates (the summer months and December) book anywhere from six to twelve months ahead.

So what if you only have two months left to plan? Don't panic. You may get lucky and find a good band or DJ with an open date. It just may take a little more legwork.

Biggest Myths About Entertainers

Myth #1 *"I'd never consider having a DJ at my wedding. All DJ's are unprofessional, dress sloppily and play disco music. Yuck."*

We often hear this refrain from parents. Yes, its true that most DJ companies owe their entire existence to John Travolta and his infamous white suit. The good news is that most DJs have moved beyond disco and, with sophisticated equipment and a broad music repertoire, have become a credible threat to live bands. We'll discuss the pros and cons of DJs later in this chapter in "Canned vs. Fresh: Should you have a DJ or a band at your reception?"

Myth #2 *"For our reception, we've decided to hire a great band that plays in several local clubs here. Is this a good choice?"*

Be careful. A great club band does not necessarily make a great wedding reception band. The main reason is variety. Playing a wedding reception requires musicians to be "jacks of all trades." Not only must they play Madonna and Aerosmith for the bride and groom but they must also satisfy Mom's and Dad's request for Elvis and Grandma's request for Glenn Miller. Switching between the Rolling Stones and Benny Goodman can be vexing for even the best bands.

While good club bands may feature competent musicians, they often play to a narrow audience. For example at one wedding, we saw one great club band that did excellent covers of 60's standards. While the bride and groom and their friends loved this music, the parents and grandparents stood in the back of the room for most of the evening.

Of course, you can't please everyone all the time. However, bands should play music for all the generations present at a wedding. Before you hire that great club band, make sure they have a wide repertoire encompassing many musical eras.

Step-by-step Shopping Strategies

CEREMONY MUSIC
❧ **Step 1:** Find out your ceremony site's policy about wedding music. Realize that houses of wor-

ship often have varying policies about what is considered "acceptable" wedding music. For example, music like the "Wedding March" is not allowed at some sites because it's deemed too secular.

❦ *Step 2:* Meet with the music director of your ceremony site several weeks before your wedding. If you need to bring in musicians, use our sources to find three good candidates. Interview the musicians and discuss your ideas for the ceremony site music.

❦ *Step 3:* Ask to hear samples of various selections. If you're getting married at a church, ask the music director if you can attend a wedding ceremony. Listen to how certain pieces sound on the organ or other instruments.

❦ *Step 4:* If you hire outside musicians, get a written contract specifying the date, time, place and selections of music. Find out if the musicians/organist will come to the rehearsal (and if there is any fee for this).

RECEPTION MUSIC
❦ *Step 1:* As soon as you have your wedding date confirmed, start your search for an entertainer. Decide what type of music fits your reception. Some important considerations include:

❦   The time of day of your reception—For example, in the afternoon, most people do not feel like dancing. Perhaps a good choice here would be a guitarist to play soft background music. But, hey, its your reception so choose the music you want.

❦   The ages of the guests—You can't please everyone but selecting a band/DJ that plays a wide variety of music will help keep everyone dancing.

❦   The size of the reception—Typically, the "reception music axiom" says the larger the crowd, the bigger the band you need to keep the event hopping. In reality, a four or five-piece band can play a reception of 500 guests as easily as 200 guests. Do what your budget allows and don't get talked into a certain size band because you have X number of guests. For DJs, the size of the crowd may determine whether extra speakers/amplification are needed.

❦ *Step 2:* After deciding on the type of music you want, identify three good bands/DJs using our sources list. Call each of them on the phone and ask the questions we outline below. Ask to see them perform at an upcoming reception.

❧ *Step 3:* When you visit the reception, don't go during dinner time. Instead plan to stop in later in the evening around 10:30 when the dancing gets going full swing. Dress appropriately for a wedding and stand in the back of the room. Look for three key factors:

1 Is the band/DJ correctly reading the crowd? In other words, are they playing the right music for the guests at the wedding? Is anyone dancing? Are they ignoring one generation?

2 How much talking does the band leader/DJ do? Is this amount of chatter helping or hurting the reception? Do you like their announcing style?

3 Is the band/DJ professional? Are they dressed appropriately? Is the volume at a good level or a deafening roar? Is the entertainer varying the tempo, mixing fast and slow selections?

❧ *Step 4:* After you preview as many entertainers as time allows, select the band/DJ you want. Get a written contract that includes the specific date, hours and place as well as the price and overtime charges. Also get the names of the exact musicians who will be there and the instruments they will be playing. If you want, specify what dress you want the band members/DJ to wear. Finally, have specific sets of music written out such as your first song, special requests, etc. You may even want to attach a song list to the contract.

❧ *Step 5:* Remember that the better you specify the music, the more likely you'll get the music you want at your reception. Don't be ambiguous here by saying you want just "rock" or "dance music." Identify specific artists and songs and then star your favorites. For some artists, specifying a certain time period may be helpful (do you want old Rolling Stones or the more current Stones material?). Don't forget to clearly mark the song you want for a first dance.

❧ *Step 6:* Meet with the band leader or DJ a couple of weeks before the wedding to go over the evening's schedule and any last minute details. Meet them at the site if they're unfamiliar with it to gauge any needs or problems. This will enable you and the entertainer to identify a problem (the stage doesn't have enough electricity, the piano is untuned, etc.) and correct it before the wedding.

Questions to Ask an Entertainer

CEREMONY MUSIC

1 WHAT IS THE CEREMONY SITE'S POLICY ON WEDDING MUSIC? Does the church or synagogue have staff musicians or soloists? What is their fee? Don't assume anything is free.

2 DOES THE CHURCH HAVE ANY RESTRICTIONS ON THE MUSIC I CAN HAVE AT MY CEREMONY? This is a particularly sticky area since some sites may have numerous restrictions on what is deemed "acceptable."

3 DO STAFF MUSICIANS REQUIRE EXTRA REHEARSALS if I bring in some outside musicians too? Will there be an extra charge for rehearsals?

4 WHO EXACTLY WILL BE PERFORMING AT MY CEREMONY? Especially when you hire outside musicians, confirm the exact performers who will be at your wedding.

5 HOW FAMILIAR ARE YOU WITH MY CEREMONY SITE? Obviously this question is only for outside musicians. Inform them of any restrictions the site has on music. A pre-wedding meeting at the site might be a good idea in case there are any logistical questions (electricity, amplification, etc.)

RECEPTION ENTERTAINMENT:

1 WHO EXACTLY WILL BE PERFORMING AT MY WEDDING? Be very careful here. The biggest pitfall couples encounter with bands/DJs is hiring one set of musicians/DJs and getting another set at your wedding. See our PITFALL section for strategies to overcome this problem.

2 HOW DO WE CHOOSE THE MUSIC? A simple but critical question. How open is the band leader/DJ to letting you select the evening's music? Do they want you to submit a song/artist list? Some bands/DJs will interview you and your fiance to find out your musical preferences. If the entertainer is evasive about this question or replies that they "have a standard set they always play," you may want to look elsewhere.

3 CAN WE SEE YOU PERFORM AT A WEDDING? The best way to gauge whether a band/DJ is worth their asking price is to see them perform live. Most entertainers should let you attend an upcoming reception, with the permission of that bride and groom, of course. We've talked to some couples who feel uncomfortable attending a stranger's party—our advice is don't sweat it. No one will recognize you. If you can't see the band/DJ live, you might be able to view a video or listen to a demo tape. Another smart idea is to call a few recently-married couples for references. Ask the reference if there was anything they would have changed about the evening's entertainment.

4 HOW MANY BREAKS WILL YOU TAKE? Will you provide a tape to play during those times? Instead of having silence during a band's breaks, consider playing a tape of dance music to keep the reception hopping.

5 DOES THE PRICE INCLUDE BACKGROUND MUSIC DURING DINNER OR COCKTAILS? Some bands and DJs throw in a free hour of background music during dinner or cocktails. One band leader we met said he always throws in a free hour of cocktail music. Besides being a nice freebie for the bride and groom, this gives the entertainer an opportunity to scope out the crowd. Then, when the dancing begins, the band is better attuned to the music the guests want.

Helpful Hints

1 FOR THE CEREMONY MUSIC, REMEMBER THAT SHEET MUSIC IS OFTEN WRITTEN FOR ANOTHER INSTRUMENT THAN THE ORGAN. Hence, give the organist plenty of time (several weeks perhaps) to transpose and rehearse the piece so it's perfect by the wedding day.

2 SHOULD YOU FEED THE BAND/DJ? Obviously, this is up to you. You may not want to provide a meal to each band member at a $50 per plate sit-down dinner. However, at least try to arrange with the caterer to provide them with some snacks or sandwiches. Remember that bands/DJs have to be at the reception a long time, and a well-fed entertainer performs better than one with an empty stomach. Whatever your decision, inform the band leader/DJ about food arrangements before the wedding.

3 TRACKING DOWN OBSCURE ETHNIC MUSIC. Unfortunately, the mall record store rarely stocks ethnic music today. Hence, DJs may find it challenging to locate certain songs. A better solution may be to let them borrow your family's records or tapes. Specifically point out the songs you want.

Pitfalls to Avoid

Pitfall #1
BAIT AND SWITCH WITH BANDS AND DISC JOCKEYS
    "My fiance and I saw this great band perform at a friend's wedding so we hired them for ours. At our reception, different musicians showed up and it just didn't sound the same."

This is perhaps the #1 problem brides and grooms have with their reception entertainment. We've known some agents and band leaders who play "musical chairs" with backing musicians—sometimes known as "pick-up bands." Here a group of musicians are thrown together at the last moment— and the lack of rehearsal shows. You might hire a certain "name brand" band but then the band leader substitutes some different (and possibly inferior) musicians at your reception. Hence, you don't get what you paid for, that is quality entertainment. Large DJ companies with several crews are also guilty of this tactic. You can prevent this deceptive practice by specifying in a written contract the exact musicians/DJ you want at your wedding. Stay away from agents, band leaders or DJ companies who won't give you a straight answer.

Pitfall #2
CHATTERBOX BAND LEADERS AND DJs

"We recently attended a wedding where the band leader incessantly talked to the crowd. No one found this constant chatter amusing and it detracted from the elegance of the reception."

Band leaders and DJs often have their own "schtick"—a certain routine they do at a wedding. It's up to you how "energetic" you want the band to be since, of course, it's your money. Don't be surprised by a chatty band/DJ. See them perform at another reception before you sign that contract. If you have any doubts, ask them about the amount of talking and tell them what you believe is appropriate for your reception.

Pitfall #3
DECEPTIVE DEMO TAPES.

"We heard a demo tape from a band that sounded great. But later we saw the same band and boy was it disappointing! What happened?"

Some demo tapes are produced in studios where a battery of sophisticated electronic equipment can make the weakest band sound like a stadium headliner. Add a little reverb to the vocals and clean up the guitar with some equalization and poof! Instant superstar band! In the harsh reality of a live performance, however, none of these studio tricks can save a lousy band. Listen to the demo tape for "style," not production quality. Beware the slick demo tape and try to see the band perform in person.

We heard about a twist on this scam from a band leader in Boston. We call it the "Milli Vanilli syndrome." Some bands don't just "clean up" their demo tape in a studio, but use *entirely different* musicians to record the tape! That's right, the band pictured on the video tape is *not* the one that's recorded the soundtrack.

Pitfall #4

KICKBACKS AND "REFERRED" LISTS.

"My wedding site recommended a musician that turned out to be lousy! Meanwhile, several great musicians in my town are nowhere to be found on their 'recommended list.' What's going on here?"

A problem with some wedding-site coordinators (as well as catering managers at reception sites) is the question of kickbacks. Believe it or not, some of these folks demand fees (we call them kickbacks) to be listed on the site's "recommended list" of musicians. A harpist in northern California told us this unscrupulous practice is rampant there. Ask the coordinator whether the site takes fees from recommended musicians. If you don't get a straight answer, be careful.

Trends in Wedding and Reception Music

So what's hot with wedding and reception music?

❦ *New technology.* Compact discs have enabled DJs to provide crystal-clear sound, replacing scratchy vinyl and mediocre cassette tapes. In the live music world, bands now have access to increasingly sophisticated computerized synthesizers and drum machines. With these computers, bands can add a phalanx of horns or a dash of strings to their "basic" sound, enabling them to compete better with a DJ in music reproduction.

❦ *DJs are replacing bands at many receptions.* To find out why, see our spotlight, "Canned vs. Fresh: Should You Have a DJ or a Band at Your Reception?"

❦ *Ethnic music and bands.* Mariachis are chic in the Southwest, while a good polka band is still in vogue in the Midwest. Couples are not only celebrating their own family heritage but also reflecting a new cultural diversity. One recently married Anglo couple in Miami had a Caribbean-flavored reception complete with a hot salsa band. When their caterer asked why they selected this theme, the couple responded that this was the music they grew up with.

❦ *Music from the 1950s and 1960s.* Reflecting radio's current fixation on "classic rock," many bands are playing more hits from the "early history" of rock 'n' roll. Motown music (à la *The Big Chill*) is still popular.

❦ *At the ceremony, the "Wedding March" is being replaced by a wider variety of classical and modern music*. This is partly due to some churches forbidding this song on religious grounds. To others, the song has become too cliched.

Special Touches to Make Your Wedding/Reception Music Unique

1 PERSONALIZE THE WEDDING AND RECEPTION MUSIC WITH YOUR FAVORITE SONGS. Of course, the type of wedding music may be restricted by your ceremony site. However, incorporating special songs that have personal meaning for you and your fiance is a great way to make your celebration unique. Before the wedding, give the band leader/DJ a list of special requests.

2 INSTEAD OF STANDARD ORGAN MUSIC, CONSIDER DIFFERENT MUSICAL INSTRUMENTS. The combinations here are endless. Many couples love the combination of harp and flute, while others attest to the regal splendor of a single trumpeter. Classical guitar (as well as violin) are beautiful alternatives.

3 USE ETHNIC MUSIC TO CELEBRATE FAMILY HERITAGE. Several weeks before the wedding, talk over the possibilities with your band/DJ. Some songs may take a band time to rehearse or DJ time to track down.

4 IF YOU'RE UNSURE ABOUT CLASSICAL MUSIC FOR YOUR CEREMONY, consider ordering "Processionals and Recessionals for Traditional Weddings." This tape has a sampling of 30 different selections, plus a booklet that explains each song. Produced by Seven Veils Records, it can be ordered by calling (512) 288-1044. The cost is $14.95 plus $2 shipping.

Spotlight

"Canned vs. Fresh: Should you have a DJ or a band at your reception?"

DJs are often the Rodney Dangerfield of wedding reception music—they just don't get any respect. For example, we've read many other books on weddings that don't even mention DJs as an entertainment alternative. Instead, *Emily Post's Complete Book of Wedding Etiquette* suggests "a full orchestra" complete with a "string section for soft background music before the dancing starts." We don't know about you, but hiring a forty-piece orchestra with accompanying string section was just a teensy bit out of our wedding budget.

According to Emily Post, if you're having a small, informal wedding, "a record player provides adequate and lovely music." Nowhere are the words "disc jockey" mentioned. Even more disturbing is the venerable *Bride's Book of Etiquette (5th Edition)* which, after talking at length about the merits of "small orchestras" at weddings receptions, says "taped, pre-recorded music is a good alternative when live music is not available." Of course, instead of mentioning DJs, the book suggests you "ask a music buff friend to pre-mix your selection on one long-playing tape."

Hey! What's going on here? Do the etiquette fanatics who write this dribble just have their collective heads in the sand or is there a conspiracy to deny the existence of DJs? If all these wedding experts are convinced that only live orchestras are appropriate for wedding receptions, then explain to us why disc jockeys dominate reception music in most major cities?

Well, let's take a look at why DJs are so popular. Of course the number-one reason is cost—DJs cost only $300 to $500 for an evening, compared to the $1000 to $2000 fees bands demand. With the cost of a wedding soaring, couples are obviously opting for the affordable alternative.

Perhaps a more subtle reason may be the state of pop music today. Almost all the music you hear on the radio is programmed on computerized synthesizers and drum machines. For a live band, trying to reproduce this music is perilous at best and embarrassing at worst. Sure, bands can play Glenn Miller and Johnny Mathis rather realistically, but many reception bands we've heard make every modern song they attempt sound like "New York, New York."

To their credit, DJs have also cleaned up their act in recent years. Many companies are now professionally-run businesses with tuxedo-clad DJs and professional sound equipment. This is a far cry from the late 1970's, when less-formal DJs spun mind-numbing disco hits complete with throbbing disco lights. Of course, disco is still with us (under the new label of "dance music") but many DJs diversified their music collection to include rock, country & western, and rap, as well as the hits from the 50's, 60's and 70's.

In fact, musical versatility is one of the top reasons couples choose DJs. Since most weddings feature several generations of guests, a good mix of music is a must. While some bands play a variety of music, many are most proficient at one or two musical genres. The lack of variety is one of live bands' biggest disadvantages.

Another plus for DJs: they never take breaks. Most DJs play music continuously, unlike bands which need to take breaks every hour. Just when the crowd gets into a particular groove, the band shuts down for five to ten minutes.

Obviously, this can kill the mood. With a DJ, the beat never stops until the party ends.

So what does Emily Post suggest if you want continuous music? Hire two orchestras, so one can play while the other is on break. We are not kidding here. That's what she really suggests. Can you believe it?

Of course, we could rattle off a million advantages of DJs over bands but that wouldn't phase those hard-line etiquette gurus. With their noses firmly planted in the air, they'd say something like "only live music such as a combo or orchestra is appropriate for a proper reception."

According to our research, DJs are now the #1 entertainment choice at receptions, with live bands a close second. Of course, bands dominate in some areas, especially in cities with a thriving live music scene (i.e., New Orleans, some East Coast cities, etc.). Also, bands are still the most popular choice for those large "society" weddings.

Sure, we admit that watching a live band crank out "Louie, Louie" is more visually interesting than seeing a DJ play the same song via vinyl (or laser with compact discs). All we are saying is don't get bullied by the etiquette police into hiring a band when a professional DJ might fit your musical (and financial) preferences better.

Spotlight

Agents: Helping Hand or Scum of the Earth?

So, what exactly is an entertainment agent? People in these businesses function as middlemen between bands or DJs and consumers. An agent's primary activity is booking bands and DJs at various engagements—in return they receive a commission. The standard commission is 15% of the band's regular performing fee.

Now, the power of agents varies from city to city. In cities with stronger musicians' unions, agents tend to proliferate. In general, we've found agents more likely to dominate older cities such as New York and Chicago than sun-belt towns like Atlanta and Dallas.

Agents cite several reasons for their existence. First, they can more effectively market the bands to engaged couples by pooling their resources. Also, many band leaders (who have other daytime jobs) hate the paperwork associated with deposits, contracts, etc. Agents do all the legwork and remove the administrative hassles.

Fine, you say, but what can an agent do for me as a

consumer? Well, agents provide "one-stop shopping," enabling you to make one call and get information on a wide range of bands and DJs. If you are in a hurry or just aren't aware of the entertainment options in your area, an agent can certainly help. Agents don't charge you a fee for their services, instead they collect a commission from the bands.

As you might imagine, some entertainers are less than enthusiastic about giving agents a 15% cut of their salary. Many of the entertainers we interviewed for this book held unanimously negative opinions about agents. And, frankly, we've met some agents who could be charitably described as "scum of the earth."

The main gripe we have with agents is their lack of "product knowledge." Too many just book a band or DJ without giving thought to whether their music is appropriate. Other agents deny brides and grooms the right to preview the band/DJ at a wedding before booking—a cardinal sin in our view.

Another major factor in this controversy: many bands say off the record they will give brides and grooms discounts off their regular rates if they book them directly. For example, one band told us they would knock off 15% (which, of course, is equal to the agent's commission) from their $2000 normal reception rate—that's a savings of $300, no small potatoes.

Agents respond to our criticism by claiming they can save brides and grooms money. One agent told us agents "can get a lower price because they do a volume of business with a band, whereas a band leader contacted directly can get very greedy." Furthermore, agents claim that legitimately professional band leaders will keep their prices the same—whether the booking comes directly or from an agent.

Well, we've "mystery shopped" dozens of bands and DJs and have yet to find any entertainer quoting a fee over their "regular rates." (After we posed as a engaged couple, we later confirmed their rates from agents and other sources). Agents have never quoted us a rate lower than the normal fee, and we often found many professional band leaders who offered a quiet discount when approached directly.

So what should you do? We recommend you try to book a band or DJ directly if you have found them from one of our sources listed above. If you are short of time or can't find any good entertainment options, call an agent. Be careful to check out any band or DJ the agent recommends before you sign that contract. You might even call the local Better Business Bureau to make sure the agent is on the up and up. Most importantly, make sure the agent lets you meet the band to talk over the music, scheduling, and other reception details.

Whether you book a band or DJ directly or through an agent, follow the tips in this chapter to make sure the reception music is everything you've imagined.

Chapter 13

Etcetera

From limousines to wedding consultants, this chapter gives you advice and tips on some fun, yet miscellaneous topics. Plus, we'll examine those new all-in-one companies: wedding-in-a-box or time saving convenience?

Limousines: Getting to the Church on Time

What Are You Buying?

 ❦ *The Limousine* A stretch limousine has several basic amenities that qualify it as a limousine. These include an extra long body, plush carpeting, a stereo, possibly a TV, sunroof and telephone, and a privacy window as well. More luxurious models have been known to contain even a hot tub or other interesting amenities.

Non-traditional forms of transportation include horse-drawn carriages, antique cars and even buses or trolleys. These options will probably not include the types of amenities mentioned above, but they will have their own versions of luxury.

❦ *The Driver* Every type of transportation you hire will include a driver. The driver should be dressed appropriately, either in a dark suit and chauffeur's cap or a black tuxedo.

AVERAGE COST: Limousines will cost approximately $60 to $125 per hour. Usually, they have a three hour minimum rental time, with the total cost for the car between $180 and $375 per car per evening. The driver is paid with an additional mandatory gratuity of about 15%. For non-traditional transportation, the cost usually starts at $100 and goes up depending on the vehicle you rent.

Sources to Find Transportation

 Some sources include the Yellow Pages under "Limousines," "Carriages-Horse" or under "Wedding Services." By all means ask a recently married friend for recommendations and look for information about transportation companies at bridal shows.

Top Money-saving Tips

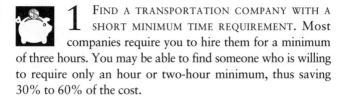

1 FIND A TRANSPORTATION COMPANY WITH A SHORT MINIMUM TIME REQUIREMENT. Most companies require you to hire them for a minimum of three hours. You may be able to find someone who is willing to require only an hour or two-hour minimum, thus saving 30% to 60% of the cost.

2 CONSIDER A "PICK UP-DROP OFF" SERVICE. Often this will cost you much less than hiring someone for three hours.

3 HAVE YOUR WEDDING ON AN OFF-NIGHT. Some companies offer deals for brides having weddings during the week.

4 RENT A LUXURY CAR. Many car rental companies rent Cadillacs and Lincoln Continentals for as little as $50 to $75 per day. While you'll need to have someone else drive, this is a big savings over a limo.

5 CONSIDER HIRING A "REGULAR LIMO." These are regular luxury cars—not the stretch variety. Many limo companies offer these cars at reduced rates.

Getting Started: How Far in Advance?

 For most limousine companies, you may not need to start looking until a month or two before your wedding date. If limos are popular in your area for weddings and you have a wedding date in the busy wedding months, consider planning three months in advance. For carriage companies, you may also have to plan farther in advance because the demand is greater and the supply smaller.

Step-by-step Shopping Strategies

 ❦ *Step 1:* Using the sources mentioned above, find two or three companies you want to talk to.

☙ *Step 2:* Find out what type of vehicle you will be hiring. See if you can visit the company and see the cars or carriages. Get details on available options, minimum required hours and the cost per hour.

☙ *Step 3:* Visit the company. Check to see how clean the cars are and what amenities they have. Find out who will be driving the car and what they will be wearing.

☙ *Step 4:* Consider calling the National Limousine Association to find out if the company you want to hire has adequate insurance and is licensed. These folks can give you that information or at least inform you of how to find it for yourself. Call the NLA at (800) NLA-7007.

☙ *Step 5:* Choose the company you like the best and get a contract detailing the car you like. Make sure the date and time are clearly written. As you get closer to your wedding day, call to remind them of your date and time.

Questions to Ask a Transportation Company

 1 WHAT AMENITIES ARE AVAILABLE?

2 WILL WE BE ABLE TO BRING CHAMPAGNE? Will you provide us with ice and glasses? Some companies will allow you to bring alcohol while others will even supply it. In some areas, it is illegal for the company to provide the alcohol, but they will bring ice and glasses for BYOB.

3 HOW MUCH IS THE GRATUITY FOR THE DRIVER? Typically, you aren't given a choice about how much the gratuity will be. Gratuities range from company to company, so check around before you buy.

4 DO YOU HAVE ANY DISCOUNTS AVAILABLE? As we mentioned above, many companies will discount their service for week nights. Other discounts may be available if you hire more than one vehicle or if you hire them for longer time periods.

5 DO YOU SPECIALIZE IN WEDDINGS? Those companies that do may have special bridal packages or other freebies.

Pitfalls to Avoid

 Pitfall #1
COMPANIES THAT DON'T SHOW UP.
This is one of the biggest problems with limou-

sine companies. We recommend you check with the Better
Business Bureau in your area if you have any questions about
a limo service. Checking with the city agency that licenses
limousines will also determine whether the company you are
considering meets local requirements.

All-in-one Companies

Wedding-in-a-box or
Time-saving Convenience?

All-in-one companies are difficult to describe because
they encompass a wide range of businesses. The term "all-
in-one" itself may be rather misleading, since we are referring to any bridal business that combines two or more elements involved in a wedding. For example, an "all-in-one"
could be merely a florist combined with a caterer. More
often these businesses provide a wider range of services such
as photography, flowers, catering and even a reception site.
Of course, there are those few businesses that literally take
on everything imaginable: apparel, invitations, cakes,
videography and so on.

Many all-in-one wedding companies are trying to provide brides with a "one-stop shopping" alternative—almost
like a wedding mall. On the East Coast, some reception
sites offer "complete wedding service:" flowers, photography, videography, catering, limos, cakes, favors, tuxedos,
gowns and even furniture. Just add a groom and poof!
Instant marriage!

Problems with All-in-one
Wedding Services

1 SPREADING THEMSELVES TOO THIN. Instead of doing one
service well, many all-in-one companies do several services poorly. For example, we met one caterer who also offered floral arrangement services. While the food looked
great, the flowers weren't impressive.

2 MASS-PRODUCED WEDDINGS. Because these companies
offer so many services, they often "standardize" their
options. While this streamlines their business, it makes for
weddings that have all the appeal of a fast-food burger.
Instead of having your wedding reflect your personal tastes,
all-in-one companies tend to fit all brides and grooms into
one mold.

Our recommendation: Use an all-in-one company for just
one or two of their services. You don't have to hire them for
the whole package. If someone recommends an all-in-one
company for their catering, realize that you don't have to use
them for their photography, etc.

How-to Waltz Videos, Mail-order Catalogs & Other Fun Stuff

The band at your reception strikes up your favorite song,
but there is only one problem: you don't know how to dance!
Well, Blanche and Emilio Liberero, dance teachers in Tampa,
Fla., have come to your rescue. They put together "Waltz at
Your Wedding," ($29.95 plus shipping), a 35 minute tape that
teaches you how to box step, turn, promenade and more. Call
(800)443-5641 to order.

Now that you know how to dance, what's the perfect
song to start the evening? If you're tired of *Daddy's Little
Girl,* Mikki Viereck, a wedding entertainer in Springfield,
Mass., has come to your rescue. She's written *A Song for My
Son* and two other ballads especially for brides and grooms.
Mikki told us she came up with the idea after hearing complaints from mothers that there was no dance that could pair
them with their sons. The songs have received rave reviews;
the *Boston Globe* said, "If *A Song for My Son* doesn't bring
a tear to your eye, turn to the obit pages. You may have
passed away already." CDs, tapes and sheet music are available from New Traditions Music at (800) 447-6647.

Looking for an affordable photo album? You might want
to order the Exposures catalog, (800) 222-4947. This
Wisconsin-based company offers a wide selection of interesting albums, picture frames, scrapbooks, and a few gift items.

Speaking of gifts, are you tearing your hair out trying to
find a nice gift for the bridesmaids and groomsmen? Tired of
the standard earrings or money clip? Here are some gift catalogs that may be able to solve this dilemma:

Anticipation	(800) 556-7376
Attitudes	(800) 525-2468
Coldwater Creek	(800) 262-0040
Hammacher Schlemmer	(800) 543-3366
Hold Everything	(800) 421-2264
Potpourri	(800) 388-7798
Smithsonian	(800) 322-0344

Bridal Shows

Fun Afternoon or Highway to Bridal Hell?

If you need a good laugh, attend a bridal show in your town. If you aren't convinced that the wedding "industry" is a joke, this is the place to give your cynical side a booster shot.

Basically, most bridal shows attempt to stage a fashion show (we use the word *show* here very loosely) and a trade fair. The latter consists of various booths with displays from merchants with names like "Brides R Us" and "Fred's Professional Wedding Photography." Like sharks smelling blood in the water, these merchants crawl out of their subterranean homes and swim circles around brides, passing out little gifts such as potpourri balls, which emit such a pleasant perfume that it takes three months to get the smell out of your purse.

The fashion show is the alleged bait to get you (the consumer) into their (the merchants') clutches for two hours of unabashed commercial plugs. During this fashion show, you will actually see live and in person many of those hideous bridesmaids' gowns that you only thought existed in the bridal magazines and in the backs of closets.

After hearing the announcer say for the twentieth time, "Here's a lovely taffeta design with PUFF SLEEVES" you'll probably be able to actually feel your teeth grind.

What's most interesting about these runway shows is the realization of how far removed the bridal apparel industry is from reality. If you look closely, you'll notice the "new design for this year" looks suspiciously like one from a wedding you attended in 1982.

After the show and the nonstop commercial plug-a-thon ("Yes, Bob, we'd love to thank Burt's Wedding Chair Rental for providing the chairs you're sitting in today! Aren't they just lovely! And they're just $3.95 plus deposit!"), you have time to walk around the booths and chat with local merchants. Many of these merchants will lunge at you from their booths and shove a brochure in your hand while simultaneously complimenting you on how LARGE your engagement ring is—all with a look of sincerely feigned sincerity. While visiting a recent bridal show, we were struck by the sheer ingenuity of wedding entrepreneurs who have invented brilliant ways to separate you from your money. Our favorite was a woman who was selling "lucky pennies" for brides to put in their shoes so brides won't break one of those sacred bridal superstitions. Each "lucky penny" was wrapped in tulle and tied with a ribbon. Cost: $5. We're not kidding.

Perhaps the best known bridal show operator is Bridal Expos, based in that state known for bridal bliss, New Jersey (just ask Bruce Springsteen). Bridal Expos mounts this massive multi-media show that admittedly is much more polished than the typical dog-and-pony show put on by locals. Slickly choreographed, the Bridal Expos are thick with plugs for the Official Sponsors.

What's most hysterical about the Bridal Expos is that these folks from New Jersey think that the world is simply dying to see what newest horror the New York bridal designers are trying to heap on us consumers. At one show in Denver, we couldn't help but notice the crowd noticeably guffawing at several bridal gowns that some designer must have dreamed up in his Manhattan office during a bad acid trip.

The biggest scam at all these bridal shows are the so-called door prizes. As you enter, most bridal shows will ask you to register for A FREE EXCITING HONEYMOON TRIP TO NEPAL. Of course, besides your name and address, the "registration card" will ask for your phone number, fiance's name, yearly income, birth place, blood type, and so on. As you wander around the booths, the wedding merchants will ask you to fill out entry forms for such tantalizing door prizes as "A FREE NAPKIN (WHEN YOU PURCHASE $1000 WORTH OF PICTURES)!"

As you fill out the forms, you'll noticed the merchants and show organizers will barely be able to keep the drool from dripping down their shirts in sheer excitement. That's because this whole thing is a big sham—what these bridal shows really want is your phone number and address. Then they can call you frequently at dinner time to inform you that they have a BIG SPECIAL this month and that if you sign up NOW you won't be killed by their bridal death squad.

Yes, bridal merchants pay hundreds of dollars to do these shows and THE BIG REASON is that list of brides, all neatly alphabetized with their home phone numbers, wedding date, bank account numbers, and more. Many brides are alarmed to find after they've attended a bridal show that they must buy a six-foot mailbox with forklift to handle the volume of mail that will give new meaning to the word junk.

The lesson? If you've got an afternoon to kill and would like to overdose on sugar from 67 cake samples, then a bridal show may be for you. But, if you value your privacy, be careful out there.

Wedding Advertising Publications

It takes approximately six to eight seconds from the time you get engaged until you get deluged with advertising publications that pretend to help you plan your wedding. Let's take a second to look at these local bridal "books" and "magazines."

We use the words "books" and "magazines" liberally here because what these things are are pure advertising masquerading as "helpful information." For example, some company in Texas actually published a "bridal resource guidebook" for a large city that claimed to be an "independent" survey of the area's best bridal merchants.

What the publisher forgot to mention was that they insisted bridal merchants pay a $200 "service fee" to be included the book. The book does say, and we quote, "many other quality and 'excellent-rated' businesses were invited to participate in our first edition. However their consent may not have reached us by the publishing deadline or they may have chosen not to be listed." TRANSLATION: the best merchants in town refused to pay our ad fee so we left them out of our "independent, unbiased" survey. Only the merchants that coughed up $200 are in here.

Of course, the publisher also forgot to say that the merchants wrote their own descriptions in this book. And that's the way it goes in bridal land—the lines between editorial and advertising are often nonexistent. Of course, considering how "ethical" the big bridal magazines are, you can understand why local publishers have no scruples.

Here are a few publications that you may come across (or have shoved in your face) during your bridal journey:

1 **The Wedding Pages.**
This Omaha, Nebraska company claims to produce the "yellow pages of the bridal industry." This slick planner is packaged in a work-book (read: large and clunky) format. Over 90 versions of the book are produced for different cities. Graphics and such insightful bridal advice as "weddings often include dancing as part of the reception festivities" are interspersed with ads for local wedding merchants.

Perhaps the best thing that can be said about *The Wedding Pages* is that it's free. Of course, there's a catch. You must fill out a card at a local *Wedding Pages* dealer (typically, a jeweler or bridal shop) and then wait a few weeks for delivery. The catch is your name (and address, phone number, wedding date and birth date) then goes on a mailing list which is sent faithfully by the company to local wedding merchants. Soon, you'll receive little love notes from such companies as "Bill's Wedding Candles" and other firms that want to sell you customized cake knife corsages. Your only clue about this comes in a sheepishly worded disclaimer at the bottom of the order form: "acceptance of this Wedding Planner may subject your name to other solicitations."

A darker side to the *Wedding Pages* is their attempts to block discounters from advertising in their book. We spoke with a Discount Bridal Service rep in one city who was blocked from advertising in the local *Wedding Pages*. Why? Well, the publishers don't want to offend those full-price bridal retailers by accepting the discounter's ads.

We spoke to Doug Russell, the VP of Marketing for the *Wedding Pages*, who said they have no official policy on discounters and "let the franchisee make the decision on who can be a *Wedding Pages* sponsor in their respective markets.

The franchisee has the right to do business with whom ever they feel will benefit them the most." In one city, after they let a discounter advertise, eight other bridal shops boycotted the *Wedding Pages*, pulling their ads. Obviously, the *Wedding Pages* is letting full-price retailers censor their publication—a practice we find disgusting, in our opinion. And the fact that the *Wedding Pages* lets their local franchisee make the decision on discounters is a cop-out. But, there's big bucks in those ads.

ONE TIP: *The Wedding Pages* asks for your phone number on their order form. Our advice is don't give it. They don't need it to send you a copy and you don't need the invasion of privacy.

2 **The Wedding Guide.**
This is the other big bridal advertising publication. Unlike the *Wedding Pages*, the *Wedding Guide* is less of a fill-in-the-blank planner and even more of an advertising vehicle for its sponsors.

In a smaller, stapled format, the *Wedding Guide* is more transportable than the *Wedding Pages*, but that's the best we can say about it. The gimmick here is the same: the Denver-based company produces a generic advice book with local ads. Merchants who advertise in the guide are provided copies to give away free. Before you can take one, however, many ask you to fill out a card to win some "prize giveaway." Don't be fooled, they want your address for the same reason the *Wedding Pages* wants it: to put you on a mailing list.

On the upside, *The Wedding Guide* has a center section of coupons that offer discounts. On the downside, the advice in *The Wedding Guide* is predictably schmaltzy. In an article titled, "Building a Healthy, Vital and Loving Marriage," the book says, "Lovely gowns, champagne bubbles, stolen kisses and parties in your honor currently fill your life and it feels wonderful." Ugh.

3   *Other Local Magazines and Books.*=

A few cities have local bridal magazines. *Best Weddings, (800) BEST-WED,* is a slick magazine that includes ads and listings for local bridal merchants. Editions are available for Washington D.C., Atlanta, Denver, Nashville, Boston, Miami, Tampa, Dallas, Houston, Chicago, Detroit, St. Louis, Baltimore, Los Angeles, and Philadelphia. Give them your mailing address (hint, hint) and they'll send you one free.

In New England, you can check out *New England Bride Magazine,* (508) 535-4186. *The Wedding Directory,* (617) 878-5931, focuses on reception sites and wedding services in Massachuesetts. For New York brides, the *Down the Aisle Directory,* (212) 779-4219 provides information on the tri-state area. *Great Locations II* is a videotape of sites in the New York City metro area. Call (212) 727-2424 to order.

Unique Meeting Places in Greater Washington, (800) 289-2339, is a book that provides site information. The same company offers a similar book for Baltimore. Also, *Washingtonian Magazine* has an annual wedding planner issue in January. Call (202) 296-1246 for the latest information.

For Midwest brides, *Planning Your Chicago Wedding Magazine,* (914) 347-2121, gives info on the Windy City. *Chicago Special Occasion Sourcebook,* (312) 828-0350 focuses on ceremony/reception sites. Iowa brides can find bridal information in the book *Des Moines Weddings* (515) 224-1358.

In California, *Here Comes the Guide,* (510) 525-3379, is a book that covers sites and services in northern California and the Bay Area. *Weddings West* is a magazine that primarily covers California (available on newsstands). If you're planning a wedding in Southern California, check out the Wedding Library in Orange, CA (714) 997-1579.

As we mentioned earlier, *Places* (212) 737-7536 has site information for major metropolitan areas. If your wedding is not in any of the above cities, check with your local bookstore or newsstand to find a local wedding magazine or guidebook.

Wedding Consultants

The 1980s saw a return of a member of the wedding not

seen for thirty years: the professional wedding consultant. Once a fixture of weddings in the 1950's, wedding consultants were hunted to near extinction in the 1970's when weddings were less formal affairs usually held on a beach.

As weddings have become more complex and formal events, professional wedding consultants have made an impressive comeback. We should note, however, that there are several types of wedding consultants. Many people who work at bridal shops or retail florists call themselves "wedding consultants." In addition to helping the bride with their own specialty, these folks pass along referrals of other bridal professionals. While they may be helpful, these are not the wedding consultants we are referring to in this section.

We define a "professional wedding consultant" as an independent business person who, for a fee, helps plan and coordinate the entire wedding. They don't actually bake the cake or sew the gown—this is done by outside suppliers. In a sense, a wedding consultant is a glorified valet or personal shopper.

So How Much Do Wedding Consultants Cost?

Most charge an hourly fee or a percentage of the wedding budget. For example, one consultant we met charges a 15% fee on the wedding expenditures. So, if you spend $10,000 on a wedding and reception, you then write out a check for $1500 to the consultant. Other party planners we met charge a flat hourly fee ($75 per hour, for example) no matter what your budget. Many consultants offer different levels of help—coordinating just the rehearsal and wedding ceremony costs a small fee, while planning the whole affair from "ground zero" will run you much more.

Sources to Find a Consultant

❦ **Call the Association of Bridal Consultants at (203) 355-0464.** This organization will give you the names of a couple wedding consultants in your area. Another new group of consultants is the Association of Certified Professional Wedding Planners. They can be reached at (408) 269-5683.

❦ **Ask your friends.** The best wedding consultants work by word-of-mouth referrals.

Questions to Ask a Consultant

1 Exactly how do you work your fees? Do you accept commissions or finder's fees from other bridal merchants? See our PITFALL section below for more information on this practice. Ask the consultant to clearly explain his/her fee schedule.

2 How will you incorporate my tastes into the wedding? If the consultant will be doing the majority of the legwork, ask them how they will account for your tastes. Will they get your approval at various stages in the planning process?

3 How long have you been a consultant? How many weddings have you planned? This is a key question. Many "consultants" we've talked to were far too inexperienced to trust your wedding to. Some have been in business for less than a year or so. We recommend you trust your wedding only to a seasoned professional with at least three years minimum experience. Sure, consultants with less experience can still plan and coordinate a beautiful wedding—but be careful. You don't want someone "learning the ropes" on your big day.

Pitfalls to Avoid

Pitfall #1
CONFLICT OF INTEREST

"I visited a wedding consultant who recommended I buy my wedding gown from a particular bridal shop. Later, I learned the shop paid her a commission for recommending me. Is this legitimate?"

Well, it certainly isn't ethical. This points up a central problem we have with some less-than-professional consultants. In a clear conflict of interest, some consultants collect "finder's fees" or "commissions" from other bridal merchants on the products and services they recommend to brides. So who are they representing—the bride or the businesses? We don't believe a consultant can negotiate effectively for the bride when they receive a kickback from bridal merchants. If you use a consultant, make sure the consultant clearly identifies how they get paid.

Pitfall #2
PERCENTAGE-BASED FEES MAY ENCOURAGE GREED.

"One bridal consultant told me she could save me hundreds of dollars. However, her fee is based on a percent-

age of the money I spend. Where is her real incentive to save me money?"

Of course, a professional consultant relies on word-of-mouth referral for new clients. If they don't deliver what they promise, word will spread quickly. However, we do agree that a conflict exists here: when their income is based on how much money you spend, less-than-ethical consultants may feel the temptation to encourage lavish spending. Or at least, the incentive to save you money comes in conflict with their bottom line. Realize that all consultants do not charge a percentage-based fee—others charge flat fees or hourly rates. This might be a better alternative.

Pitfall #3

COUNTERFEIT CONSULTANTS.

"I called a so-called 'wedding consultant' from the phone book. Instead of offering a consulting service, she pitched me on her wedding chapel and reception site."

Yes, many "all-in-one" wedding companies deceptively advertise themselves as wedding consultants. Don't be fooled—these businesses aren't interested in consulting on your wedding. They just want you to book their wedding and reception site, photography and so on.

Pitfall #4

LACK OF REGULATION.

"I contacted a wedding consultant to talk about my wedding. Boy was I surprised! This person knew nothing about weddings. Aren't these guys suppose to be licensed?"

Unfortunately, very few laws regulate wedding consultants. When you think about it, wedding consultants are quasi-financial planners—they advise people on how to spend money. Unlike other financial planners, however, there is very little regulation. Anyone can call themselves a wedding consultant. Just print business cards and poof! Instant expert! Some cities do require wedding consultants or party planners to be licensed. In most areas, however, the industry is left to police itself. Consider hiring a consultant who is a member of a professional association. Many require the members to subscribe to a basic ethics pledge. Other groups offer on-going training through seminars and workshops.

Advantages of Consultants

❦ *Bridal consultants can save you time.* If you and your fiance are working too many hours to plan your wedding, you may find a wedding consultant to be worth the expense. Frankly, planning a wedding is very time-intensive. Realistically evaluate your schedules and time commitments to decide if you can handle it alone. Brides planning large and expensive wedding may find consultants a necessity.

❦ *Long-distance weddings may require such help.* Planning a wedding in another city is quite challenging. Having a local bridal consultant to coordinate the details may be prudent.

❦ *Seasoned experts may be able to negotiate more effectively, getting you a better deal.* Now we aren't talking about novices here but wedding consultants with years of experience. These people are on a first-name basis with catering managers and other bridal professionals. Some consultants are tough negotiators who can make sure you get the best price. Other consultants claim that other bridal professionals have a vested interest in doing their very best work for their clients—if they don't, they may lose future business. We are not sure to what extent these claims are true but we do believe one thing: a talented, experienced consultant may be worth the extra expense.

Disadvantages of Consultants

❦ *The Association of Bridal Consultants does have a few problems.* One bridal consultant told us she didn't belong to the ABC because "my dog can join that group." Lack of rigid membership standards have soured some wedding planners on the group. Also, the group's training amounts to optional home-study courses that some call "simplistic."

Another bridal consultant in California told us she dropped out of the ABC because she found their workshops disappointing. The workshops were more applicable to the Northeast, she said. (The ABC is headquartered in Connecticut.)

We spoke to the ABC about these problems. They admit that anyone can join the group, but they must subscribe to the code of ethics on the application. While this is nice, it probably explains why we have met several ABC wedding consultants who just didn't know what they were doing.

As for the complaint about workshops, the ABC told us they try to make their training as generic as possible.

Regional questions are handled by the state coordinators (of which there are 16). State-wide newsletters also address regional issues.

On the upside, the Association of Certified Professional Wedding Consultants requires in-depth training, two years of experience plus recommendations from brides and wedding professionals *before* planners can be "certified." While the group is newer, this approach may yield better results for brides.

So what does this mean for you? If you interview a consultant who is a member of the ABC (or any professional group), don't assume they are all-knowing "experts." Check references and ask some tough questions to weed out the amateurs.

If you have any questions or comments about this chapter, please feel free to call the authors. See the "How to Reach Us" page at the back of this book!

PART III

Weddings
Across America

Chapter 14

Weddings Across America

Here's a quick quiz. If you are at a wedding and encounter a Mandelringstarta, what would you do? If you answered "run like hell," guess again. The correct answer: eat it. That's because a Mandelringstarta is a Swedish wedding cake made from rings of almond pastry. If you don't live in Minnesota (with its large Scandinavian population), you probably have never come to face to face with a Mandelringstarta. Which brings up a point: weddings in the U.S.A. are anything but uniform.

Weddings vary greatly from region to region, state to state and even city to city. What's a time-honored tradition in one town is a major social gaffe in another.

Take the relatively straight forward concept of a "wedding reception," for example. In the Northeast, this means a formal sit-down dinner. Suggest such a reception in Texas (or for that matter, anywhere in the South or West) and you'll get weird looks from caterers. Cocktail receptions with "heavy hors d'oeuvres" are the norm in those regions.

You get the idea. While the "wedding press" often reports on nuptial traditions in New York or Los Angeles, there's nary a word on wedding customs in places like Memphis, Denver, or Seattle. We wondered, hey, how are couples tying the knot in the U.S.A.?

In order to find out, we conducted telephone interviews with nearly 30 bridal consultants across the country. (Our special thanks to the Association of Bridal Consultants, whose members graciously shared their insights with us). What follows is a city-by-city look at weddings in the U.S.A.

Atlanta, Georgia

Weekend Weddings Popular
in Gateway City of the South

Spring is the most popular time to tie the knot in Atlanta. "In April, the blooming dogwood trees, tulips and azaleas make this an extremely impressive time of the year, especially for out of town guests," said Michele La Motte, a wedding consultant in Atlanta for two years. Another big wedding month: October. The beautiful fall weather makes that time popular as well.

"A real highlight of Atlanta weddings are all the unique sites to have wedding ceremonies and receptions," Michele said. Among the top spots is the Callanwolde Mansion. Also known as the Coca Cola Mansion because it was built by the family that founded that little soft drink company, the Callanwolde is a Tudor-style mansion that has beautiful gardens as well as a rare organ inside. The site is so popular that it books at least a year in advance.

Another popular spot is the Atlanta Botanical Gardens. While you can't get married in the gardens, you can have a ceremony and/or reception in the large exhibit hall which holds 350 seated. The large, beautiful room has huge windows that look onto the gardens.

Atlanta is blessed with many Antebellum homes that can used for ceremonies and receptions. Popular Bulloch Hall is where Teddy Roosevelt's mother was born and raised. Other homes "are loaded with history from the Civil War," she said.

"We're suggesting that families totally budget $125 to $150 per guest for a wedding in Atlanta," said Sue Winner, another Atlanta bridal consultant who has done many Jewish weddings in the area. Hence weddings cost anywhere from $15,000 to $30,000 with an average of about 150 to 225 guests.

There is good news on the cost front: our sources in Atlanta say that many sites are willing to negotiate on prices for weddings during "off-peak times." Examples include weddings at noon, Sundays and slower months like January, February, March and July. For those off-peak weddings, hotels often throw in extras like complementary honeymoon suites or hospitality rooms. At other sites, that $60 bottle of champaign may come down in price by $20 or more.

Sue Winner, who is also the Discount Bridal Representative for Atlanta, said that brides are selecting more formal, elegant gowns. Sheath gowns and the "off-the shoulder look" are currently in vogue. Popular designers include Galina, Christos, Ilissa and the Diamond Collection.

Traditional flowers such as roses and stephanotis are often incorporated into cascade and presentation bouquets. "One popular style for bridesmaids bouquets are lace fans decorated with silk and fresh flowers," Michele added.

Receptions in Atlanta often feature buffets with carving stations of country ham or roast beef. Cheese straws, a Southern favorite, are perennial hors d'oeuvres. Other popular buffet dishes include Greek phyllo pastries (perhaps because of Atlanta's large Greek community) and various fish and salmon dishes.

Sit-down dinners at local hotels are a close second in popularity. "We are very much into the nouvelle cuisine," Sue said. "There is a lot more fish being served but we still see a fair amount of chicken."

Wedding cakes are often three-tiered confections of vanilla cake, decorated with fresh flowers. Other favorite flavors include amaretto as well as raspberry and peach fillings. Cheesecake weddings cakes (with each tier a different flavor) are also popular. Of course, the Southern tradition of groom's cakes (with strawberries cascading down the side) is prominent in Atlanta. With the recent recession, however, some couples have forgo the groom's cake and incorporated chocolate into the wedding cake.

Formal bridal portraits taken before the ceremony are not popular in Atlanta. Instead of a portrait on display at the reception, Michele said "many couples have at the sign-in table a display of photos from childhood as well as their dating days." Videos are in but party favors aren't. At most, satin roses filled with birdseed are given to the guests.

At the ceremony, "programs are real popular. These list who's who in the wedding party and a background of how the couple met each other." Also at the ceremony, Michele told us that the father of the groom is the best man at the majority of weddings. Large wedding parties are currently in vogue. "It's not unusual to see eight bridesmaids and twelve to fourteen groomsmen at an Atlanta wedding," she said.

"Weekend weddings, with events arranged from Thursday evening to a brunch on Sunday morning, are quite popular today," Michele said. Since there are so many things to see in Atlanta, out-of-town guests are often given a hospitality bag with brochures and maps for sightseeing.

A trend in rehearsal dinners is toward a casual picnic that features Southern fare: fried chicken, barbecue, and biscuits. And for dessert? Pecan pie, of course.

Special thanks to Michele La Motte, 864 Cinderella Ct., Decatur, GA, 30033, (404) 299-6091. Sue Winner, 333 Sandy Springs Circle, Atlanta GA 30308 (404) 255-3804.

Boca Raton, Florida

Putting on the Ritz for Weddings in Boca Raton

Boca Raton, Florida. Beach front weddings? Informal gatherings of friends at sunset? Think again.

The average wedding in Boca Ration costs $20,000. And, as you might imagine, those weddings and receptions are not on the beach. So says Dona Rayne, a former wedding planner in Boca Raton.

"The winter months are quite popular for weddings," Donna said. "When you're inviting many out-of-town guests its wonderful to bring them from the cold climate" to sunny Florida. Unlike the rest of the country, summer weddings are not as popular because of the summer heat.

The "in" reception sites? The Boca Raton Hotel and Club (a five star hotel) is popular as well as the Count Hoernle Pavilion, a restored train station. Other favorite sites include the tony Polo Club and Addison's, a local restaurant. Yachting receptions at sunset are quite popular alternatives to hotels.

Whether on land or at sea, black-tie, sit down dinner receptions are the norm, Dona said. Popular dishes include exotic veal, chicken and fish entrees. Besides a dessert like chocolate mousse, the wedding cake is typically a stacked confection covered with fresh flowers. Preferred flavors in Florida include amaretto, strawberry, pineapple, white chocolate mousse and even cheesecake. The cake is often put on a riser to be the focal point of the reception. After dessert, guests dance the night away to five or six piece orchestras.

Dona said Boca Raton brides are selecting apparel that is "classic, sophisticated and yet traditional." Favorite designers include Priscilla and Bob Mackie. For flowers, contemporary cascades of exotic flowers like calla and rubrim lilies are quite popular as are European country looks.

Favors are still given to guests at many weddings, "though not as popular as they used to be," Donna said. Potpourri-filled sachets and bags filled with chocolates are the most popular gifts.

With most wedding traditions, Southern Florida is less like its Dixie neighbors and more like the Northeast. For example, groom's cakes (the Southern dessert staple) are a rare sight in the Sunshine State.

Finding a good videographer is almost more important than a photographer, Dona told us. The video productions are "marvelous," she said, adding that the tapes often feature snazzy special effects.

Other wedding trends in Boca Raton: "bridal presentations" before the ceremony. Here, the bride and the groom see each other before the ceremony, exchange gifts and take pictures. Then the couple can go directly to the reception without the usual delay for photography.

Boston, Massachusetts

Moving Away from the Sit-down Dinner Reception

Estates and hotels are the most popular places to tie the knot in Boston, says consultant Elizabeth Gemelli of Weddings by Elizabeth, a Boston-based wedding consultant.

"Friday night is becoming a fun night to have a wedding," Elizabeth said. While Bostonians still adore June weddings, October is quickly gaining in popularity.

Weddings in Boston are somewhat smaller than in other cities, averaging about 150 guests. Nevertheless, Elizabeth said her clients spend $20,000 to $25,000 for a wedding reception. While Bostonians invite fewer guests, they tend to spend more per guest for the reception, according to one hotel catering manager who worked in Boston for eight years.

A large part of the wedding budget is for a sit-down dinner, still the mainstay of Boston receptions. However, Elizabeth told us she's noticed a new trend.

"Many of my clients don't want that typical, sit-down boring dinner," she said. "Now, they're doing cocktail receptions where they have heavy hors d'oeuvres and food stations. They might have a wok station, a pasta table, a roast beef station and so on," she said.

For apparel, Boston brides are still wearing traditional gowns "no matter how young or old they are," Elizabeth said. Popular designers include such hometown favorites as Bianchi and Priscilla. One hot custom designer is Pat Tatiana, who has a shop on Newberry St.

Tradition is less popular in wedding flowers, Elizabeth said. "Many brides are having a range of colors in their bouquet, just not the all-white ones." Fresh flowers are less popular as decoration for wedding cakes. Instead flowers made from marzipan icing are popular.

"Years ago, wedding cakes here tasted awful. Now they're so good that they are often served as dessert. Not many people are sending the cake home in boxes anymore."

While the flavor has improved, the prices of wedding cakes in Boston have increased. Elizabeth told us the average cake that serves 200 guests costs $500 to $600, but that can go even higher. One cake at a reception she did last year cost $1800.

"No one has that standard white cake anymore," she

said. "Chocolate has become very popular—many people also have dessert tables here."

Wedding photographers in Boston are doing more candid and creative pictures than posed shots, she said. Bridal portraits are rare but wedding videos that cost $900 on the average are quite popular.

Special thanks to Elizabeth Gemelli, Weddings by Elizabeth, 621 Main St., Waltham, Mass., 02154, (617) 932-2580.

Cleveland, Ohio

Ethnic Foods Add Spice to Cleveland Weddings

Food, glorious food! That's one of the most unique items at a Cleveland-area wedding. And are the options incredible! Thanks to the large Polish, Slovenian and Italian populations in the area, you might find dishes like pieroghis (potato or sauerkraut filled pastries), keifles (rolled dough filled with nuts and fruit) or cannolis (Italian pastries filled with cream). Sausages and stuffed cabbages are other favorites that might appear.

Ethnic traditions are making a comeback in other areas of Cleveland weddings, according to Donna Pincura, a wedding consultant in Avon Lake near Cleveland. Donna told us "a lot of the young people are going back to their roots." This may include special ethnic dances at the reception such as the "Dollar Dance," where guests have to pay to dance with the bride.Many weddings take place in reception halls rather than in restored homes or hotels. One such hall is the American Slovenian Hall; another is De Luca's Place in the Park. Balloons are among the most popular decorating options according to Donna. For her son's recent wedding they had balloon arches decorating Wagner's Country Inn.

Most Cleveland brides are choosing to hire DJs rather than bands for their wedding receptions. Weddings are usually rather large, topping 250 to 300 guests. But what most surprised us were the bridal showers. Donna told us many ethnic showers invite 100 to 200 guests! And every guest takes home a plate of pastries and cookies from the shower! Wow!

Dessert tables are also popular at the wedding along with the wedding cake. Wedding cakes are no longer traditional white cakes, but may be marble or chocolate and often include a filling. Guests also receive favors in Cleveland, according to Donna. Usually they are small items such as mini champagne glasses filled with almonds and wrapped with tulle.

Special thanks to Donna Pincura, Timeless Traditions, 32795 Briarwood Ct., Avon Lake, Ohio, 44012, (216) 933-9400.

Weddings in Texas

Big Weddings in the Lone Star State
(Dallas, Houston, Austin, San Antonio)

As Texans like to point out, everything is big in Texas. And weddings are no exception.

"The average wedding in Texas has between 200 to 300 guests—and weddings with over 500 guests aren't uncommon," said Denise Coopwood, co-author of consumer wedding guides to Dallas, Houston, Austin and San Antonio.

In the state's capital, Austin, brides have several lovely reception sites to choose from. The Caswell House is a beautifully restored Victorian home built in 1900. Another popular spot is the Texas Federation of Women's Club, an elegant mansion that oozes Southern hospitality. The Green Pastures Restaurant and Four Seasons Hotel are two other favorite sites.

Elegant hotels are popular for receptions in the Dallas/Fort Worth Metroplex. Among the best include the Crescent Court, the Grand Kempinski and the Mansion on Turtle Creek. Another favorite site in Big D is the Camp Estate at the Dallas Arboretum, a beautiful home that overlooks White Rock Lake. Of course, you can even get married at the famous Southfork Ranch.

In Houston, brides prefer to have receptions at many of the city's beautiful country clubs and restaurants. The Junior League Tea Room and the River Oaks Garden Club are two standouts, as well as the lush grounds at the Rainbow Lodge and Vargo's restaurants.

Private clubs are also popular in San Antonio. Many of the city's most popular reception sites are located along the picturesque River Walk downtown. Other romantic sites in the Alamo City include the majestic Black Swan Inn and the grounds at the Witte Museum.

Most Texas brides choose traditional bridal gowns with detailed trains. Popular designers include Bianchi and Galina, as well as local favorites like Watters and Watters in Dallas and P.C. Marys in Houston.

Bridal bouquets in Texas are often cascades of orchids, lilies and roses. Native wildflowers like bluebonnets are favorites for spring weddings, a florist in Austin told us. Contrary to popular belief, however, yellow roses aren't common in Texas weddings!

Most wedding receptions in Texas feature hors d'oeuvre buffets; sit-down dinners are rare. One caterer in Dallas told us Texans like to eat things they can identify. Hence, barbecue and Mexican food is "in"; gourmet dishes with

French names are "out." "The most popular wedding cake flavor in Texas has to be Italian Cream," an Austin baker told us, adding that chocolate groom's cakes are a staple at receptions. To match those big weddings, Texas bakers are often called upon to create cakes that tower six feet in the air. A Taste of Europe in Fort Worth, for example, has a seven-foot cake that serves 500 people! Covered in hand-sculpted hard-sugar flowers, this cake costs $1250!

Wedding photographers in Texas often take a formal portrait of the bride prior to the wedding. This is then displayed at the reception. Video is extremely popular in the Lone Star State—nearly three-quarters of all receptions are taped.

June is still the biggest month for tying the knot in Texas, despite the summer heat. December and October are a close second, however. Christmas and New Year's Eve weddings have become increasingly popular over the last few years.

The cost for a wedding in Texas varies from city to city. In smaller cities like Austin and San Antonio, most weddings cost $7000 to $12,000. Those costs can soar to more than $15,000 and $25,000 in Dallas/Fort Worth and Houston.

Denver, Colorado

Weddings in Mile High City

As you'd expect, weddings in Colorado are closely entwined with the beautiful scenery. Carla Harbert, a Denver wedding planner, told us that while "most of my brides want to go to the old mansions," they often schedule a half hour between the wedding and reception to have pictures taken in a local park. Equally popular among Carla's brides are weddings in the foothills and even in mountain towns like Vail or Aspen.

Carla told us that her average wedding consists of about 100 to 150 guests on a Saturday evening. "September is usually one of the nicest months," she told us because the weather is at its best. August is another popular month.

Most brides are traditional in their choices, she told us. The most popular bridal gown styles in Denver are sophisticated, heavily beaded gowns with plenty of lace. Designers like Ilissa, Bill Levkoff and Watters & Watters are popular. Some brides, especially those who get married at the Museum of Western History, opt for Jessica McClintock styles to continue the western theme of the wedding.

Wedding flowers are also incorporating more sophisticated looks. Elegant flowers such as calla lilies, iris and cattleya orchids are popular, especially designed in contemporary, high-style bouquets. Carla told us that some exotic varieties like bird-of-paradise and anthurium are also popular.

Brides in Denver also tend to prefer heavy hors d'oeuvres for reception food rather than sit-down dinners. Sliced beef with rolls, poached salmon, crab wontons and shishkebobs are among the more popular items served. Carla mentioned that Denver brides are trying to offer more healthy foods instead of the typical meatballs in sauce.

Carrying through the healthy theme, brides prefer to serve beer, wine and champagne at Denver weddings and are moving away from hard alcohol. An interesting note: among younger brides in Denver, a cash bar is often seen.

"Very customized" is how Carla describes wedding cakes in Denver. She has seen varieties ranging from lemon cake with raspberry filling to poppyseed with cream cheese icing. Cheesecakes are also increasing in popularity. Designs tend to be tiered with basket weaves or other simple looks and fresh flowers are the usual final touch.

Finally, Denver brides are developing some new traditions of their own. Since many ceremony sites prohibit birdseed or rice, balloon releases are becoming a popular alternative.

Indianapolis, Indiana

Balloon Releases and September Brides in Hoosier Capital

September weddings and balloon releases are popular in Indianapolis, Indiana, according to former Indianapolis wedding planner Mary Smith.

The beautiful fall foliage makes September and October very popular months to tie the knot in Indianapolis, Mary said. The average wedding has 125 to 150 guests and costs $3000 to $6000. While Indianapolis has few outdoor locations for weddings and receptions, several restored homes and mansions are popular. One local favorite, the Schnull-Rauch House, is booked up to a year in advance. Eagle's Crest and Hideaway at Eagle Creek Reservoir are two other popular spots.

Indianapolis brides are choosing many contemporary designs for bridal gowns. "This year we have seen a real increase in mermaid and sheath-style gowns—I think this reflects the sophistication of local brides," Mary said. What's out? "The ruffled, Southern belle, Scarlet O'Hara look is not popular." Ilissa is a popular designer "because they have so many sophisticated styles. Unfortunately, Ilissa also has a sophisticated price tag." Many Ilissa-knock-off labels, Alfred

Angelo, and San Martin are top designer requests.

Floral motifs can be summed up with one word: roses. Beside appearing in bridal bouquets, many bridesmaids carry single, long-stem roses. White cascade bridal bouquets are favorites; specific flowers that are also popular include gardenias, carnations and orchids.

Indianapolis wedding receptions are most often light buffets that feature hors d'oeuvres, regardless of the time of day. Swedish meatballs are the #1 favorite. Chicken wings, veggies, finger sandwiches and shishkebobs are also popular. Jewish and Greek weddings often feature a colorful mix of ethnic foods.

Fountains are the favorite decoration of wedding cakes, Mary said. Satellite cakes connected by bridges and staircases are still in, while the traditional "white cake" remains the fave rave flavor. Chocolate wedding cakes (iced white) are a close second (however, groom's cakes are a rarity).

DJs are the most popular entertainment choice and most receptions are videotaped (though mainly by a relative). Instead of throwing rice or birdseed at the end of the reception, balloon releases have gained in popularity.

Mary's advice to Indianapolis brides: Plan in advance. Many sites book up to a year in advance, though many brides try to plan a wedding in just six months.

Kansas City, Missouri

Nuptials in Heart of America

With home-town designer Paula Varsalona setting the tone for wedding gowns, it's no wonder that Dodie Jacobi, local Kansas City wedding consultant, told us that "fairy-tale" gowns are the rule. She said that the typical bridal gown is "very detailed with a full train and veil." Many brides choose Varsalona's high-style gowns especially since her company has a big promotion every year in Kansas City.

To complement such stylish gowns, Kansas City brides stick with traditional floral arrangements like all-white cascades with roses and gardenias. Dodie told us that the trend is toward less church decoration which helps brides save money. Popular bridal colors include pink, teal, peach and electric blue. Black and white are popular among couples who choose them as "statement colors."

A trend toward smaller ceremonies is giving Kansas City weddings a more intimate feel, Dodie said.

Flowers are also coming into vogue as decorations on wedding cakes. Cakes are becoming more creative, with exotic flavors like amaretto and Grand Marnier.

If brides don't use fresh flowers to decorate the cake, they stay with traditional icing flowers for decorations.

For the rest of the reception food, Dodie sees a majority of cake, punch and light hors d'oeuvre receptions. Gaining in popularity are seated dinners, which caterers are pitching as a better value. Common hors d'oeuvres include canapes, roast beef on rolls, fresh fruit and veggies. "Most people are sticking to basic approaches" with reception food and many brides serve beef or barbecue, she said.

Dodie told us about two very unique wedding sites in Kansas City. The first is the Swope Memorial Monument in Swope Park. This beautiful hilltop memorial overlooks the entrance to the park. Another popular site is the Loose Park Rose Gardens.

Most Kansas City brides prefer the "journalistic approach" to wedding photography because "they want more candid shots," she said. Overall, couples are hiring photographers who offer fewer posed pictures and more action shots. As opposed to years past, more couples are opting for have a professional video of the wedding.

Kansas City does have three large ethnic communities (Italian, Jewish and Hispanic) that have traditions of their own. One common Italian tradition is to have a dessert smorgasbord with Italian cookies and pastries. What isn't eaten, the guests take home!

Dodie, also a local wedding columnist for *Kansas City Star*, offered some of the best advice we received during our interviews. Primarily she suggested that brides "look for ideas in unusual places" rather than relying on traditional outlets. Brides should decide what parts of the wedding are their highest priorities and spend their money on those things. She also offers this advice about etiquette: making people comfortable is the idea of etiquette rather than following Emily Post word for word.

Special thanks to Dodie Jacobi, Designs & Details, 6880 Sni-A-Bar Rd., Kansas City, MO, 64129, (816) 923-0198.

Louisville, Kentucky

Mixing Southern and Midwestern Traditions in Bluegrass Country

Kentucky weddings are an interesting blend of Southern and Midwestern traditions. For example, June, August and September are big wedding months (like their neighbors to the North) but many foods at the receptions are decidedly Southern in character: groom's cakes are a common sight, especially in the southern part of the state.

Buffet receptions are standard for most Kentucky weddings, according to Jo Ann Smith, a wedding consultant for three years in Louisville. "Rumaki (an interesting combination of chicken liver and water chestnut wrapped in bacon) is a popular hors d'oeuvre," she added. Other popular dishes include, of course, Kentucky ham served on biscuits, various pâtés, miniature quiches and pastry shells filled with chicken salad.

Dancing is popular at many receptions, with disc jockeys the preferred entertainment choice. "People like to boogie down here," she said.

Jo Ann told us the typical wedding in Louisville costs $8000 to $9000, with an average of 200 guests. Saturday afternoon weddings from 4 to 6 PM in a local church are most common, with a reception site following in a local hotel. Other popular reception sites include the Star of Louisville (a cruise ship on the nearby Ohio River) and the Water Tower Association (run by the Louisville Visual Arts Foundation), which offers a beautiful view of the city. Several other restored homes of Victorian architecture are choice spots. In nearby Lexington, the Marriot's Griffin Gate Resort is the quintessential Southern Mansion.

Sunday weddings are also a new trend, Jo Ann told us. Many informal and second weddings are held on Sundays as well as Friday nights, she said.

For the bridal gowns, "everyone wants a long train," Jo Ann said. Full skirts, beading and intricate designs are in; the "fairy-tale ruffle look" is out. "Brides are also going more for the sleek, elegant look, I've noticed," she said. Kentucky brides' most favorite designers include Demetrios (Ilissa), Alfred Angelo and Eve of Milady.

Roses and stephanotis are popular flower choices, Jo Ann said. "The basic style would be a cascading bouquet for the bride and a nosegay for the bridesmaids," she said, adding that attendants sometimes will carry a single long-stem rose. Silk flowers are also big.

Flowers often decorate the wedding cake, which is typically a three or four-tier white confection. Satellite cakes are common. The most popular flavor is white cake. At some receptions in Kentucky, dessert tables also feature walnut squares, chocolate-dipped strawberries and, of course, bourbon balls.

Memphis, Tennessee

Serenading the Bride in Volunteer Country

If your looking for an unusual ceremony tradition, check out what's going on in Memphis, Tennessee.

According to Pat McKenzie, one groom in Memphis started a unique tradition when he dropped to his knee during the ceremony and serenaded the bride with a love song. Perhaps this is Elvis' legacy.

"The guests loved it. He did an excellent version of the song. Now, more grooms have done it. It certainly breaks the monotony of the same old thing," she said.

December is the big month for weddings, which typically have about 250 guests. "Weddings used to be held here at six or seven in the evening. Now, afternoon weddings are most popular. Most people get married here at 2 PM so they can party all night," Pat said.

Most weddings in Memphis are in churches—the weather is too unpredictable to do outdoor weddings, Pat said. Hotels are increasing in popularity as reception sites. Other unique sites in Memphis include the Goldsmith Gardens and the Fountain House, a restored home.

"The Cinderella look is in here," Pat said. "Many Jessica McClintock gowns are also popular." She added that Memphis brides are selecting more contemporary looks for flowers. "The open, airy look is coming back in here for flowers," Pat said, "but most of my brides go for the back-to-the-basics look and get more elaborate for the bridesmaids." Popular flower choices include lilies of the valley, stephanotis, lilacs and Casablanca lilies. As always, white roses are also traditional.

Receptions in Memphis are hors d'oeuvres affairs. Swedish meatballs and ham in a biscuit are popular dishes. Sit-down dinners are "out", while DJs and harpists are "in." Overall, the average wedding and reception in Memphis costs $3000 to $5000.

Wedding cakes in Memphis are often spice, strawberry, or chocolate. Satellite cakes, fountains and heart-shaped cakes are quite popular. Groom's cakes are a common sight, usually a single sheet of chocolate cake decorated to reflect the groom's occupation. Often that means a motif of Federal Express or International Harvester.

Wedding favors are in, typically tiny champagne glasses filled with rice or birdseed. Satin roses are also favorites. Pat's advice to Memphis brides: "Organization. Call people whose work you've seen at other weddings. Also, plan at least six to eight months ahead."

Minneapolis, Minnesota

Nuptials in the Land of 10,000 Lakes.

If you walked into a wedding reception in Minneapolis-St. Paul, you might marvel at the wedding Kransekaki or Mandelringstarta.

Perhaps you're saying right now, hey what are those things besides the ultimate spelling nightmare? Well, quite simply, Kransekaki (as the Norwegians call it) or Mandelringstarta (as the Swedes refer to it) is a traditional Scandinavian wedding cake. With its large Scandinavian population, Minneapolis (and the rest of Minnesota for that matter) sees a lot of these cakes. Taking their inspiration from the French croquembouche, these cone-shaped cakes are stacked layers of almond pastry rings topped with powdered sugar. In addition to a standard, traditional cake, couples often have this almond ring cake too.

We spoke to Joan Kalpiers, a Minneapolis consultant who has been in the wedding business for 20 years. Besides providing the spelling for those Scandinavian cakes, Joan told us the average wedding there costs $12,000 to $14,000 with an average of 200 guests.

"The Twin Cities are a very traditional and conservative area for weddings. We are seeing larger weddings than in the past and less 'nuts, mints, very small church receptions.' Now there are more elegant hotel and country club receptions," Joan said.

The area's many lakes are a popular backdrop for local weddings and receptions. The "Outdoor Chapel," in a wooded area with a pond and waterfall is a popular site, as is the Jonathan Padelford Paddleboat on the Mississippi River. Edinborough Park is an "outdoor facility that is inside: its a completely enclosed park with trees, indoor pool, ice rink and amphitheater," Joan said.

In the past few years, several unique wedding sites have become available. Now Minneapolis brides can get married or have receptions at a restored movie theater downtown or on the Minnesota Zephyr train. You can even have a wedding and reception at the Mall of America, the country's largest shopping mall.

Minneapolis brides are big on traditional apparel; gowns with sweetheart necklines, long sleeves, and basque waists are favorites. In a change from year's past, however, many brides are also opting for sheath dresses with detachable trains.

The most popular wedding flowers in the Twin Cities "are still roses," Joan said, "but I see brides breaking away from traditional looks to more hand-tied English garden bouquet styles." Lilacs and lily of the valley are two other floral favorites. A big recent trend are bouquets with bold and bright colors, instead of the all-white look.

For receptions, the buffet dinner is most popular. Joan said Minneapolis is basically a meat and potatoes town— beef, turkey, chicken, potatoes and salads are common sights on the buffet table. More brides are opting for "healthy" menus featuring chicken in various sauces. The Twin Cities ethnic communities often add their own favorites: the Polish favor sausages and sauerkraut, the Italians like pasta and the Swedes prefer, of course, a smorgasbord.

In a switch from years past, the most popular entertainment options are disc jockeys with light and sound shows. Dance bands are somewhat in vogue, as couples opt for the more affordable DJ services. Chamber groups or a harpist are common for ceremony music.

"September is the most popular month to get married here," Joan said, adding that this probably due to the pleasant weather at that time of the year.

Special thanks to: Joan Kalpiers, 2021 128th Ave NW Minneapolis, 55433, (612) 757-8590.

Oklahoma City, Oklahoma

Second Weddings are OK in Oklahoma.

Oklahoma has one of the highest divorce rates in the country, but that hasn't deterred couples from taking the plunge again.

"Second weddings are big here—especially from Thanksgiving to Christmas," said Felicia Moghbel, a formal bridal consultant in Oklahoma City for 14 years.

A typical wedding costs $10,000 and has between 200 to 250 guests, she said. "Although traditional June weddings are most popular, August and September are real close," Felicia said.

Thanks to the unpredictable Oklahoma weather, most weddings are indoors. Popular reception sites include the Renaissance Building and the Botanical Gardens downtown. The Myriad Gardens Convention Center is also a favorite. Next in popularity are many area restaurants that have banquet rooms.

Ethnic weddings are on the rise in Oklahoma City. Besides the city's large Hispanic community, Iranians, Lebanese, Greek and Vietnamese weddings have mixed their customs with American traditions.

"Big Iranian weddings are grand scale here, " Felicia said. "Couples are married on a sophra, a satin cloth. The women then gather around the couples and rub sugar cones together—similar to our tradition of throwing rice."

Vietnamese brides will wear a white gown to a morning ceremony and then change into a red gown (their color for formal weddings). "All of the ethnic groups here have introduced something new to Oklahoma City—the sit-down dinner reception," she said.

"The traditional Oklahoma reception is just cake, nuts, mints and coffee," Felicia said, adding that "in the last five years we have seen a new trend toward hors d'oeuvre buffets." Popular reception foods include fruit and cheese displays in the summer and hot hors d'oeuvres like roast beef sandwiches in the winter. "Pigs in a blanket" with smoked sausages is the #1 choice, she said.

Another unusual aspect of Oklahoma City weddings is the Friday night ceremony. Why not Saturday night? Felicia explained that "churches here don't allow weddings on Saturday evenings to make sure the sanctuary is cleaned up for Sunday services." Hence, formal weddings in the evening must be on Friday night (if they want a church wedding). In the summer, 2 PM Saturday weddings are common, too.

Oklahoma brides are choosing ruffles and lace in wedding gowns, Felicia said. Older brides opt for traditional satin gowns and imported gowns that sell for $700 to $1500. "The traditional looks are strong," Felicia said. Above all, San Martin and Bonny are the most popular designers.

Folks in Oklahoma City have discovered a unique solution to the alcohol question. To keep guests from overindulging, many restaurant banquet halls now give guests who want to drink two tickets that can be redeemed at the bar. Hence guests are kept to a two-drink limit. In rural areas, alcohol is nonexistent at receptions since churches (where most receptions are held) prohibit it.

For wedding cakes, basic vanilla is most popular, Felicia said. Many brides today also have different flavors for each tier: strawberry and banana walnut are both favorites. Groom's cakes (a separate cake served at the reception) are often exotic chocolate confections "with Tootsie Roll icing," she said. For the bride's cake, staircases and fountains are "out" as decorations—fresh flowers are "in."

"In fact, brides are using the flower bouquet cake topper as their throw-away bouquet," she said. "Roses are the #1 flower choice." Orchids and rubrim lilies are also favorites, while cascades are the bouquet shape preferred by most brides. Bridesmaids often carry a single long-stem rose or an arm bouquet wrapped in tulle and ribbons.

Bands are the most popular reception entertainment in Oklahoma City—DJs, by comparison, are scarce. If a band is not selected, many other receptions feature a pianist, harpist, or violinist.

Phoenix, Arizona

Just Like East Coast but Add Some Sand

Believe it or not, weddings and receptions in Phoenix are much like those on the East Coast.

"Most of the people who live in Phoenix are not from Phoenix—most moved here from the East Coast and Midwest," Jacque Carman, a former wedding planner in Phoenix, said. "Therefore, most of the couple's relatives don't live in the Phoenix area and must fly in. So I don't think weddings here are as large as other areas of the country where people have lived (in one city) all their lives."

Jacque said most weddings and receptions cost $6000 to $10,000 with 125 to 150 guests. "The largest wedding here I have ever seen was 300 people." The exception to this rule is Phoenix's large Hispanic and Indian communities, who generally have larger weddings and receptions.

The extreme summer heat in Phoenix dictates some changes in wedding traditions. For example, unlike the rest of the country, the summer is not the most popular time to tie the knot in Arizona. "March, April and May are the most popular months to get married," Jacque said. "When its 118 degrees (in June) and you got Grandma and Grandpa in from Detroit passing out—it's not a pretty scene."

One recent change Jacque has noticed is a shift from Friday and Saturday night weddings to Saturday afternoon. "Most couples now get married at 11 or noon on Saturday with a luncheon reception following," Jacque said.

Next to churches and synagogues, the most popular wedding and reception sites in Phoenix are the area's many resort hotels. "Some of my clients don't want to get married in churches anymore," she said. "First of all, they're expensive. Also, most Phoenix churches require engaged couples to take classes. Couples simply don't want to be bothered." Instead, the Camel Back Inn and La Posada are two popular sites, as well as an historical district in downtown.

Most receptions start with a cocktail hour with hors d'oeuvres "served Butler style." Perhaps due to the influx of Easterners and Midwesterners, the sit-down dinner (or luncheon) is most popular. "Also, buffets (in Phoenix) are also more expensive, believe it or not," Jacque said. Typical dishes include a choice of London broil, a chicken breast in wine sauce, or a fish entree."

Younger brides often choose to have a cash bar, while

older couples will host a bar, Jacque said. Beer, wine and champagne are most common but recent local campaigns to stop drunk driving have also reduced the amount of alcohol served at Phoenix wedding receptions.

Wedding cakes often have tiers with different flavors like German chocolate or banana with a mousse or fruit filling. "They don't go for the plain old white cake anymore," Jacque said.

Fresh flower decorations are the most popular cake toppers. Since they have to be flown in to Phoenix, flowers in general are quite expensive. "Of course, roses are always popular. I'm seeing a lot of pink tiger lilies (alstroemeria)." As you might expect, flowers that aren't as heat-sensitive (carnations and daisies) are also common.

Wedding photographers in Phoenix are often taking formal group pictures before the wedding, instead of the traditional after-ceremony session. Hence brides and grooms are seeing each other before the ceremony. Formal bridal portraits are out.

"Videos are big productions here, with two or three cameras (covering the ceremony). Many tapes have a montage of the couple's baby pictures as well as family interviews," Jacque said. For entertainment, bands that play anything from country and western to reggae music are popular.

Jacque told us Phoenix brides are choosing white, traditional bridal gowns with long trains. What's "out?" Veils, she said. "Hats or headpieces are most popular."

Planning in advance is critical for Phoenix brides. "A year is good since the hotel resorts book up very fast. This is a convention center town. They don't want to fool around with a wedding for 150 guests when they can book a big convention for thousands."

The biggest time for conventions in Phoenix is November and December. During those months, "you can hardly find a place," she said.

Pittsburgh, Pennsylvania

Traditional Nuptials Popular in Pittsburgh

A trend toward spring and fall weddings (instead of the summer) is the latest news in Pittsburgh weddings. So says Valerie Martin, a wedding consultant in Pittsburgh for the past two years.

"Many of the older churches in Pittsburgh, which are most popular for weddings, do not have air conditioning. This probably accounts for the shift away from the summer," she said, adding that Memorial and Labor Day weekends are still the most popular times.

Most weddings in Pittsburgh are held on Saturdays at 4:30 PM. For receptions, "what's becoming more popular in Pittsburgh are restored estates. The Slaugherty House near the airport is one example. People just like that style. The only problem with estates is they will only accommodate 100 people," Valerie said. The average wedding in Pittsburgh is 175 guests.

Pittsburgh brides are opting for wedding gowns with traditional detailing. The puff shoulder, high neckline and full-length skirt is popular. For bridesmaids, the high-low hemline has also been a hit this year, she said. One favorite designer is Demetrios.

For color motifs, brides are choosing more jewel tones than pastel colors, Valerie said. To match these designs, floral designers are using many calla and rubrim lilies. "The most popular choice is, of course, roses," she said. A new floral style gaining acceptance is the European-inspired bridal bouquet.

Wedding receptions in Pittsburgh are typically sit-down dinners with open bars and dancing. Most menus feature a chicken dish and a meat dish. For dessert, the wedding cake is traditionally served with French vanilla ice cream.

"A lot of people this year have gone with fresh flowers on the wedding cake. A simple icing like basketweave is popular. I've even seen a few wedding cheesecakes," she said.

Disc jockeys are the most favorite entertainment at receptions. "Another popular musical choice here is to have a strolling violinist during dinner," she said. Favors are still popular with Pittsburgh's large Italian community.

"One tradition we have up here that is so popular is the balloon releases. Couples will have these instead of throwing rice since most churches prohibit it. The balloons are usually ordered in the same color as their wedding party. There is usually a separate, heart-shaped balloon for the bride and groom. In other cases, there is a little paper attached to the balloon so everyone can write a wish to the bride and groom."

Portland, Oregon

Romance on the Willamette River

May has almost replaced June as the most popular month to wed in Portland, Oregon, according to Melanie

Perko, a bridal consultant and Portland native. And, while Portland weddings are large (averaging 250 guests), their cost is somewhat more affordable than national averages. Melanie told us the average wedding in Portland costs $10,000. Portland also boasts several unique wedding sites. "Local vineyards west of Portland are popular reception sites," Melanie said. Other popular sites include local hotels and several area private clubs.

Portland brides are choosing gowns without much bead work. "Many brides are wearing their mother's gowns with some small alteration to make them more timely," Melanie said.

Bridesmaids colors range from deep teal to amethyst. "Lately, we've seen several black and white weddings," Melanie added. For flowers, the "European garden" bouquets are popular. Calla lilies, peonies, and long-stem French tulips are favorite floral choices.

Most Portland wedding receptions feature heavy hors d'oeuvres. "Quite a few weddings I've seen are staying away from the sit-down dinner. The food is more healthy—lots of pasta, fresh fruit, shrimp, and chicken wings. Since we're close to the coast, there are always quite a few seafood dishes, too," Melanie said. Asian cuisine and capuccino bars are hip.

For dessert, "wedding cakes are going toward the real unusual," she said. "I've seen many French cakes with Marzipan icing and layers of flowers and icing ruffles." Banana, chocolate and poppyseed are the most popular flavors for wedding cakes in Portland.

Melanie also told us couples in Portland are breaking with tradition in one way—most see each other before the ceremony to take all the formal photographs. Of course, that doesn't mean weddings there are informal by any means. "In fact," Melanie said, "quite a few weddings are optional black tie."

Special thanks to Melanie Perko, RSVP Melanie, 4120 SW 55th Dr. Portland, OR, 97221, (503) 291-7083.

Poughkeepsie, New York

Tradition and Romance in the Hudson River Valley

Hudson River Valley is blessed with many unique wedding and reception sites, according to bridal consultant Jeannie Greene of Party Planning Service. The area's many mansion and hotels are popular picks for brides and grooms.

Among the best sites are the Hotel Thayer at the West Point Military Academy, the Troutbeck Mansion (in Anenia), the Valeur Mansion and the Bear Mountain Inn in Bear Mountain State Park. The area also boasts the oldest inn in America, the Beekman Arms in Rhinebeck, NY, which is a popular spot for receptions.

Local wineries are also a favorite choice for weddings and receptions. Among the best are the Regent Champagne Cellars, the Cascade Mountain Winery, and the Westpark Wine Cellars on the Hudson River. If that isn't enough, brides and grooms can celebrate their wedding on a river cruise.

Jeannie told us the average wedding in her area has 150 to 200 guests and costs between $8,000 and $13,000. May and October are the most popular months to tie the knot in the Hudson River Valley. As in many parts of the Northeast, most receptions have sit-down dinners.

"Chicken and prime rib are the popular dishes here in the Hudson Valley," Jeannie said. A several course sit-down dinner with wine starts at $30 and can go up to $75 per person. For dessert, the wedding cake is served with ice cream. The most popular cake flavors are white cake with strawberry/vanilla custard filling and chocolate cake with mousse filling. "Most cakes are very elaborate with stair-cases and fountains," she said. "Some bakeries put fresh flowers on the cake or they put a photograph of the bride and groom in a frame as a cake topper."

For entertainment, "disc jockeys are being used here instead of expensive bands. The advantage is that they play continuously and also provide the special dances like the circle dance, the limbo, the conga and many ethnic dances."

In fact, ethnic weddings are quite big in Poughkeepsie. "We do have Hungarian, Italian, Jewish, Polish, German, Greek and Russian weddings—it's a melting pot here since we are so close to New York City. So, ethnic foods are big. Usually the grandmother will bring in special breads and cakes for the reception," Jeannie said.

Brides in the Hudson Valley are choosing both fresh and silk flowers for their weddings. "Silk is running a close second here since they don't wilt and can be given as mementos at the wedding." Jeannie's survey of local florists turned up several floral favorites: calla lilies, roses and stephanotis are the most popular varieties. Also popular lately are Victorian-inspired floral designs and invitations.

Special Thanks to Jeannie Greene, Party Planning Service, 31 Briarwood Dr., Poughkeepsie, New York, 12601, (914) 462-4858.

Raleigh-Durham, North Carolina

Basketball Court Cakes and Brunswick Stew in Tar Heel Country.

"Shagging and Pig Pickin'" are what's hip for weddings in Raleigh-Durham, North Carolina. So says Marci Fricke, a local wedding consultant for two years in the Raleigh-Durham area.

So, what are shagging and pig pickin'? Marci told us shagging is a popular dance at wedding receptions that resembles the jitterbug. Pig pickin' is the time-honored North Carolina tradition of having a roasted pig at the rehearsal dinner, which is more a picnic than a dinner.

June is the most popular month to get married, though Christmas is also a favorite time. "The big tradition here is that at most weddings the father of the groom is the best man," Marci said. A late afternoon ceremony on Saturday is the most popular time of day.

Many weddings and receptions in Raleigh-Durham are held either in a church or in a relative's home. Other interesting sites include the historic Arrowhead Inn, the restored Nello Teer House and the elegant Fearrington Restaurant. For those alumni of Duke University, the campus gardens and the beautiful Gothic chapel are quite popular.

"The tradition here is to wear your mother's gown," Marci said. If the mother's gown is not available, simple, classic styles by designers like Priscilla are in vogue. For flowers, daffodils, iris, gardenias, white roses, and stephanotis are popular choices.

Brides in Raleigh-Durham also stay close to tradition food choices at the reception. A white bride's cake and a chocolate groom's cake are standard. "Fruit fillings and carrot cake are starting to make inroads here," she said. Icing flowers are a popular decoration for the bride's cake while groom's cakes normally reflect the area's passion for basketball. "At many weddings I've seen, the groom's cake is (decorated like) a basketball court," she said.

Most receptions in North Carolina feature hors d'oeuvres; sit-down dinners or buffets are rare. (The exception are Jewish weddings that often feature a sit-down dinner reception at a local hotel.) Stuffed tomatoes and mushrooms, as well as mini-meatballs, are popular hors d'oeuvres. After dinner, the guests usually dance to "beach music," Marci said, "which is more like the Four Seasons and the Four Tops than the Beach Boys or Jan and Dean."

At rehearsal dinners, chopped barbecue and Brunswick

stew (a popular regional dish with beef, chicken and vegetables) are common sights. The average wedding in Raleigh-Durham, North Carolina has 150 guests and costs $5000 to $10,000.

Sacramento, California

Combining Old and New in California Capital

Outdoor weddings are all the rage in Sacramento California, according to bridal consultant Lorie Worman. "We have many parks in Sacramento that have specific areas set aside just for weddings," Lorie said. McKinnley Park Rose Garden is particularly popular.

With all those outdoor weddings, August and September (instead of June) have become the busiest months for weddings in Sacramento since the weather is predictably nice then. For receptions, the Delta King, a newly restored paddle-boat on the Sacramento River is extremely popular. "For one fun wedding, we decorated up a speed boat that the couple used as their get-away after the reception," Lorie said. Other popular sites include restored mansions like the Grand Island Mansion and the Sterling Hotel. At the Sterling, a European-imported glass conservatory is a unique ceremony or reception site. Best of all, Sacramento brides have a wide variety of choices: both the beach and mountain sites are relatively close in proximity.

Few Sacramento couples (as few as two in 10 couples) belong to the church they get married in. Lorie said couples spend $400 to $800 to get married in a church as non-members. The nearby wineries in Nappa Valley are also very popular alternatives for ceremony and reception sites.

For apparel, Lorie told us Sacramento brides are wild over the mermaid-style gown. Taffeta and big bows are also "in." Popular designers include Alfred Angelo and San Martin, she said.

To complement these gowns, many brides are choosing flowers in asymmetrical and unstructured bouquets. "I'm seeing a lot of calla lilies and anthurium and even exotic tropical flowers like bird of paradise," she said.

Availability and prices of flowers are excellent, thanks to Sacramento's close proximity to California's big flower growers. Also, Lorie told us that flowers as table centerpiece decorations common, while some couples choose balloons to fill up a cavernous reception site. Overall, "jewel tone" weddings are definitely in vogue.

At the reception, buffets are most popular. Teryaki chicken and baron of beef are the "all time favorites," Lorie said. Hors d'oeuvres are less popular as is hard liquor. In fact, Lorie said several weddings she is doing this year are completely non-alcoholic. Most other brides are opting for just beer and champagne (for the toast); some are now requesting a bottle of chilled wine at each table. For the wedding cake, the most popular flavor is chocolate with a raspberry filling. Lorie has even done several carrot cake and fruit cake wedding cakes. Rolled fondant icing is quite popular.

Wedding favors are big— "especially items with pot-pourri instead of almonds," Lorie said. After the reception, many couples have a portrait taken in one of Sacramento's parks, sitting on the grass with the river in the background. Almost all weddings in Sacramento are also videotaped. "Many wedding photographers in Sacramento offer video in their packages, " Lorie said.

The average wedding in Sacramento costs about $13,000. One great savings tip: many Sacramento brides have discovered several bridal outlets (including Jessica McClintock's Gunne Sax) in San Francisco.

Overall, Sacramento brides are combining the old and the new. For example, many brides use their mother's head-piece with their own bridal veil.

Special Thanks to Lorie Worman, "Wedding World," 4753 Manzanita Ave., Carmichael, CA, 95608, (916) 486-0909.

Salt Lake City, Utah

Wedding Breakfasts and Spun Taffy in Salt Lake State.

Wedding breakfasts are "what's in" in Salt Lake City, Utah, according to Gail Wathen, owner of Danielle's Bridal Shop. Gail, who is also a bridal consultant to Salt Lake City brides, explains that many Mormon ceremonies are at nine or 10 in the morning. Following the ceremony, a wedding breakfast is held for the immediate family and the bridal party. Later in the evening, a reception is held for all the guests.

"As far as receptions, there are quite a few reception centers in the Salt Lake Valley that cater to weddings," Gail said, adding that "in the summer, we are seeing a trend toward garden weddings in a home." Several popular reception sites that also have a gazebo for ceremonies include the McCueon Mansion, the Murray Mansion, and the Old Meeting House Chapel.

June is still the biggest month for weddings in Salt Lake City. For the apparel, Bianchi and Demetrios (Ilissa) are top requested designers. "More brides are turning away from the ruffle-ruffle look and instead are into more contemporary, simplified fashion. The finer fabrics like silk are gaining popularity," Gail said.

The average wedding in Salt Lake City costs between $7000 to $12,000. The wedding breakfast or brunch (traditionally paid for by the groom's family) is followed in the evening by a larger reception, which typically features a light buffet. "Little finger sandwiches, fruit kabobs and pastries are the most popular foods at Utah receptions," Gail said.

And those receptions are big. "On the average, 500 invitations go out for a typical Mormon wedding," Gail said. "We're a little more conservative here in Utah with wedding (spending). The contributing factor is because the average family has at least four or five children. Some have as many as eight or nine children. And that's a lot of weddings to pay for."

Another unusual feature of Salt Lake City weddings: taffy wedding cakes. "The cake is also covered with taffy flowers, for a unique look." Other unusual wedding cakes include a replica of the L.D.S. temple. With the preponderance of Mormon weddings, liquor is virtually non-existent at Salt Lake wedding receptions.

"What used to be big were those invitations with a picture of the bride and groom. Now, its definitely out." Dancing is not as big for receptions, with less than half of the couple's opting for a band as entertainment. Instead of musical entertainment, a video is often played that chronicles the couple growing up.

Special Thanks to Gail Wathen, Danielle's Bridal, 4098 S. Highland, Salt Lake City, UT. 84124, (801) 272-1146.

San Diego, California

Outdoor Weddings Big in Southern California

Outdoor weddings during August and September are what's popular in San Diego, according to local wedding consultant Kathy Januario. Balboa and Presidio Park are two local favorites.

Kathy told us the average wedding in San Diego costs

$13,000 to $17,000 with 200 guests. The ceremony typically is at 2 or 3 PM on a Saturday afternoon followed by a sit-down dinner reception at a local hotel. Chicken, prime rib and Cornish game hen are popular dishes.

"Brides are choosing very simple but elegant gowns. They are really into long trains," Kathy said. Preferred designers include Galina and the Diamond Collection. White roses and lilies of the valley are chosen for the bridal bouquet.

Receptions are often elegant, three course sit-down dinners. Buffets are popular for afternoon wedding receptions or for smaller weddings. For the wedding cake, a white cake with lemon or strawberry filling is decorated with white chocolate shavings.

San Diego has a large population of Portuguese, who have a unique tradition with wedding photography. "The bride and groom both have a portrait made separately in their formals before the wedding. These are then displayed at the reception," she said. Portuguese weddings are quite big with anywhere from eight to 18 attendants.

Favors are quite popular in San Diego, especially in the Portuguese, Italian and Hispanic communities. Scrolls, almonds and mints are most common as well as heart-shaped candies and specialty chocolates.

San Francisco, California

Surprise Chocolate Truffles in City by the Bay

Outdoor weddings are what's "in' with San Francisco brides, according to Terri Revelli, a Bay Area wedding planner.

We spoke to Terri recently about what's popular for nuptials in the City by the Bay. She said many area mansions like Ralston Hall and the Flood Mansion make for spectacular reception sites.

The average wedding in the Bay Area has 200 guests and costs $15,000 to $20,000. For apparel, San Francisco brides are choosing striking gowns by the Diamond Collection and Priscilla of Boston. To match those gowns, free-flowing bouquets of roses and tulips are hand-tied for a garden effect.

At the reception, brides and grooms are choosing "seated buffets," a cross between hors d'oeuvres and seated dinner receptions. Popular dishes include pasta bars, cracked crab and many other varieties of fresh seafood.

For dessert, wedding cakes are sometimes supplemented by a separate dessert table. The wedding cake itself is often a chocolate confection with a surprise: Terri told us bakers hide chocolate truffles inside the cake—sounds wonderful! Wedding photographers in San Francisco have moved toward more candid, spontaneous pictures. As in other parts of the country, photographers who do formal posed pictures are less popular.

Favors are a common sight at Bay area receptions. Terri told us one popular favor she's seen is a chocolate truffle in a small box. The box, which is colored in the same motif as the wedding party, is wrapped with a ribbon that has the couple's names imprinted on it.

San Francisco's large ethnic communities have their own wedding traditions. For example, Terri told us that Asian brides often wear more than one gown during their wedding day, changing into two or three gowns that are sewn by various family members. Of course, ethnic foods and family traditions also play a big role in Asian weddings in San Francisco.

Seattle, Washington

Three Staples of Seattle Receptions: Salmon, Salmon, Salmon

Don't go to Seattle in June and expect to see many weddings. Unlike the rest of the country, June is not the most popular wedding month in Seattle, thanks to that month's usually wet weather. Instead, dryer August is the number-one choice.

So says Carole Haney of Carole's Elegante Weddings, a bridal consultant for several years in the Seattle area. She told us the average wedding in Seattle costs $10,000 to $12,000 with an average of 150 guests. Saturday at 7 pm is the most popular time to tie the knot, although other days (Friday and Sunday) are becoming more common as a cost-savings alternative.

"People like to plan outdoor weddings here. August is the safest month here to plan an outdoor wedding as opposed to June," Carole said.

Favorite reception sites in Seattle include the famous Space Needle and several restored mansions. "Another popular site is the Kiana Lodge, which is noted for its beautiful salmon barbecues and surroundings with native American carvings," she said. If you want to wed at sea, over 15 charter boats are available for wedding cruises. One boat can hold 600 people on three decks with dancing and dining!

Northwestern wines and foods are popular at weddings in Seattle. For example, salmon is the most popular dish at wedding receptions, as are other seafood dishes. Buffets with pasta stations are common sights. For wedding cakes, Carole told us brides choose flavors from traditional white to exotic flavors like mocha or carrot cake.

Seattle brides are choosing bridal gowns that range from "fancy gowns with sequins and ruffles to simple linen suits." Jewel tones are the most popular wedding color motifs for bridesmaids.

Flowers for Seattle weddings include a generous mix of fresh roses and orchids. In photography, Carole said Seattle brides are preferring more candid approaches "like Denis Reggie. Less formal photography and more casual pictures. Brides don't want to spend their whole day posing for the photographer." One new trend: black and white photography, in addition to color shots.

A recent influx of Californians into the Seattle area has changed local wedding traditions somewhat. For example, Carole said boudoir photography is now much more popular in Seattle. "We're very conservative up here. And, now, with more Californians, we are becoming less conservative."

Seattle's large Filipino community has their own wedding traditions, including a roasted pig for the buffet and a "money dance," where guests pay to dance with the bride and groom. This money helps pay for the honeymoon, etc.

Overall, Carole said that Seattle weddings are more informal than other parts of the country. While the bride may wear a long gown, most mothers wear short dresses, for example. "We have our fancy weddings, too. But the attitude is more casual here."

Special thanks to: Carole's Elegante Weddings, 500 Aurora Ave. North B-3, Seattle, WA 98109, (206) 329-8893

Chapter 15

Last Minute Consumer Tips

Okay, let's assume you're the perfect consumer. Instead of using cash or a check, you've put your deposits on a credit card. All the agreements with each service are in writing. You've dotted all your "i's" and crossed all your "t's."

But what if your wedding day arrives and, for example, the florist delivers dead flowers? Or the photographer sends a surrogate "stand-in"? Or the wrong wedding cake is delivered? What can you do to prevent this?

Meet the Surrogate Bad Cop

No matter how careful you are, things can still happen at your wedding and reception that are not according to plan. That's why you need a Surrogate Bad Cop as an "enforcer" to fix last minute problems and correct wayward merchants.

Who can be a surrogate bad cop? Anyone you believe is trustworthy and reliable. This can be your best friend, your mother or a close relative. Of course, if you're hiring a professional wedding planner, they would play this role typically.

What does the surrogate bad cop actually do? *Their job is to make sure you enjoy your wedding.* While you're greeting guests and having fun, it's the surrogate bad cop's role to tell the florist to fix the flowers. Or track down the photographer who is running late. Or find out why the wrong wedding cake was delivered and see if it can be fixed.

In addition to major problems, the surrogate cop also handles any minor situations. One bride told us she was upset with the band she hired when the musicians launched into an unscheduled set of heavy metal music. While she was taking pictures, she had her surrogate bad cop (her sister) talk to the band leader. She informed him of the band's mistake and said the bride had requested they change the tempo. And the band complied.

The Surrogate Bad Cop's Bag of Tricks

Any good enforcer needs the tools at their disposal to do

their job effectively. Here's a look into their "bag of tricks," a special folder or notebook that you give to them on the wedding day (or shortly before):

1 PHONE NUMBERS OF EVERY SERVICE (HOME, BUSINESS, MOBILE/CAR PHONE). Okay, it's Saturday night, the wedding is in one hour and the florist is nowhere to be found. You call the shop and, of course, it's closed. Now what? That's why you also need a home phone number for the key contact at every service. Even better: get the car/mobile phone number and/or a pager number as well. These numbers will be crucial if your surrogate needs to track down an errant florist, photographer, DJ, etc.

2 COPIES OF EACH CONTRACT AND PROPOSAL. Let's say that florist has shown up, but she's missing several arrangements. Or a special orchid corsage for your grand-mother. But the florist claims you never ordered that. What can you do? Well, if you're smart, you'll put copies of every contract and proposal into your surrogate cop's bag of tricks. That way she can whip out the florist proposal and tactfully point out that, yes, there is suppose to be an orchid corsage. Usually, florists carry a few extra flowers with them (or they can perhaps pop back to their shop and pick up the missing pieces). One hopes that you won't have to resort to producing written contracts to correct prob-lems, but it's a nice back-up just in case. Also, it helps the surrogate bad cop figure out just what you ordered.

3 AUTHORITY TO ACT ON YOUR BEHALF. This "invisible" tool is important. You must tell each service (photog-rapher, florist, caterer DJ, band, etc.) that this special per-son will be acting on your behalf during the wedding and reception. If they come to them with a request, they should know it is your wishes.

The Final Check-Up

A week or so before your wedding, you should set up a "final check-up" with each merchant and service. Whether an in-person meeting or a telephone consultation, you should discuss the following:

❦ *Confirm all dates, days, times and locations.* You need arrival or drop-off times from such services as the florist and baker. Be careful if you're not getting married on a Saturday—make sure the merchant knows your wedding is a Friday or Sunday, for example. We've heard stories of "no-shows" since the merchant assumed all weddings are on Saturday.

❦ *Get all the phone numbers we mentioned above.*

❦ *Tell them the identity of your "surrogate bad cop."* While you may not use those words exactly, let the companies know that this one special person will be helping you that evening. They should treat any request from this person as your direction.

❦ *Confirm the order.* Now is the time to make sure that the florist can do bird of paradise flowers in your bouquet. Or that the wedding cake will be a certain flavor. Go over the menu with the caterer and fix any problems. Make sure they have your special requests in writing in their file.

❦ *Pay the Balance.* Many services and merchants will require the payment of the balance due at this time. Try to pay by credit card.

Strategies for Dealing with Problems that Crop up on the Wedding Day

We find these problems fall into one of three categories.

1 IMPROPER DELIVERIES. What can you do if the wrong cake is delivered or the caterer serves the wrong main course? While you (or your surrogate cop) may be able to contact the company before the wedding, there may not be enough time to fix the problem. Solution: Ask the company to make an "adjustment" in your final bill. This doesn't mean you get the item for free—but a discount or partial refund may be in order.

2 NO SHOWS/LATE ARRIVALS. If the photographer is late, use the contact phone numbers to track him/her down. Solution: anyone who charges by the hour should make an adjustment in their bill if they run late. Or they may be able to make up the time by staying later.

3 INFERIOR QUALITY. You were promised big, beautiful roses, but the florist has delivered half-dead, sweetheart roses. The DJ said he had an extensive collection of country music, but it turns out that it's just one Garth Brooks album. Honestly, there isn't much you can do on the day of the wedding if a company has deceived you about the quality of their products or services. However,

after the wedding, you may want to dispute the charge on your credit card (which you used for deposits and final payments) if what was delivered didn't live up to the promises. If you paid by check or cash, you may have to take the merchant to small claims court to recover your money. Document the problem with pictures or video. Also, complain to the Better Business Bureau and your city/county's consumer affairs office.

Many of the so-called wedding "disasters" are due to the lack of written agreements or ambiguous contracts. You can stop this problem by simply getting everything in writing.

Another source of problems are "early deliveries." One bride in Texas told us about a wedding cake that was delivered *six hours* before her reception. As the hotel was setting up the ballroom, someone with a ladder wacked the cake. The lesson: don't have the flowers, cake or other items delivered *too early*. There's just too much of an opportunity of something happening.

Finally, some goofs are due to a lack of organization on the businesses' part. Whether the mix-up is an honest mistake or an intentional fraud, it doesn't matter. As a professional, the service should act to correct the mistake or give you a refund. Sadly, not all wedding merchants are professionals and you must take steps to protect yourself as a consumer.

The Bottom Line

While there's no such thing as a perfect wedding, there is such a thing as a consumer-savvy bride and groom. With credit cards, complete written agreements and a well-armed surrogate bad cop, you can get the quality that you're paying the big bucks for at your wedding and reception.

Chapter 16

What Does It All Mean?

After reading through all the tips and advice in this book, your first thought may be "Let's elope!" And, if you didn't question your sanity in this process at least once, we would be worried.

Of course, it's easy for us to sit here in our Ivory Tower and tell you that you need to keep your "perspective" while you plan your wedding. In truth, perhaps many married couples take perverse joy in seeing engaged couples go through the anguish of planning a wedding. It's almost like a boot camp for marriage: if you can survive this, then you are fit to join the rest of us on the other side of the fence of marital bliss.

Even if weddings are some sinister plot to initiate the single into the married world, this doesn't excuse the fact that the entire U.S. wedding industry, your friends and relatives are trying to convince you that YOUR WEDDING DAY IS THE SINGLE MOST IMPORTANT DAY OF YOUR LIFE. And, of course, unless you get everything perfect, the wrath of the WEDDING GODS will be on your head.

Complicating this process is that green stuff with the presidents on it. As you are probably now well aware, weddings are darn expensive. Worse yet, as a consumer, planning a wedding puts you in a sometimes hostile environment. In a very short time, you must shop for products and services that you've never bought before and probably will never buy again.

We hope this book is useful as you plan your trip down the aisle. We sincerely appreciate your purchase of this book and we want to help you any way we can. If you have any questions about this book or just want to chat, see the "How to contact us" page at the end of this book.

In the face of all this, our message to you is quite simple: have a good time. Don't take this stuff too seriously. Remember that you are planning a party to celebrate you and your fiance's relationship. And, theoretically, people are suppose to have fun at parties. Even the guests of honor.

Appendix

Setting the Budget

T he first step in setting the budget is prioritizing your needs. That's what the first section of this chapter is about. Next, you will set the overall budget you want to spend. Finally, we will show you how to budget money for each category according to your priorities.

Prioritizing Your Needs

We suggest that both you and your fiance or you and your parents (depending on who will be contributing to this event) sit down together with separate sheets of paper and make a list like this:

APPAREL..	$ _____
FLOWERS...	$ _____
CAKE..	$ _____
RECEPTION/CATERING	$ _____
PHOTOGRAPHY...	$ _____
VIDEOGRAPHY..	$ _____
INVITATIONS	$ _____
MUSIC...	$ _____
MISCELLANEOUS..	$ _____

Once you've each made up priority worksheets, rank each category in order of importance from one (most important) to nine (least important). Be sure not to confer on your choices until everyone is finished.

In order to understand exactly what each category entails, the following is a brief explanation, including average costs.

1 APPAREL. This includes the bride's gown, veil, shoes, accessories, undergarments, and alterations. It may also include a separate going-away outfit. The groom's formal

wear is also part of this category. The average cost for apparel is $1175 ($1100 for the bride and $75 for the groom's formal wear rental).

NOTE: For parents who are paying for the wedding, include the price of your gown and/or tux in this section. Also, some couples or their parents may pay for siblings' formal wear. Include such extra apparel expenditures in this category if necessary.

2 FLOWERS. Of course, this category includes "personal" flowers such as bouquets, boutonnieres, corsages or even hairpieces. Ceremony flowers may include candelabrum, altar arrangements and aisle decorations. For the reception, flowers may be used as table and buffet centerpieces, and even to decorate the wedding cake. If it's alive and blooming, include it in this category. Most weddings average about $750 but elaborate floral decorations can cost $1000 to $2000 or more.

3 WEDDING CAKE. The wedding (or bride's) cake is the obvious item we're talking about. However, in some parts of the country, a groom's cake or a dessert table may also be included. Using our example of 200 guests, the average cake costs about $400.

4 RECEPTION/CATERING. Basically, this category includes all food (except the cake), beverages, labor and rental items. Charges to rent the reception facility are included here, when applicable. For a basic sit-down dinner or hors d'oeuvre buffet, we've budgeted about $35 per person—that includes beverages and gratuities. This average can be deceiving—in Boston, for example, a sit-down dinner reception can cost $125 per guest. On the other hand, a simple "cake and punch" reception in a smaller city can cost just $5 per person.

5 PHOTOGRAPHY. The bride and groom usually only need to budget for their album and possibly a bridal portrait. The average couple spends about $1500 for professional wedding photography. Parents should include a separate album in their budget as well as any additional photos they will want.

6 VIDEOGRAPHY. If you want your wedding and reception videotaped by a professional cameraman, add in this category. Also budget for extra copies for parents if necessary. A rough estimate for a professionally-shot video is about $500 to $1000. However, prices can range from $200 up to $4000.

7 INVITATIONS. First, you buy the invitations and announcements. Add on any extras like reception or

response cards and other enclosures. Don't forget napkins, printed matches, programs, scrolls and favors if you want them. You'll need informals (a.k.a. thank you notes) for all those gifts, and you may want to add in calligraphy. Don't forget to account for postage too. When you account for all these details, the average expenditure here is about $350.

8 MUSIC. Ceremony music may consist of as little as a church organist or as much as a string quartet and a soloist. As for the reception entertainment, choices range from a pianist to a professional DJ or band. Music costs average out at $1000 for entertainment at both the ceremony and reception.

9 MISCELLANEOUS. This isn't actually a fair category because it covers many things, but we mention it anyway. Some areas to think about are ceremony fees, blood tests and/or marriage license fees, accessories like guests books, beauty make-overs, transportation, or even lodging for members of the wedding party. A fair average for this category is about $1000—that figure can also cover cost overruns in one of the other categories if necessary.

Two other items not included in our calculations are the engagement and wedding rings. For the curious, the average engagement ring costs about $2000 and wedding rings now average $800 for the pair.

Now compare worksheets. Are everyone's priorities the same? Probably not! In fact, by using the priority worksheet, you may be able to spot possible conflicts before you get started.

For example, Mom may think that flowers are extremely important to make a wedding festive; the bride may be more concerned about her dress, while the groom's priority is the reception music. Now is the time to discuss differing opinions before they cause major problems with your wedding planning.

The Overall Budget

As you read in the introduction, the average wedding in the U.S. today costs about $18,000! But, of course, your wedding doesn't have to.

The cost involved is dependent on several items: how far in advance you can plan, what time of day and day of week you want your wedding, where (in the U.S.) you get married, what time of year you choose, and what your priorities are.

❦ *How far in advance.* When you have little or no time to plan in advance, you may have to accept what is available regardless of quality or price. Bridal gowns are a good example. Many wedding gowns in traditional bridal shops require from three to six months to special order. If you don't have that much time, you may have to settle for a sample gown that is not in the best condition. The more time you allow yourself, the more choices you will have and the more flexibility for your budget.

❦ *Time of day, day of the week and time of year.* Typically throughout the U.S., the most popular day of the week to have a wedding is Saturday (there are exceptions, see our last section for more details). If you choose a Saturday to get married, you will have to compete with many more brides than if you choose a Friday evening or a Sunday. Weekdays will be even more open. Some bridal businesses will even offer discounts for non-traditional days. For example, bands and DJ's will often accept work on Friday night or Sunday and give you a discount at the same time.

Time of day is also an important factor with your budget. If your budget is very tight, consider having your wedding in the morning or the afternoon instead of the evening. Food is the largest expense for most wedding receptions and dinner is the most expensive meal to serve. A late morning brunch or afternoon tea reception may save considerable money. These options and even a cake and punch reception are perfectly acceptable alternatives to the high expense of evening receptions.

❦ *Time of the year.* If you plan on having a holiday reception (such as Christmas or New Years), you should also plan on higher expenses. For example, flowers are more costly during December because of high demand and limited availability. Caterers are also busy with corporate parties at this time of year, as are bands and DJ's. As a result, prices are higher than at other times of the year. Other holidays such as Memorial Day, Valentine's Day, Labor Day, and Thanksgiving weekend may be similarly more expensive.

❦ *Number of people invited.* Since we noted above that food is your highest expense, it makes sense that cutting down on your guest list will save money. Enough said.

❦ *Your priorities.* When you look at your priority list, remember that you want to spend a larger part of your budget on the highest priorities. For example, if the reception catering is a high priority, this could be as much as one-third of your total budget. Even more if you are serious about food.

And that leads us to our next section: allotting money. First, before we do that, you need to come up with a total figure you want to spend on your wedding. We do not recommend that you go into debt to have the kind of wedding you want. In fact, there is no reason you should have to. There is also no magic formula for determining an overall amount. Look at what you can **afford** and determine the total from there.

Allotting Money

Again, take up your illustrious priority worksheet. At the top write in your total budget figure. Begin to allot your money to correspond with your priorities. Spend money where you think it is important. The following is a sample priority worksheet with a budget.

TOTAL BUDGET: **$10,000**

	Priority	Your Budget
APPAREL	1	$1,000
FLOWERS	5	600
CAKE	6	350
RECEPTION/CATERING	3	4,500
PHOTOGRAPHY	2	1,000
VIDEOGRAPHY	7	500
INVITATIONS	8	300
MUSIC	4	900
MISCELLANEOUS	9	850
	TOTAL	**$10,000**

With this sample, the reception, the photography and the dress are the highest priorities therefore, we are going to spend $6500 or 65% of our budget on these three items. You may decide you don't want to spend this much on the dress for example, and you will order a gown through Discount Bridal Service. Instead you may want to spend more money on the flowers because you want a bright garden-like wedding. And so on. The choices are up to you! That's what makes planning a wedding both exciting and challenging.

Tradition vs. Reality

Traditionally, the bride's family paid for nearly the entire wedding and the groom's family paid for the rehearsal dinner. Of course, that was in 1955. Today, couples are writing their own rules. In some cases, families split the expenses 50/50. Other wedding budgets are split three ways among the families and the couple. Still other couples pay for the entire wedding themselves. Obviously, this is a personal decision.

ONE MORE THING WE'D LIKE TO ADD: We believe that it is too easy to get caught up in the planning and paying for a wedding. Even with our own wedding, we found ourselves having to step back from the event and remember why we were getting married in the first place. In fact, it's good to keep in mind that all you really need to get married is a license, a bride, a groom and an official. All the rest is fluff. If you keep this in mind and remember that the wedding is the beginning of your lives together, instead of a huge social event used to impress your friends and family, it will be easier to keep calm and cool throughout the planning period.

About the Authors

Typically, this part of any book describes how the authors are cousins of really great writers like Stephen King and Dave Barry and the authors (since age 7) have always dreamed of being authors. Of course, we could say all that about Denise and Alan Fields, except for the fact that it wouldn't be true.

The reality is that the authors decided to write books on weddings after having a near-death experience trying to plan their own. Not that they had a particularly challenging wedding to plan—both sets of parents were in favor of the union. No, to really see what drove two allegedly sane people to make a living writing wedding books, we need to explore their sordid backgrounds.

Denise Fields (a.k.a. Denise Coopwood) originally wanted to be a ballerina when she grew up. At age 13, Denise switched career paths and decided to become a doctor. She later abandoned this goal after learning that to become a doctor you had to dissect cats at some point along the way.

Growing up in Loveland, Colorado, Denise developed an appreciation for the outdoors, the mountains and the absurd. She decided to attend college at the University of Colorado at Boulder—a place that has all three of the above qualities. Denise received a degree in European History, specializing in Elizabethan England. Only after graduation did Denise learn that the unemployment rate for Elizabethan scholars was approximately 132%. Sensing an impending financial crisis, Denise called a career audible: hey why not write books for a living? Denise had written some poetry in college and newspaper articles before that—so she did have writing experience.

Which is more than we can say about the second author of this book: Alan Fields. Alan had authored a newspaper column for the University of Colorado's student newspaper—but no one who ever read the libelous tripe he produced had ever described it as writing. This is probably explained by the fact that Alan's career ambition was originally to become a television weatherman. This dream came to an abrupt end when someone pointed out to Alan that to be on TV, you couldn't look goofy.

Alan grew up in Dallas, Texas—which probably explains his particularly warped sense of humor. In high school, Alan was voted as "Most Likely to be a Defendant in a Major Lawsuit." Fields was admitted to the University of Colorado in an administrative error, according to a university official who refused to be identified.

While in college, Alan met Denise in a chance encounter in the hallway of Kittridge West Dormitory. Two years later, Alan popped the question to Denise. While trying to plan their wedding, the couple came to the conclusion that this whole process is TRULY INSANE. After talking to other engaged couples, Denise and Alan realized that what the world really needed was a consumer guide to planning a wedding.

After five books and five years of working together, it is a miracle the Fields haven't killed each other yet. Although they might after they see this "about the authors" section.

Index

How to Reach Us

Have a question
about this book?

Want to make
a suggestion?

Discovered a great bargain
you'd like to share?

**Contact the Authors,
Alan and Denise Fields**

Call us.
(303) 442-8792

Or write to:
Alan and Denise Fields
Windsor Peak Press
1223 Peakview Circle, Suite 7000
Boulder, CO 80302

Join Our "Preferred Reader" List!

We've got lots of new books and special reports coming out over the next few years! Just jot down your name and address below, mail in the coupon and we'll keep you up-to-date!

Best of all, we have "early bird" DISCOUNTS especially for BRIDAL BARGAINS preferred readers!

- -

Name _____

Address _____

City _____ *State* _____ *Zip* _____

Wedding Date _____

How did you hear about our book? _____
_____

How can we improve this book? _____
_____

Mail To:

BRIDAL BARGAINS
1223 Peakview Circle
Boulder, CO 80302